The Global Housing Crisis

"It is high time that we found a way to pool our savings in order to invest in national housing inventories, thereby providing affordable homes for our people. Levent Sümer's book is a valuable contribution to the momentum that this idea deserves to generate."

— Andrew Baum, *Senior Research Fellow, Green Templeton College, Emeritus Professor, University of Oxford, UK*

"We need to think out of the box to provide sustainable solutions and this book exactly does so. Dr. Sümer asks a wise question: Shall we wait to use the money in pension funds until we retire or use it for our current needs, such as purchasing a house now? The answer calls for a much-needed shift in our thinking and in our models of finance. Dr. Sümer's sustainable financing models deserve to be carefully examined towards a fairer world for societies."

—Vedat Akgiray, *Professor of Finance, Boğaziçi University, Türkiye*

"An inspiring book that triggers many new ideas about sustainable home financing models structured on new paradigms. After reading the book, as a banker, I started to think about the new role of the banks in the new decentralized sharing economy. I'm sure all readers, from policymakers to bankers, will be excited and want to take action immediately."

— Hakan Aran, *CEO and Board Member, Türkiye İş Bankası*

"The Global Housing Crisis: A Sustainable New Home Financing Model" gives insightful, practical and statistically supported plans for governments to make house ownership an important National Policy Goal to increase the loyalty of the citizens leading to economic prosperity for the future generations. The author, Dr. Levent Sümer, elaborates in his book on the psychology of homeownership, dynamics of the mortgage financing industry, causes and consequences of past housing crises, lessons not learned from past mistakes, the outlook of the housing sector based on market data, statistics, and forecasts, past and ongoing housing policies, funding mechanisms and schemes, best practices, their pros, and cons. The book offers an excellent reference for strategic planning for a better future for many growing economies."

—Dr. Yahia AbdulRahman, *Founder and CEO of LARIBA—American Finance House and Riba Free Bank of Whittier, USA*

"Everything you wanted to know about housing, but you couldn't find in one place—now you can, thanks to Dr. Levent Sümer. Dr. Sümer's book "The Global Housing Crisis: A Sustainable New Home Financing Model" is one of those books that keeps you engaged from the start to the end with interesting facts and a richness of data with a global outlook on market dynamics, statistics, and forecasts, past and ongoing housing policies, funding mechanisms and schemes, best practices, their pros, and cons—all explained in a comprehensive way. Can we (governments, developers, banks, consumers)/and have we learned from past mistakes to avoid crises that affect housing or that are caused by housing? How to make sure housing is affordable for most of the population? Dr. Sümer proposes a Sustainable Home Financing Model that is worth reading and implementing."

—Doris Andoni, *Previous Director of Housing Policy in Albania, Housing Policy Expert*

Levent Sümer

The Global Housing Crisis

A Sustainable New Home Financing Model

palgrave
macmillan

Levent Sümer
Boğaziçi University
Istanbul, Türkiye

ISBN 978-3-031-72603-3 ISBN 978-3-031-72604-0 (eBook)
https://doi.org/10.1007/978-3-031-72604-0

This Palgrave Macmillan imprint is published by the registered company Springer Nature Switzerland AG
The registered company address is: Gewerbestrasse 11, 6330 Cham, Switzerland

I dedicate this book
***to my father*, *Hıdır Sümer*,**
who taught me to live my life by following my moral values and principles,
&
***to my mother*, *Sevgi Sümer*,**
who taught me love, mercy, and forgiveness

Foreword

Since the beginning of life, food and shelter have been the primary needs of humankind. Whether it is a one-bedroom apartment, single-family house, condominium, or luxury villa, a home is a need and dream for everyone. Despite the continual growth of the global economy, transformational advances in technology, new construction techniques, and the vast land size of the earth, it is still a big dilemma that 150 million people are homeless, and shelters for 1.6 billion people do not qualify as homes. By 2030, UN-Habitat estimates that 3 billion people, about 40% of the world's population, will need access to adequate housing.

The main reasons for this impasse are the increasing inequality in wealth and income, the debt-obsessed financial system, and policy-makers' untimely and wrong decisions. Monetary expansion policies, which inevitably result in high inflation, late decisions of central banks to tackle inflation, and political conflicts resulted in mass migrations and consequent interest rate increases, making it difficult to access finance, causing a housing affordability problem for billions of people. Obviously, the current bank-credit-dependent home financing systems are insufficient to break this deadlock in any sustainable way.

We need to think out of the box to provide sustainable solutions; this book exactly does so. Capital markets provide several useful tools such as real estate investment funds and trusts, real estate certificates, and many variants of these as sources of financing for residential development. However, the usefulness of all these models inherently depends on the overall monetary conditions in general and the level of interest rates in particular. It is totally irrational for a person who already has money in a pension fund not to be able to afford a house because of temporary unfavorable credit conditions. Dr. Sümer then asks a wise question: Shall we wait to use this money until we retire or use it for our current needs, such as purchasing a house now? The answer calls for a much-needed shift in our thinking and our finance models.

This book touches on every aspect of the housing industry, including the psychology and economic evaluation of homeownership, the reasons behind the past housing crises and their consequences, and the current housing financing models, policies, and schemes. It offers a new sustainable housing financing ecosystem using new digital technologies on yet untapped vast amounts of data. Dr. Sümer's sustainable financing models deserve to be carefully examined toward a fairer world for societies.

Prof. Vedat Akgiray
Boğaziçi University
Istanbul, Türkiye

Preface

When I published my first book last year, I was not planning to write this second book that soon, but the current situation of the global housing industry made me share my ideas faster. *The World Economy and Financial System* was a challenge against the current flawed capitalism-driven economic and financing system. The model I proposed in that book aimed to replace the erroneous system with a new sustainable approach structured on four pillars: ***developing, balancing, saving, and sharing***. The practical implications of the theoretical framework outlined were generally discussed in the first book, and different books were aimed to be published for each industry, including housing, finance, pension, and insurance.

As the second piece of the Book Series, I wrote this book during the peak of the current housing affordability crisis that most of the world's population is struggling with. The affordability-related indices and ratios, the total volume of the loans granted, the expensive cost of financing, the inadequate supply, the increasing number of homeless households, and decreasing homeownership rates are all signals of another global housing crisis.

Under the high inflationary period and high interest rates market conditions, financing became extremely difficult for homebuilders and homebuyers. The land is expensive, construction costs are high, and the wages are not satisfactory enough to afford a house. Due to increased prices, the renting or buying dilemma is not the case for millions of people, yet it is critical to understand the psychology of home purchasing.

The housing schemes and policies implemented in different countries are partially successful with all their criticized deficits, including the long duration needed to save enough money for down payments, the disintegration of the affordable houses built with the city work and social lives, bureaucracy of the application processes, and the dilemma for qualification requirement for subsidized houses. The strong relationship between politics and policies is also an important factor regarding the success or failure of such policies and schemes. In addition, political conflicts in many parts of the world are increasing global economic risks, which puts additional pressure on the housing industry.

Undeniably, bank loan-dependent housing financing does not provide a sustainable solution to the industry's boom-and-bust cyclical nature. We can clearly say that one of the primary reasons for this cycle is the flawed financing system structured on debt. Since the system creates financial crises due to its nature, the housing industry's problems also trigger an economic crisis, remembering the 2008 Global Financial Crisis. We are in a vicious circle or, in other words, walking on Penrose Stairs.

We have two choices: either continue with the same systems, sweep the problems under the rug, use temporary solutions, expand the issues, or think out of the box and create alternative, innovative, and sustainable systems.

In that context, this book chooses the second one and offers a new sustainable financing model structured on new paradigms. Before discussing the details of the financing model, on a broader scale, we need to start by planning the cities based on their potentials and capacities, developing sustainable cities, and initiating a reverse migration from metropolitan cities to small towns. Balancing the life standards of cities is crucial. Designing eco-villages where the comfort of cities is provided, but the spirit of the villages is not spoiled, is a serious option to consider. Living on smaller scales may decrease household consumption and increase savings. The increase in savings may shift the paradigm from a banking-oriented financing approach to a collective, participating, and sharing economic system where the people become the funder and the investor of the investment projects. The role of the banks in the financial system is redefined.

At this stage, we can shift the mindsets from a conventional loan-oriented housing financing system to a collective and cooperative approach. Pooling the savings of the household saved in different pension and saving accounts into a real estate investment fund and using this money for housing purposes may trigger a new housing investment and financing ecosystem. In that case, we may contribute to the price stability of the housing market, increase the affordability and homeownership rates, decrease the financing costs, and help more people live in better conditions.

In a digitalized world, no solution can be separated from digital technologies. The real estate industry shall also use digital platforms. Tokenization of the housing industry is the way that the navigation will eventually take us. The model proposed in this book also offers the tokenization of fund shares or real estate certificates.

This book covered many aspects of the housing industry, including the psychology of homeownership, dynamics of the industry, causes and consequences of past housing crises as well as lessons not learned from past mistakes, the outlook of the housing sector based on the market data, statistics and forecasts, the past and ongoing housing policies, funding mechanisms and schemes, the best practices, their pros and cons, and proposed a sustainable home financing models with different alternatives.

I hope the policymakers implement these ideas and the models proposed in this book and trigger better and more sustainable housing policies.

Istanbul, Türkiye

Dr. Levent Sümer
Founder, Chairman
SMR Strategy

Acknowledgments

I thought writing this second book would be faster and easier than the first one. I was wrong. Although rapidly developed technology is helping us in many aspects, perfectionism is the enemy of the good and slows us down. Providing a reference book for practitioners and academicians takes time, but it is definitely worth it. When you look back and feel the support you have, everything flows smoother and quicker.

This book is an outcome of the collaborative efforts of the writer and the publisher. I extend my profound thanks to Tula Weis, who fully supported me throughout the writing and publishing process. I also thank Supraja Yegnaraman and Kanchan Latambale for putting great work into publishing this book. I thank my brothers Mehmet and Gökmen and my friends, who have always supported me at each phase of my life.

My daughter, Rana, deserves special thanks for her patience. She always asked me why I was working too many hours while I was spending hours on the screen. Although she wanted to spend more time as she grew up, she acted very maturely and supportively.

The most special thanks go to my beloved wife, Nur, for always being there for me at every step of my life.

Contents

About the Author

Dr. Levent Sümer is a strategist, author, and scholar. He is the Chairman of SMR Strategy, an international investment and management consultancy company and teaches at Boğaziçi University in the Executive MBA and Construction Engineering and Management Masters Programs. Before establishing the SMR Strategy, Dr. Sumer worked for reputable real estate companies at C-level positions. Dr. Sumer is the co-founder and the Chairman of the International Project Management Institute (UPYE), founded in 2010 to extend project management knowledge in Türkiye. He is also a PMP certificate holder from PMI, Project Management Institute, and a professional member (MRICS) and assessor of the Royal Institution of Chartered Surveyors.

As a guest lecturer and a keynote speaker, he has also given lectures and speeches at many reputable organizations and written articles for newspapers and international journals. Dr. Sümer is also an investment committee member of various real estate and venture capital investment funds.

Dr. Levent Sümer graduated from Istanbul Technical University, Civil Engineering Department. He got his master's degree in Construction Engineering and Management from the Illinois Institute of Technology, and he holds a Ph.D. from Boğazici University with the interest-free financing model he developed for large investment projects by combining interest-free real estate capital market instruments with pension funds.

Dr. Sumer is the author of "The World Economy and Financial System: A Paradigm Change Offering a Sustainable Approach" book. His areas of interest and research include project management, real estate finance, Islamic funds, pension funds, sovereign wealth funds, and political economy. His studies mainly propose alternative sustainable economic and financial systems to replace flawed capitalism. Dr. Sümer is married and the father of a lovely daughter.

List of Figures

List of Tables

CHAPTER 1

From Lehman Brothers to Evergrande: Is Another Housing Crisis on its Way?

On September 15, 2008, Lehman Brothers, one of the largest investment banks in the United States (US) with USD 613 billion in debt, declared bankruptcy. Its failure was primarily caused and accelerated by the subprime mortgage crisis, which turned out to be the Global Financial Crisis (GFC) (Lioudis, 2023; Mamudi, 2008). The crisis significantly impacted the housing market, and within a short period, foreclosures and evictions started. In response, the stock market collapsed, large companies worldwide went bankrupt, unemployment rates increased rapidly, access to loans became difficult, and the global economy went into recession. 2008 GFC was considered the most significant financial crisis in history, initiated by a housing crisis (Kenton, 2022).

On August 17, 2023, Evergrande, a Chinese real estate giant that develops more than 1,300 real estate projects in more than 280 cities, struggled to pay off its USD 340 billion debt by the end of 2022 and filed for bankruptcy protection (Delouya, 2023). The company failed to pay its debts in 2021 despite its recovery efforts. The story did not end well for them, leading to serious real estate risks in China. Evergrande was founded in 1996, overgrew, and became the world's most valuable real estate company in 2018, but faced a dramatic collapse just three years later, in 2021. This downfall indicated the onset of a broader real estate crisis in China, impacting consumer confidence and investor's attitude. A USD 6.7 billion loss declared by another large real estate developer,

L. Sümer, *The Global Housing Crisis*,
https://doi.org/10.1007/978-3-031-72604-0_1

Country Garden, increased the country's real estate industry risks (The Guardian, 2023). The Chinese developer is facing a liquidation petition, and its shares in the stock market are in decline. The collapse of Evergrande and the situation of Country Garden is jeopardizing the future of the real estate industry in China.

Although the reasons behind the collapse of Lehman Brothers 15 years ago and the Evergrande debt case are different, their effects on the global housing market are critical to compare and observe closely. We witnessed a global financial crisis in 2008 following the subprime mortgage crisis, which we can define as the default of high-risk mortgages caused by the low-interest rates home loans provided to borrowers with poor credit scores where Lehman Brothers had underwritten the most amount of mortgage-backed securities accumulating a USD 85 billion portfolio which was four times of its shareholders' equity.

Let's remember what Ed Royce, who served in the US House of Representatives for 26 years and identified systemic risk in the housing finance system before the 2008 GFC, said about the crisis:

> Let us not forget, the financial crisis had its roots in the decision by Congress to embark on a course of social justice to get everyone that wanted a home into one, regardless of whether or not they could afford it. (Quote Fancy, 2024)

Now, we are also witnessing another risk of a new housing crisis caused mainly by high sales and rental prices, low affordability in the US and European housing markets, and additionally, defaults and losses of real estate giants of the Chinese real estate market, which is struggling with deflation and decreased demand.

Indeed, the global housing industry, in general, is experiencing tough days. According to a Goldman Sachs analysis, the state of the housing industry in 2023 is worse than in 2008, with a declining affordability rate (Lake, 2023). On October 10, 2023, the National Association of Home Builders, the Mortgage Bankers Association, and the National Association of Realtors asked the Federal Reserve (FED) to stop increasing interest rates as the housing industry suffers through rising housing costs and decreased supply of homes for sale (Cox, 2023).

Many citizens in the US lost their jobs during the Coronavirus disease (COVID-19) pandemic, and millions of US homeowners and renters have experienced difficulties in making mortgage and rental payments.

Congress and federal agencies placed a moratorium on foreclosures and residential evictions to assist homeowners in these challenging periods and suspended their mortgage payments. In addition, Congress granted USD 46.55 billion to help low-income renters and their landlords (Gao.gov, 2024). In 2021, nearly 22 million American households were troubled by the cost of housing. House prices have increased even faster than rents. In 2022, the average household in the US did not make enough money to qualify for a mortgage, and only about 15% of renters could afford to purchase the median-priced home (Statista, 2024a).

The increase in rental and sales prices and unaffordable housing due to the decreased household income compared to the sales and rental prices are also severe problems in the European Union (EU). The housing prices/average income ratio in the US and the United Kingdom (UK) is now higher than in the 2008 Global Financial Crisis. Homeownership rates are in decline, and the rate and the number of homeless people are on the rise globally. In that context, the risks of homelessness, financial insecurity, and inadequate housing supply are also increasing in Europe. Providing accessible housing for its population is a common difficulty, especially for Portugal, Türkiye, and even wealthy Luxembourg (Adhem, 2023).

On the other hand, in the third quarter of 2023, housing prices started declining for the first time since 2014 in 9 EU countries, including Germany, Denmark,, and Sweden, which had the sharpest decline over the quarter with 9.9%, 7.6%, and 6,8% respectively. In the other EU member states, house prices keep increasing. Croatia, Bulgaria, and Lithuania are the top three countries where the price rise is above or close to 10% (Katanich, 2023).

The situation in China is different but critical. From the 1990s onward, China's shining rise as an economic powerhouse has brought significant urbanization and changes in its housing market. As a result of migration to urban areas, cities were developed and expanded, and new towns were established. Infrastructure and real estate development were considered tools to trigger and drive economic growth, resulting in a surge in housing prices in cities like Beijing, Shanghai, and Shenzhen. Housing sales prices rose higher than incomes (Chen et al., 2022). By the 2010s, concerns of a housing bubble began to surface. The debt of giant real estate developers also put much pressure on the Chinese economy. Oversupply and incomplete constructions created ghost cities, increasing social problems within the country.

We can evaluate the current housing problems in China from a mortgage repayment perspective. The COVID-19 pandemic increased China's non-performing loan (NPL) rates (Kryzanowski et al., 2022). After its peak of 1.95% in July 2020, the NPL rates declined and were observed as 1.65% at the end of the third quarter of 2023 (Reuters, 2023). The country's construction crisis may lead to mortgage payment defaults and increase the NPL rates. The Chinese government intervened to stabilize the sector and eased the restrictions for first-time homebuyers, reduced down payment limits, and decreased the minimum mortgage rates.

Furthermore, purchasing unsold homes from troubled developers and converting them into affordable housing was also planned as a direct involvement of the government to resolve the problem (Globaltreasurer.com, 2023). Despite all the measures taken, the industry is still far from recovering, as the collapse of Evergrande is considered the consequence of a systemic problem in the Chinese housing sector rather than a single incident. The default of the company revealed that the financing strategy of the company, which uses the advance payments of homebuyers, is unsustainable. Too much borrowing, speculative investments, and a mismatch between supply and demand were considered the main reasons that triggered the crisis in China.

The collapse of banks in the 2008 GFC crisis and the default of Evergrande clearly show that the housing industry's financing is structured on slippery ground. The housing industry is highly dependent on the banking industry, and any ups or downs in interest rates deeply affect the housing market. If the interest rates are declining, home prices are increasing, and the rise in interest rates results in difficulties in accessing finance, affordability problems, and a decrease in sales (Sümer, 2023).

Political developments also have a profound impact on economies and financial markets. The continuing war between Russia and Ukraine resulted in rising energy prices and high inflation rates in many developed and developing countries. That was one of the main reasons for the increase in housing prices as the construction costs surged. The ongoing political conflict between Israel and Palestine, which recently turned out to be a disproportionate and unfair cruel attack on Palestinian civilians, increased the tension in the Middle East, opened the door for new conflicts that many countries may be involved in, and put additional risks to the global economy. During 2023, energy prices were volatile due to the instability of the political relations (Aecom, 2024). An upward trend in oil prices may impact the inflation remaining high longer.

Another major factor that affects the housing sector is the increasing number of refugees all around the world. According to the United Nations Refugee Agency (UNHCR, 2023), as of 2023, there are 117.3 million forcibly displaced people worldwide. The housing needs of these people also create additional housing, infrastructure, security, cultural integration, and socioeconomic problems for the host countries.

Going back to economic reasons, inflation and the interest rate spiral force many countries to balance their market conditions. Despite the monetary tightening policies of the Federal Reserve (FED), European Central Bank (ECB), and many other central banks, the potential increase in commodity and energy prices and the consumption trends of people may keep the inflation rates high longer than expected. Since the rising income level rates are slower than those inflation rates, the housing affordability problem becomes greater and heavier.

The UK housing market is one of the severely affected markets by the soaring inflation. Back in history, due to the financialization of the London economy, foreign investments in luxury properties, and shortage of supply, the UK market experienced property booms in the late 1970s, late 1980s, and most recently, from the early 2000s onwards (Mulheirn, 2019; Samuel, 2024). Indeed, the wording that defines the problems of the UK housing market as a "housing crisis" is not new. Heslop and Ormerod (2020) criticize UK housing policies and explain the crisis due to supply constraints and policymakers' overregulation.

Several crashes were also observed in the UK housing market in the early 1990s and during the 2008 financial crisis. Then, the prices went up, and the UK housing price index hit 154 in November 2022, with a 54% increase compared to 2015 due to easy access to financing with low rates and some tax incentives applied. While the two-year fixed mortgage rate was 1.2% in September 2021, this rate rapidly increased to over 5% in September 2023. As a result, the growth rate of housing prices slowed down in 2022 and turned negative in 2023. In December 2023, house prices declined by 1.4% percent (Statista, 2024a). Today, London covers 23% of the total value of the UK's housing stock, exceeding GBP 7.5 trillion in 2020 (Dianati, 2022). Affordability problem, inadequate supply mostly relied on private sector developments, focusing on developing units for sale but not for rent, the decline in social renting, the upward impact of foreign investments in property prices, money expansion policies, developing houses without focusing on housing need but as a response to money supply, and the potential implications of Brexit on the housing market are the main challenges of the UK housing market (Gallent, 2019; Watt & Minton, 2016).

Australia is also struggling with housing problems due to the supply shortage caused by underinvestment. The number of social housing constructions has also declined over the years. This shortage makes it difficult for Australians to buy houses or rent (Aihw.gov, 2024). This issue is not new, as Mitchell (2017) pointed out the affordability problem in 2017, and Dufty-Jones (2018) underlined that numerous housing crises have occurred throughout Australia's housing history. Housing supply has been a persistent political concern ever since white settlers arrived in the country. Viforj (2024) also points out that despite the impacts of post-COVID factors, including the preference for more space, the return of international migrants, and increasing interest rates, the affordability crisis has been a chronic problem for decades due to the failure of government policies that could not provide affordable shelters for low-to-moderate income Australians.

In 2022, the average housing supply in the Organization for Economic Cooperation and Development (OECD) countries was 468 per 1,000 inhabitants. This level was 517 for EU countries but only 420 per 1,000 people in Australia (OECD, 2024). The vacancy rates in the market are also below 1.5%, which is far lower than the stable market equilibrium, commonly accepted as 3%. The housing supply shortage impacted the rise of housing prices, and affordability declined. In Australia, within the last 22 years, the price-to-income ratio rose from 4.9 to 8.6, and while it was taking less than seven years to save a 20% down payment, this duration went up to 11.4 years in 2024 (Hutchens, 2024). It is estimated that the affordability problem will worsen further over the next six years, and it is essential to change the housing system in Australia (Karp, 2024).

Brazil, the largest economy in South America, has also been experiencing housing problems. During the 2000s, strong growth was supported by high commodity prices, growing domestic consumption, and foreign investment. The 2014 FIFA World Cup and 2016 Olympics, organized by international sports bodies, positively impacted infrastructure and real estate development, increasing property prices, especially in major cities such as São Paulo and Rio de Janeiro (Samuel, 2024). Factors such as urbanization trends, availability of financing, and the expansion of Brazil's middle class were critical drivers of the real estate boom. Additionally, construction activities were boosted by affordable housing programs like "Minha Casa, Minha Vida" (My House, My Life).

Presently, the housing situation is critical, with almost 6 million homes needed as approximately 25 million families live in inadequate housing conditions in Brazil. In urban areas, 35 million people and 39% of the rural population do not have access to drinking water, and 100 million people are not connected to sewage systems (UN-Habitat, 2024).

On the contrary, 11 million units are vacant, and 600,000 of them are in São Paulo alone. In addition to the Minha Casa and Minha Vida programs, other government programs aim to support municipalities and states in taking the required steps to access housing. (Synergia, 2023).

The housing market in African countries also faces challenges. While South Africa struggles with affordability problems despite its efforts on low-income housing initiatives for disadvantaged groups, Nigeria, Kenya, and Ethiopia, which are experiencing high urbanization, lack adequate infrastructure and housing to meet the skyrocketing demand for residential properties. Income inequality is a problem on the continent, yet the middle classes of Ghana, Nigeria, and Kenya seek modern housing and amenities, which drive demand for new residential developments. Political instability is also a significant threat to a stable economy, which is needed for sustainable housing market development.

The Turkish housing market is also suffering from the untimely interest rate decisions of the Central Bank of Türkiye (CBRT). During the periods when inflation rates were climbing rapidly, the CBRT decided to decrease interest rates. This decision resulted in a rapid devaluation of the Turkish Lira against many currencies, the inflation rates and the construction costs skyrocketed, and the housing prices surged. Türkiye became the country where the housing sales and rental prices increased the most in Europe. Although the rental price was legally limited to 25% yearly (which also caused social problems and many conflicts between the tenants and landlords), renting a house in metropolitan cities like Istanbul became almost impossible.

Similarly, rent caps were used in Dublin, Ireland, in 2016 alongside private rental subsidies. Limiting rental prices was a temporary solution that hindered supply growth (Lima, 2018). Türkiye also experienced a devastating earthquake in February 2023, which affected 11 cities and more than 15 million people in Türkiye, resulting in more than 50,000 deaths. The dynamics of the housing industry were severely impacted. The housing prices in Türkiye are still increasing, but they have lost their ability to hedge the monthly inflation rates.

The policy of CBRT was reversed in the second half of 2023, and the interest rates rose to 50% to their current level. The rise in interest rates cooled the market, and the speed of the price increases slowed, but the high level of the prices reached and access to finance due to high interest rates deepened the affordability problem in Türkiye.

Indeed, according to the research conducted by Coupe (2021), the global housing affordability problem is not new. The results of his analysis, which covered 500,000 respondents from over 140 countries, exhibited a standard idea about the existence of the housing affordability problem. The situation got worse during and after the COVID-19 pandemic, and thus, there is an urgent need for alternative home financing models to overcome the problem. While the widely used mortgage system works well in low-interest environments under stable economies, financing through bank loans creates significant problems when the economies are not in good shape and when the income levels are unstable. Considering the more frequent and heavier financial crises and the Global Financial Crisis (GFC) initiated by the mortgage crisis, bank loan-dependent home financing models are no longer sustainable.

Besides the GFC, several historical housing crises triggered a financial crisis or were affected by an ongoing economic crisis. For instance, the Panic of 1837 was caused by the speculative lending standards, the real estate bubble, and a decrease in cotton prices. Suspended payments and loans turned into seven years of recession, resulting in the bankruptcies of thousands of firms and high unemployment rates (Stevens, 2024).

In 1929, with the onset of the Great Depression, caused by overconsumption, the speculative boom in the 1920s, the stock market crash in 1929, oversupply, and overproduction problems, the housing industry was affected destructively (Sümer, 2023). Before the 1929 Great Depression, housing prices reached their highest level in the third quarter of 1929 but declined by 67% until the end of 1932 (Nicholas & Scherbina, 2013). Many homeowners could not pay their mortgages, foreclosures started, and inner-city slums were increased. 273,000 people lost their homes in 1932, and thousands of mortgages went into foreclosure the following year daily. Around 50% of all home mortgages in the US defaulted in the same year.

After a stable period in the post-World War II era, due to the high inflation of the 1970s, the cost of building new houses almost doubled in the second half of the twentieth century. Home prices kept increasing over the next 20 years, and the size of mortgage loans also increased.

With the rise in interest rates during the savings and loan crisis, new home constructions slowed down, and housing prices were flat until the end of 1997. Between 1997 and 2003, housing prices went up in the US and the rest of the world, and the rate of mortgage fraud rose steeply. However, the mortgage denial rate decreased during this period (Stevens, 2024). Then, as we all know, the world experienced the global financial crisis.

After the GFC, many economists suggested decreasing debts and relaxing the pressure on the banking sector urgently in order not to face further crises. Unfortunately, from 2008 to 2024, parallel to the global debt, which rose from USD 175 trillion to more than USD 300 trillion within 16 years, the total outstanding mortgage loans in the US rose from USD 14 trillion to USD 20 trillion. The case in Europe is not different. The UK, Germany, and France carry Euro 1.9 trillion, Euro 1.8 trillion, and Euro 1.3 trillion outstanding mortgage loans as of the second quarter of 2023 (Statista, 2024b).

A potential default in the repayment of mortgages may trigger another crisis in the housing industry, which is currently struggling with an affordability problem mainly due to an imbalance between the rise in wages and the increase in housing prices. The income and welfare of people melted down against inflation thanks to the monetary policies of central banks. For instance, in London, housing prices are 13 times higher than earnings (Rees, 2024). The lack of supply and the rise in construction costs due to inflation rates are important factors that increased housing prices and widened the gap. Construction costs rose by around 23% in the European Union, which continued in 2022 at 11.9%. Türkiye was listed as the country with the highest construction cost increase in Europe in 2022, at 99.6% (Eurostat, 2023).

Tax incentive programs, launching low-interest rates for affordable housing developments, free or cheaper land allocations, and grant programs are used in different countries, including the US, Canada, the UK, Australia, France, Germany, Türkiye, and Luxembourg. The US Government National Mortgage Association (Ginnie Mae), the Federal National Mortgage Association (Fannie Mae), the Federal Home Loan Mortgage Corporation (Freddie Mac), German Bausparkassen, Malaysian Cagamas Berhad, Singapore Central Provident Fund, China and the Philippines social housing financing initiatives (Pag-IBIG Fund), the Netherlands Central Housing Fund and the social housing guarantee fund, Mexico National Workers' Housing Fund Institute (Infonavit), cooperative housing finance schemes of Uruguay and Sweden, Brazilian

Minha Casa, Minha Vida" (My House, My Life) affordable housing program, Turkish Housing Development Administration (TOKİ) initiatives, Turkish Myhome-Evim models are some of the home financing institutions, entities, funds or programs that are actively used in different countries. These programs were sometimes successful but are criticized from various aspects, such as the type of houses developed, the legal framework, the risks taken during construction.

Housing cooperatives, lease-purchase programs, co-ownership, and public–private partnership (PPP) models are alternatives to bank loan home financing models. Depending on the conditions, these programs or entities are sometimes partially successful but do not provide long-term permanent solutions. Sometimes, a policy implemented in a country has a successful outcome, but the same model copied and used in another country does not result in the same success story. It is a fact that there is no single model that fits every country. Still, the primary approach to overcoming general problems is changing mindsets and replacing traditional policies that have been tried many times but have not yielded concrete results with sustainable, innovative techniques.

The new *sustainable approach* shall be structured on *new paradigms* in that context. First, we must stop insisting on the capitalism-driven bank loan financing models and shift to a partnership-based approach. Last year, in my previous book, I proposed a new and sustainable economic and financial system based on four pillars: *developing, balancing, saving, and sharing*. This new approach is aimed at being applied in many different sectors, including the housing industry, which is currently struggling with high affordability, financing, and debt problems. In this book, I focused on implementing the model in the housing industry to contribute to resolving the never-ending global housing affordability problem.

The first step shall be using people's money to match their needs. Under the regulations of capital market boards, establishing a real estate investment fund (REIF) that both the real estate developers and the homebuyers become fund participants, linking it with pension funds by directing the savings of the people who are willing to use their savings to purchase their houses to the real estate investments funds, creating a co-ownership mechanism between the homebuyers and the real estate developers, and implementing a diminishing partnership mechanism within the REIF may provide a sustainable solution both from financing of the construction and the home purchase perspectives.

Several alternatives or derivatives can be developed by following the main principles on which the model is structured. For instance, a real estate investment fund can be linked with a real estate investment trust (REIT) , and they can invest in each other. This approach may help REITs find funds to invest in more projects.

Another option can be a combination of real estate certificates with real estate investment funds. A real estate certificate is an innovative instrument that enables homebuyers to purchase their houses by investing in the houses in square meters and accumulating the certificates until the completion of the construction. This may give the developers finance the construction and help the homebuyers purchase their houses gradually without a bank loan. Linking the real estate certificates with real estate investment funds may also include institutional investors involved in the funding process and increase the fund's volume, which may help finance more units.

Crowdfunding is another source of financing that may help the homebuyers and the constructors meet in a platform to finance the purchase of land and the construction cost. Suppose a real estate investment fund or a housing crowdfunding platform is used as a tool that enables land and construction financing. In that case, it may help decrease sales prices, increase affordability, and help homebuyers purchase their houses faster without a bank loan. Land certificates that enable investors to invest in large amounts of land with small portions and timeshares used for co-ownership of properties with the right of use in a predetermined period may also be integrated into the model.

Technological developments are changing many industries. While developing new models, digitalization is a must. A model without a digital wing does not provide a long-term solution and is a strong candidate for failure. A digital platform is an essential tool to match all the stakeholders of the housing industry. Homebuyers, developers, portfolio management companies, regulators, valuation companies, financial institutions, and other investors need to have access to data online and need to make transactions easily. In that context, tokenization of the model under a reliable platform and regulated by laws may enhance the model's success and make the whole process more liquid.

The global economic and political conditions are signaling a new housing crisis. Although another secondary mortgage crisis is not considered a high probability risk due to the regulated borrowing market, the high inflation rates alongside high interest rates, difficulties in accessing finance, and loss of purchasing powers due to insufficient rise in wages may prolong the affordability crisis in the west side of the world. On the other hand, the high debt, unfinished construction projects, and decrease in demand raise the risk from the east side. The disrupted supply and demand balance due to the decline in new housing construction and the increasing refugee impact on this balance, especially from a rental market perspective, enhance the risks of the global housing industry. The south side, mainly Africa and Southeast Asia, is struggling with poverty, income inequality, and homelessness. Providing alternative housing financing solutions is essential.

This book provides insight into the sector's current situation by analyzing the facts and figures of the global housing market. It also deeps into the causes and results of the past housing crisis and bubbles, lessons (not) learned, mistakes repeated, and the best practices and successful policies used globally. As a case study, the affordability problem in Türkiye, which is the 10th least affordable country in the world, with the highest housing sales and rental prices alongside the highest inflation and interest rates in Europe, is also analyzed in the book. The psychology of homeownership is also examined, and the buy or rent decision is discussed from homebuyers' level of income, financial literacy, social and economic conditions perspectives.

By introducing an alternative sustainable home financing model, this book also provides recommendations to policymakers with the hope of being implemented.

References

Adhem, J. (2023). *Europe's housing crisis: Portugal, Turkey, and Luxembourg struggle to find solutions*. https://www.euronews.com/business/2023/10/07/europes-housing-crisis-portugal-turkey-and-luxembourg-struggle-to-find-solutions. Last Accessed on July 21, 2024.

Aecom.com. (2024). *Middle East property & construction handbook*. https://publications.aecom.com/MEH/static/69a84a66cc94f48d41d456bfc959f519/4714f9cc02b32c869d15d7378fcb142e.pdf. Last Accessed on July 21, 2024.

Aihw.gov. (2024). *Housing assistance in Australia 2024*. https://www.aihw.gov.au/reports/housing-assistance/housing-assistance-in-australia/contents/social-housing-dwellings. Last Accessed on July 21, 2024.

Chen, J., Chen, Y., Hill, R. J., & Hu, P. (2022). The user cost of housing and the price-rent ratio in Shanghai. *Regional Science and Urban Economics, 92*, 103738. https://doi.org/10.1016/j.regsciurbeco.2021.103738

Coupe, T. (2021). How global is the affordable housing crisis? *International Journal of Housing Markets and Analysis, 14*(3), 429–445.

Cox, J. (2023). *Housing industry urges powell to stop raising interest rates or risk an economic hard landing*. https://www.cnbc.com/2023/10/10/housing-industry-urges-powell-and-fed-to-stop-raising-interest-rates.html. Last Accessed on July 21, 2024.

Delouya, S. (2023). *China's evergrande files for bankruptcy*. https://edition.cnn.com/2023/08/17/business/evergrande-files-for-bankruptcy/index.html. Last Accessed on July 21, 2024.

Dianati, K. (2022). *London's housing crisis—A system dynamics analysis of long-term developments: 40 years into the past and 40 years into the future*. PhD Thesis. University College London, UK.

Dufty-Jones, R. (2018). A historical geography of housing crisis in Australia. *Australian Geographer, 49*(1), 5–23. https://doi.org/10.1080/00049182.2017.1336968

Eurostat.com. (2023). *Construction producer price and construction cost indices overview*. https://ec.europa.eu/eurostat/statistics-explained/index.php?title=Construction_producer_price_and_construction_cost_indices_overview. Last Accessed on July 21, 2024.

Gallent, N. (2019). *Local pathways to crisis*. https://discovery.ucl.ac.uk/10093993/1/Gallent_4.%20Local%20Pathways%20to%20Crisis%20v4%20FINAL.pdf. Last Accessed on July 21, 2024.

Gao.gov. (2024). *Affordable housing*. https://www.gao.gov/affordable-housing. Last Accessed on July 21, 2024.

Globaltreasurer.com. (2023). *A Deeper dive into China's housing sector crisis*. https://www.theglobaltreasurer.com/2024/05/23/a-deeper-dive-into-chinas-housing-secto-crisis/. Last Accessed on July 21, 2024.

Heslop, J., & Ormerod, E. (2020). The politics of crisis: Deconstructing the dominant narratives of the housing crisis. *Antipode, 52*(1), 145–163.

Hutchens, G. (2024). *Australia's housing crisis in 10 graphs, from the federal budget*. https://www.abc.net.au/news/2024-05-15/federal-budget-housing-crisis-in-10-graphs/103847336. Last Accessed on July 21, 2024.

Karp, P. (2024). *Australia's housing crisis to worsen with 'significant shortfall in supply', labor's expert council says*. https://www.theguardian.com/australia-news/article/2024/may/03/australias-housing-crisis-to-worsen-with-significant-shortfall-in-supply-labors-expert-council-says. Last Accessed on July 21, 2024.

Katanich, D. (2023). *European house prices drop for the first time in almost a decade*. https://www.euronews.com/business/2023/10/03/european-house-prices-drop-for-the-first-time-in-almost-a-decade. Last Accessed on July 21, 2024.

Kenton, W. (2022). *Lehman brothers: History, collapse, role in the great recession.* https://www.investopedia.com/terms/l/lehman-brothers.asp. Last Accessed on July 21, 2024.

Kryzanowski, L., Liu, J., & Zhang, J. (2022). Effect of COVID-19 on non-performing loans in China. *Finance Research Letters, 52*(103372). https://doi.org/10.1016/j.frl.2022.103372.

Lake, S. (2023). *Goldman is back with a 16-years-later look at the housing market crash of 2008—And finds affordability is even worse right now.* https://fortune.com/2023/10/11/goldman-sachs-housing-crash-affordability-2008/. Last Accessed on July 21, 2024.

Lima, V. (2018). Delivering social housing: An overview of the housing crisis in Dublin. *Critical Housing Analysis, 5*(1), 1–11.

Lioudis, M. (2023). *The collapse of lehman brothers: A case study.* https://www.investopedia.com/articles/economics/09/lehman-brothers-collapse.asp. Last Accessed on July 21, 2024.

Mamudi, S. (2008). *Lehman folds with record $613 billion debt.* https://www.marketwatch.com/story/lehman-folds-with-record-613-billion-debt. Last Accessed on July 21, 2024.

Mitchell, H. (2017). *Australia must face some home truths about housing affordability.* https://www.smh.com.au/business/the-economy/australia-must-face-some-home-truths-about-housing-affordability-20170223-gujpy1.html. Last Accessed on July 21, 2024.

Mulheirn, I. (2019). *Tackling the UK housing crisis: Is supply the answer?* https://housingevidence.ac.uk/publications/tackling-the-uk-housing-crisis-is-supply-the-answer/. Last Accessed on July 21, 2024.

Nicholas, T., & Scherbina, A. (2013). Real estate prices during the roaring twenties and the great depression. *Real Estate Economics, 41*(2), 278–309.

OECD.com. (2024). *Housing stock and construction.* https://www.oecd.org/content/dam/oecd/en/data/datasets/affordable-housing-database/hm1-1-housing-stock-and-construction.pdf. Last Accessed on July 21, 2024.

Quotefancy.com. (2024). *Top 10 Ed Royce quotes.* https://quotefancy.com/ed-royce-quotes. Last Accessed on July 21, 2024.

Rees, T. (2024). *London's sky-high home prices are most affordable in decade.* https://www.bloomberg.com/news/articles/2024-01-29/london-s-homes-haven-t-been-this-affordable-in-a-decade. Last Accessed on July 21, 2024.

Reuters.com. (2023). *Chinese banking sector's npl ratio at 1.65% at end of Q3.* https://www.reuters.com/world/china/chinese-banking-sectors-npl-ratio-165-end-q3-2023-10-20/. Last Accessed on July 21, 2024.

Samuel, N. (2024). *The complete history of housing bubbles around the world.* https://pictureperfectportfolios.com/the-complete-history-of-housing-bubbles-around-the-world/. Last Accessed on July 21, 2024.

Statista.com. (2024a). *U.S. affordable housing—Statistics & facts*. https://www.statista.com/topics/5081/affordable-housing-in-the-us/. Last Accessed on July 21, 2024.

Statista.com. (2024b). *Mortgages in Europe—Statistics & facts*. https://www.statista.com/topics/3926/mortgages-in-europe/. Last Accessed on July 21, 2024.

Stevens, R. (2024). *History of housing market crashes in the US*. https://newsilver.com/the-lender/history-of-housing-market-crashes/. Last Accessed on July 21, 2024.

Sümer, L. (2023*). The world economy and financial system: A paradigm change offering a sustainable approach*. Palgrave Macmillan.https://doi.org/10.1007/978-3-031-27530-2

Synergiaconsultoria.com. (2023). *Housing deficit: Even with growth in the number of households, the population still does not have access to decent housing*. https://www.synergiaconsultoria.com.br/en/fique-por-dentro/access-to-housing/. Last Accessed on July 21, 2024.

The Guardian.com. (2023). *Chinese developer country garden reports $6.7bn loss amid fears of another evergrande*. https://www.theguardian.com/world/2023/aug/31/country-garden-chinese-property-developer-reports-half-year-finanical-loss-fears-default-risk. Last Accessed on July 21, 2024.

UN-Habitat.org. (2024). *Scaling-up affordable housing supply in Brazil*. https://unhabitat.org/scaling-up-affordable-housing-supply. Last Accessed on July 21, 2024.

UNHCR.com. (2023). *Refugee data finder*. https://www.unhcr.org/refugee-statistics/. Last Accessed on July 21, 2024.

ViforJ, R. O. (2024). *Our housing system is broken and the poorest australians are being hardest hit*. https://theconversation.com/our-housing-system-is-broken-and-the-poorest-australians-are-being-hardest-hit-228511. Last Accessed on July 21, 2024.

Watt, P., & Minton, A. (2016). London's housing crisis and its activisms. *City, 20*(2), 204–221. https://doi.org/10.1080/13604813.2016.1151707

CHAPTER 2

The Psychology of Homeownership: Does Owning a House Really Matter?

Is purchasing a house an investment? Or is it just where you hang your jacket, relax, and feel safe rather than risking your savings? Knowing that homes are not very liquid investment instruments, especially in the periods you urgently need to sell, buying a house can be a long-term investment if you feel the sales price is reasonable, the financing cost is optimum, and in addition to a monthly rental income you aim a capital gain on the long run. Home is also an assurance for retirement periods where you do not want to feel the stress of being a lessee as your regular income diminishes.

On the other hand, a residential property investment may not be reasonable as it could be costly during high inflationary periods when the prices skyrocket, and the cost of borrowing is high due to the rise in interest rates. Renting the house you purchased to a family or an individual may also be considered an investment that brings additional monthly income. However, considering the long payback periods, dealing with lessees, being responsible for insurance and maintenance costs, and paying the mortgage for many years may decrease the appetite for home investment. Having said that, deciding to buy or rent a house is a dilemma for many people, and owning a home is always considered a dream for almost everyone.

Homeownership is anticipated as a wealth creation tool, providing security and residential stability, enabling people to live in better physical

L. Sümer, *The Global Housing Crisis*,
https://doi.org/10.1007/978-3-031-72604-0_2

and social quality neighborhoods, and providing better-quality housing for a feeling of social status and achievement. On the other hand, owning a house may restrict mobility, cause load stress for mortgage payments and foreclosures, and increase the cost of maintenance and repair (Rohe & Lindblad, 2013).

Homeownership is traditionally and primarily defined as fulfilling people's safety needs by providing shelter. This definition corresponds to the second level of Maslow's (1954) Hierarchy Pyramid, which consists of 5 layers: psychological, safety, social, esteem, and self-actualization. However, homeownership also responds to people's social needs by creating a space for families and friends to socialize. Through homeownership, esteem needs are also fulfilled by giving individuals a sense of financial achievement (Hew et al., 2020). Homeownership indicates independence and economic stability, an important milestone in many people's lives. After owning their houses, many individuals or families start a new chapter. Although it is a dream for Americans and citizens of many other nations, the road to becoming a homeowner is a thorny garden full of challenges, obstacles, and uncertainties.

Home buying is a personal journey with emotions, goals, and memories. Compared to renters, who might not have as strong of an interest because they are more temporary residents, homeowners are more likely to be involved in community concerns and encourage civic engagement. Homeownership, which enables people to be more responsible for their living environment, is considered a commitment that strengthens families, fosters love, enhances good citizenship, and increases communication, social interaction with neighbors, and the sense of belonging in a community (Blum & Kingston, 1984). Owning a home may make individuals physically and psychologically healthier, build a more robust family unit, increase life satisfaction, self-esteem, and happiness, and enhance control over their lives.

Considering the relationship between the landlords and the lessees, especially in countries where the rental market is not well-regulated and landlords are not professional property management companies but primarily individuals, dealing with sudden rent increases and demands of property owners brings a psychological load on the shoulders of the lessees. Thus, being a homeowner in that context provides psychological relief for renters in terms of feeling comfortable now and then, even after retiring without fearing sudden eviction due to rent hikes or lease termination, declaring the freedom of using the property as wished to, decorating it as liked and make it *feel like home*. The comfort of owning their own space increases the homeowners' happiness and self-esteem and reduces stress. Indeed, *a home is a place of peace and tranquility for people*, and people feel this peace more when they become homeowners.

The sense of identification, belonging, security, and stability are critical emotional factors when considering purchasing a house. Yet, deciding on buying a home, one of the most expensive financial decisions, is not easy, as it adds a heavy economic burden on potential homebuyers. Besides the house's sales price, potential homebuyers should also consider the property taxes, insurance, maintenance costs, and income tax if the property is rented to others. Hence, while homeownership brings psychological relief, it also requires a sustainable income that will not jeopardize the monthly payments of the mortgage loans.

Homeownership also limits the mobility of people. One of the most critical determinants of selecting the house's location is where people earn their income. Climate, neighborhood, and religious groups may also be important factors but not as significant as the location of employment (Blank & Winnick, 1953).

A house is not a liquid asset that can be readily cashed as stocks and bonds, so it is not a simple issue to sell a unit and purchase a new one very frequently. Sudden decisions on this issue may result in selling the property below its value, which may cause a financial loss for the homeowners.

On the other hand, the financial aspects of homeownership can greatly influence mental well-being. Monthly payments secured for home buying do not necessarily need to be a loan, but a monthly installment paid based on the monthly income may regulate the cash flow of the homebuyers. Furthermore, although buying a house to live in is not considered an investment since a home is a primary necessity for people to protect themselves, in the long run, the rise in housing prices due to inflation and market trends may help homeowners make a return over this price increase in the case they sell the property. Even though they do not sell, such an increase may mentally relieve the homebuyers in terms of future financial stability. Owning an asset whose value increases over time may bring a sense of security and comfort.

Beyond the economic benefits, every payment fosters emotions of accomplishment and progressivity in both people and families by helping to reduce debt and increase personal assets. In that sense, secured housing situations help improve all households' mental health. Homeownership

Fig. 2.1 The psychology of homeownership (By Author)

also positively impacts the academic performance of children who grow up in their own homes as they are not disrupted due to moves during the mid-school periods.

Moreover, young adults' capacity to imagine a cohesive future is linked to having secure housing. A fulfilling life is primarily associated with owning a home (Kubala & Samec, 2021). The factors that impact the decision to buy a home are shown in Fig. 2.1.

Homeownership and Satisfaction

The relationship between homeownership and satisfaction is interesting. For instance, renters' standpoints on housing satisfaction change after becoming homeowners, and they experience different benefits from the same housing context (Diaz-Serrano, 2009). Even though homeownership positively impacts well-being and increases life satisfaction of low-income groups, as Rohe and Basolo (1997) point out, the high financial cost of homeownership may result in negative life satisfaction (Zumbro, 2011). In addition to the house needing to be paid for many years, maintenance costs decrease satisfaction over time. In that context, the affordability stress also diminishes the impact of homeownership on life satisfaction (Park & Kim, 2022). Housing-related life satisfaction is also linked with the characteristics of the individuals, the housing unit itself (architecture, decoration, materials used, location, etc.), and the neighborhood. People are also more satisfied when living in new units (Galster, 1987; Rohe & Stewart, 1996).

Homeownership and Self-esteem

Self-esteem is the individuals' perception or judgment of their worthiness (Coopersmith, 1967). It is also their opinion and beliefs about their abilities, achievements, and limitations. Thus, in the US, homeownership brings a higher social status increasing self-esteem. Homeownership also triggers self-esteem as people think that being able to afford a house makes them do better than the renters. Achieving the purchase of a home is also a sign of increased self-esteem, as its definition points out the individuals' self-assessment (Rohe et al., 2007).

Homeownership and Happiness

The relationship between homeownership and happiness is also worth discussing. Homeownership raises the level of joy for low-income families since these families are concerned about their rental costs, especially during their retirement years when their income decreases. The result is not the same for high-income people in Switzerland, and people who own their houses are not happier than those who do not own their units (Hofmann & Umbricht, 2019). On the other hand, the study of Ruprah (2010) over seventeen Latin American countries revealed a positive link between homeownership and happiness. Another study conducted in 2011 in Ohio homeowners exhibited that homeowners weren't any happier than renters as they had less time to spend on leisure activities. The disintegration of homeownership and happiness in China was also exhibited by Fong et al. (2021). In Germany, where the rate of homeownership is the second lowest after Switzerland in Europe, the result of 16 years of observation concluded a diminishing satisfaction after the first five years of owning a new home, and the participants did not feel happier due to homeownership (Stieg, 2020). Owning a home may make the owners feel more comfortable and less anxious, but the main thing that brings happiness in a house is not the title deed you have but what memories and experiences you accumulate in that house. The neighborhood, the climate, the design, and the decoration of the house also come behind the memories that make the dwellers of that house happy. Then, the house turns into a home where the people find peace.

The Reasons for Buying a House

People have different reasons when deciding whether to purchase a house or replace the existing home with a new one. The most essential factor about buying a house is getting rid of being a lessee. Living in a rented place undoubtedly limits the abilities of the lessees, and people want freedom.

The aim of living in a more comfortable house, a will to change the neighborhood due to safety or any other reason such as the change of income level, structural security concerns, especially in earthquake regions, threats of climate change such as floods and hurricanes, the need for a more prominent place due to the increased population of the family or vice versa, relocation due to job change, providing better social amenities for kids, enforcement of family-related responsibilities, the rent cost, the sales price of the house, security concerns, tax benefits, and investment purposes are essential factors for the decision of buying or replacing a house.

How to Finance a House?

Despite everybody wanting to live in their own house without thinking about the stress of the monthly rent, it isn't easy to afford it with their financial power. In the US, a first-time buyer's average down payment on a house is 8%. While a larger down payment may decrease the cost of borrowing due to lower interest rates applied, a high amount of initial payments may also risk the homebuyers' cash flow since it consumes all the emergency funds. For a home valued at USD 400,000, individuals must pay 32,000 USD, which is not easy to save quickly (Goff, 2024).

Thus, people seek sources to make the down payment while considering applying for a mortgage loan. As exhibited in Table 2.1, savings proceeds from the sale of a primary residence, a gift from a relative or friend, and cashing other investments such as stocks and bonds are the most preferred sources of the down payment for potential homebuyers. Older people use fewer savings, but since they already own a house, they use the income from the first house to buy a new one, which means replacement is more common for upper-age groups. Pension funds and individual retirement accounts are other down payment sources for purchasing a house (Sandhu, 2024).

Traditionally, after making the down payment, people use mortgage loans to pay the remaining sales price. When the interest rates are low, and the prices are more predictable, conventional financing methods work and people can afford to repay their mortgages by using some portion of (ideally around 30%) their monthly incomes. Still, life is not straightforward, and the conditions are unstable. Especially in the last century, the global economy faced many repetitive recessions and crises that impacted people's lives badly.

Dire economic conditions result in the loss of jobs and income decrease, and homebuyers, mostly mortgage loan holders, feel anxious about paying their installments. The exciting, emotional journey of home buying turns into complete dissatisfaction and sadness. For instance, in 2008, during the global financial crisis, millions of houses went into foreclosure, which disrupted lives and families and had a profoundly negative impact on the physical, emotional, and mental health of people. While some of them were able to recover, many others could not stand up, and even some of them went to death.

The study of Chang et al. (2013) exhibited 4,900 excess suicides in 2009 compared with the forecast based on the previous 8-year trends. Another study conducted in the US also revealed that the number of suicides due to evictions or foreclosures doubled between 2005 and 2010, where 79% of suicides occurred before the actual housing loss, and 37% of them experienced eviction or foreclosure within two weeks of the suicide

Table 2.1 Sources of Down Payment for Purchasing a House (National Association of Realtors [by Sandhu, 2024])

Age groups/ Sources of down payment	*All buyers (%)*	*24 to 32 (%)*	*33 to 42 (%)*	*43 to 57 (%)*	*58 to 67 (%)*	*68 to 76 (%)*	*77 to 97 (%)*
Savings	47	64	57	49	38	41	28
Proceeds from the sale of the primary residence	38	22	29	33	46	54	61
Gift from a relative or friend	7	19	12	7	2	1	2
Sale of stocks or bonds	7	9	7	5	7	10	6
401 k/pension fund, including a loan	5	4	6	5	7	2	0
Inheritance	4	4	5	3	4	3	1
Tax Refund	3	6	6	2	1	0	0
Proceeds from the sale of real estate other than primary residence	3	1	2	1	4	6	1
Individual retirement account (IRA)	3	2	2	1	5	3	1
Equity from the primary residence buyer continues to own	2	1	1	3	1	4	4
Loan from a relative or friend	2	3	4	1	1	0	1
Loan from financial assistance from sources other than employer	1	2	2	1	1	0	0
Loan from a financial institution other than a mortgage	0	1	3	0	1	7	2
Other	3	0	0	0	0	0	0

(Fowler et al., 2015). In addition, low-income adults in the US experienced a reduced risk of depression when they had family savings and owned a home (Ettman et al., 2021).

Thus, a house purchased at the wrong time and under dire economic conditions may turn the peace-seeking homeownership journey into a disaster for many families.

Then, we must answer the question: "*Does homeownership really matter?*".

Buy or Rent Decision

There is no particular answer about whether owning or renting a home is better. Buying or renting a house mainly depends on the financial situation, but people's future expectations, plans, goals, and lifestyles also matter. You must pay rent or make a mortgage repayment each month if you financed the house by borrowing money from banks. When you prefer to rent a house, you are not responsible for the insurance, repair, and maintenance costs, and you are more flexible as you may move out after giving a notice based on your contract. Moreover, despite its tax benefits, the potential capital gain of the property over time by considering the house as an investment and the mental well-being it brings, the down payment, and the monthly mortgage payments you make may limit your financial independence.

Renting doesn't necessarily mean you're spending your money for nothing every month, and owning doesn't always create wealth in the long run. Based on the financial analysis, it is possible to invest the savings you are considering using for the down payment in other investment tools such as real estate investment funds, stocks; by paying rent, you can have a stable cash outflow and have the freedom of mobility by living in a rented house. Germany, together with Switzerland, is one of two countries with the lowest homeownership rate in Europe. In Germany, the private rental market is robust. At the same time, there is tight control on mortgage lending and borrowing, and the tax and subsidy system seems to support rental housing in general, especially private rental (Kofner, 2014; Voigtländer, 2014).

On the other hand, homeownership helps people build equity and credit and brings more stability and tax benefits. The homeowners do not have to deal with the landlords; they can decorate, improve, or upgrade their homes to their taste. Therefore, there is no *one-size-fits-all solution*, as both options have pros and cons.

From a financial analysis perspective, households shall also consider the price-to-rent ratios while deciding whether to rent or buy a house. The lower price-to-rent ratio indicates a better option to purchase instead of rent.

To conclude, the psychology of homeownership depends on many factors, including the income level, financial situation, neighborhood, the individual's life expectations and personal characteristics and choices, the local and economic conditions, the monetary policies and ease of access to finance, the size and lifestyles of families, and the physical conditions of the housing units, and each factor has an essential impact on the decision of owning or renting a house.

It is also important to note that analyzing and understanding the current and future market conditions impact such a significant decision. Thus, in the next chapter, we will focus on the housing market dynamics and interpret recent global trends and threats from a housing affordability crisis perspective.

References

Blank, D. M., & Winnick, L. (1953). The structure of the housing market. *The Quarterly Journal of Economics, 67*(2), 181–208.

Blum, T. C., & Kingston, P. W. (1984). Homeownership and social attachment. *Sociological Perspectives, 27*(2), 159–180.

Chang, S.S., Stuckler, D., Yip, P., & Gunnell, D. (2013, September 17). Impact of 2008 global economic crisis on suicide: Time trend study in 54 countries. *BMJ, 347*, f5239. https://doi.org/10.1136/bmj.f5239. PMID: 24046155; PMCID: PMC3776046.

Coopersmith, S. (1967). *The antecedents of self-esteem*. W.H. Freeman.

Diaz-Serrano, L. (2009). Disentangling the housing satisfaction puzzle: Does homeownership really matter? *Journal of Economic Psychology, 30*(5), 745–755. https://doi.org/10.1016/j.joep.2009.06.006

Ettman, C. K., Cohen, G. H., Vivier, P. M., & Galea, S. (2021). Savings, home ownership, and depression in low-income US adults. *Social Psychiatry and Psychiatric Epidemiology, 56*, 1211–1219. https://doi.org/10.1007/s00127-020-01973-y

Fong, E., Yuan, Y., & Gan, Y. (2021). Homeownership and happiness in urban China. *Journal of Housing and the Built Environment, 36*, 153–170. https://doi.org/10.1007/s10901-020-09728-6

Fowler, K. A., Gladden, R. M., Vagi, K. J., Barnes, J., Frazier, L. (2015, February). Increase in suicides associated with home eviction and foreclosure during the US housing crisis: Findings from 16 National Violent Death Reporting System States, 2005–2010. *American Journal of Public Health, 105*(2), 311–316. https://doi.org/10.2105/AJPH.2014.301945. PMID: 25033148; PMCID: PMC4318323.

Galster, G. (1987). *Homeowners and neighborhood reinvestment*. Duke University.

Goff, K. (2024). *What is the average down payment for first-time homebuyers?* https://www.bankrate.com/mortgages/down-payment-for-first-time-homebuyers/. Last Accessed on July 21, 2024.

Hew, W. W., Tan, C. L., & Yeo, S. F. (2020). Determinants to homeownership and/or leasing intentions: A review and proposed framework. *International Journal of Law, Government and Communication (IJLGC), 5*(21), 22–33. https://doi.org/10.35631/IJLGC.521003

Hofmann, R., & Umbricht, R. (2019). Homeownership and happiness: Evidence for Switzerland. *Swiss Real Estate Journal, 19*, 4–12. https://doi.org/10.21256/zhaw-18640

Kofner, S. (2014). The German housing system: Fundamentally resilient? *Journal of Housing and the Built Environment, 29*, 255–275. https://doi.org/10.1007/s10901-013-9383-0

Kubala, M., & Samec, T. H. (2021). The pace of "the good life": Connecting past, present, and future in the context of a housing affordability crisis. *Time & Society, 30*(2), 198–222.

Maslow, A. H. (1954). *Motivation and personality*. Harpers.

Park, G. R., & Kim, J. (2022). Trajectories of life satisfaction before and after homeownership: The role of housing affordability stress. *Journal of Happiness Studies, 24*(1), 1–12. https://doi.org/10.1007/s10902-022-00601-7

Rohe, M. W., & Stewart, L. S. (1996). Home ownership and neighborhood stability. *Housing Policy Debate, 7*, 7–81.

Rohe, W. M., & Basolo, V. (1997). Long-term effects of homeownership on the self-perceptions and social interaction of low-income persons. *Environment and Behavior, 29*, 793–819. https://doi.org/10.1177/0013916597296004

Rohe, W. M., & Lindblad, M. (2013). Homeownership built to last: Lessons from the housing crisis on sustaining homeownership for low-income and minority families. A National Symposium held on April 1–2, 2013. Harvard Business School in Boston, Massachusetts.

Rohe, W. M., Quercia, R. G., & Van Zandt, S. (2007). The social-psychological effects of affordable homeownership. In W. M. Rohe & H. L. Watson (Eds.), *Chasing the American dream: New perspectives on affordable homeownership*, pp. 215–232. Cornell University Press. https://doi.org/10.7591/9781501731136-011

Ruprah, I. J. (2010). *Does owning your home make you happier? Impact evidence from Latin America* (Inter-American Development Bank Office of Evaluation and Oversight Working Paper: OVE/WP-02/10). https://doi.org/10.18235/0011137

Sandhu, C. (2024). *The road to homeownership in 2024: navigating five common challenges for first-time homebuyers*. https://www.linkedin.com/pulse/road-homeownership-2024-navigating-five-common-challenges-f34ue/. Last Accessed on July 21, 2024.

Stieg, C. (2020). *The psychology of buying a house: Is it a key to happiness or just a source of stress?* https://www.cnbc.com/2020/10/27/does-buying-a-home-make-you-happier-psychology-of-home-ownership.html. Last Accessed on July 21, 2024.

Voigtländer, M. (2014). The stability of the German housing market. *Journal of Housing and the Built Environment, 29*, 583–594. https://doi.org/10.1007/s10901-013-9366-1

Zumbro, T. (2011). *The relationship between homeownership and life satisfaction in Germany* (CAWM Discussion Paper, No. 44). Westfälische Wilhelms-Universität Münster, Centrum für Angewandte Wirtschaftsforschung (CAWM), Münster.

CHAPTER 3

Housing Market Dynamics: Understanding the Recent Global Trends and Threats

"The housing shortage is getting worse, and demand is rising steadily," said Alexis Alban, the president of a real estate agency in France. If you live in Paris, you must wait around six months to rent a furnished studio apartment.

Rising difficulties in accessing finance made people stay longer in their houses because they did not have the financial power to purchase one (Duboust, 2023). The situation in Istanbul is not different, even the worst among all OECD countries, where the housing rental price index rose from 100 (2015) to 519 as of the last quarter of 2023 (OECD, 2024a). On the other hand, homeownership rates are declining in many countries, including the US. After its peak rate of 69% before the global financial crisis, around 65.7% of US citizens own a house as of 2023.

Real estate and the housing industries are significant indicators of the healthiness and stability of the global economy. The size of the real estate market worldwide is expected to reach a value of USD 634.90 trillion by 2024. This value is over six times the world's total gross domestic product (GDP). With its USD 132 trillion projected value in the real estate market in 2024, the US is leading the industry despite its housing affordability problems. The global real estate industry is estimated to reach USD 727.8 trillion by 2029, with an annual rate of 2.77% (CAGR 2024–2029). The size of the housing market covers more than 81% of the total global

L. Sümer, *The Global Housing Crisis*,
https://doi.org/10.1007/978-3-031-72604-0_3

real estate market, and its value will reach USD 516.8 trillion by 2024 (Statista, 2024a).

The dynamics of the housing market are dependent on many factors, such as general and global economic conditions, including income growth, employment rates, inflation rates, consumer confidence, demographic trends, government policies, political developments, local market conditions, monetary policies, interest rates, construction costs, land availability and costs, zoning regulations, building codes, development policies, generation trends, population growth, age distribution, migration patterns, homeownership rates, supply–demand balance, and even the post-pandemic hybrid working styles, etc.

The healthier the housing market in a country is, the better the performance of the general economy. However, the housing industry is also one of the main reasons for weaknesses and economic crises. While the primary need for housing matches the basic needs of people living in a safe shelter, it is also considered an important investment tool and an indicator of wealth. People tend to buy houses instead of investing in financial instruments. For instance, while the rate of homeowners in France is around 63%, less than one-quarter of people invest in stocks in France (Zhu, 2014).

The housing market is one of the main determinants of consumer spending. While the rise in housing prices makes homeowners feel more confident as they can use the value of their house as leverage to borrow more or spend more money, the value decrease in house prices makes people cut down on their spending and hesitate to make investments, which may slow down the economy.

On the other hand, a potential default on mortgage loans, which currently is the primary financing source of the housing sector, may jeopardize the banking sector and initiate a financial crisis.

The start of new housing construction is also vital for the GDP growth. Buying a new house stimulates economic development by creating jobs and producing new materials and equipment. For example, the number of employees reached 1 million at the peak of the housing bubble in 2006 and declined to 560,000 in May 2011 due to the recession in the US. Except for the lockdown period during the 2020 COVID-19 pandemic, the number of individual employees in the residential real estate sector increased and reached about 903,000 by November 2022, according to Bureau of Labor Statistics data (Congressional Research Service, 2023). Secondhand home sales also affect the economy through legal and agent fees or renovation expenditures. Thus, it is essential to analyze these dynamics in detail to understand the current conditions of the market, determine the risks and threats, and see the big picture of the housing industry in order not to face heavy financial crises triggered by the housing industry-related problems.

Homelessness

Around 150 (2% of the world population) million people in the world are homeless due to political conflicts, wars, natural disasters, poverty, rising prices and rents, economic difficulties, and financial crises. In addition, 1.6 billion people (20% of the global population) live in poor housing conditions worldwide. Homelessness rates have risen in the past ten years in most European countries. At least 700.000 homeless people are living on the streets on any given night in Europe (FEANTSA, 2022).

According to the United Nations Refugee Agency 2023 report, the number of forcibly displaced people exceeded 117 million, and this number is increasing by 15 million each year. Nigeria, with around 25 million homeless, is ranked the country with the highest number of homeless people living in (Obasi & Anierobi, 2021). As of 2022, this number is around 582,000 (18 out of 10,000 people) in the US (De Sousa et al., 2022). With 30% of the (6,6 million) population, the country with the highest homelessness rate per population is Syria. The war demolished the infrastructure of the country, leaving millions of people lacking sufficient food and potable water and 90% of the population in poverty. On the other hand, Iceland, Finland, and Japan are the countries where the number and the rate of homeless people are the lowest (Filipenco, 2023).

While millions of people suffer from homelessness, ironically, the vacancy rates for rental apartments in many countries are high. OECD reports that 42 million of 426 million homes (almost 10%) are vacant (Betterdwelling, 2021). Generally, a vacancy rate of about 3–5% indicates a healthy housing system in a country. As of May 2024, the vacancy rate in the US is 6.7% (Statista, 2024b). This rate is between 6.9 and 11.5% in İstanbul, Türkiye, which is struggling with a severe affordability problem (Massink, 2023).

The number of vacant houses and homeless people reveals that one-third of the homelessness problem can be fixed independently from the location of the vacant units. These figures show how housing development is distributed unfairly among societies and cities. Getting into details of the homeownership rates may give better insight into the problems of the global housing market.

Homeownership Rates & Housing Quality

Homeownership

Living in a house you own is the *American dream*, symbolizing success in finance and the sign of independence. According to a survey by Fannie Mae 1994, 74% of Americans believe that buying a house is essential as soon as it becomes affordable (Huduser.gov, 1994).

Americans are not the only nations that dream of becoming homeowners. Chinese, Turkish, and even the residents of Switzerland, who have the lowest homeownership rate at 36%, dream of owning their houses (Fuller, 2023).

Turks consider owning a house as the assurance of their retirement periods. One of the former Prime Ministers of Türkiye, Süleyman Demirel (who later became the 9th President), had promised to *give his voters two keys: one for a house and the other for a car* if he was elected. Yes, he won the elections, but people did not own a home or a car, and they experienced another economic crisis in 1994 (Çağlar & Aslan, 2019).

The homeownership rate in the US was 64% at the beginning of the 1990s, and it rose to more than 69% in 2004, before the global financial crisis initiated by the mortgage crisis in the US. As of March 2024, the homeownership rate fell to 65.2%, almost back to its value in the 1990s (Statista, 2024c). Figure 3.1 shows the homeownership rates in the US.

On the other hand, homeownership also changes based on age groups. Unsurprisingly, 79.1% of people over 65 own a house in the US, but this rate is 39% for people below 35 (PropertyShark, 2024). Figure 3.2 exhibits the homeownership rates by age of household. Young households are more likely to feel and struggle with the affordability problem in the US.

Homeownership rates also vary considerably from state to state. Education opportunities, job openings, social activities, lifestyles, migration trends, population density, and cost of living are critical factors for homeownership. As shown in Fig. 3.3, the high-density population states like New York and California have the lowest rates, with 54.1% and 55,8%,

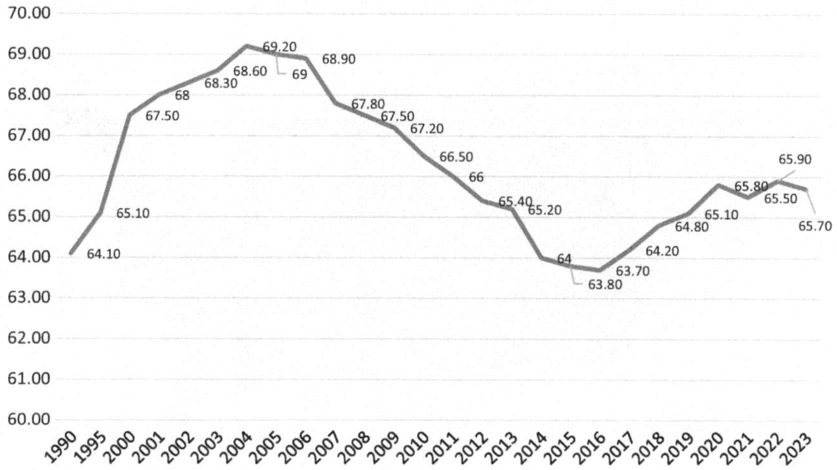

Fig. 3.1 Homeownership rates in the US 1990–2023 (Statista, 2024c)

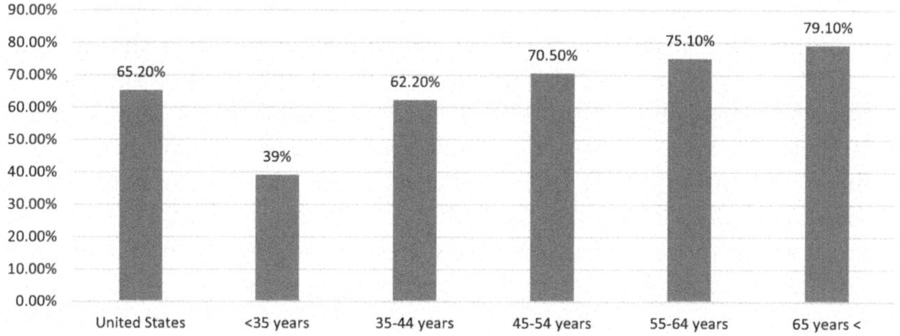

Fig. 3.2 Homeownership rates by age of household (PropertyShark, 2024)

respectively. In contrast, the states with fewer populations and less expensive housing prices, such as West Virginia (74.5%), Delaware (74.1%), and Maine (74.1%), have higher homeownership rates. Among the US states and territories, Washington, D.C. has the lowest rate of homeownership, 41% (PropertyShark, 2024).

Analyzing the homeownership rates globally, as shown in Fig. 3.4, Kosovo is listed as the country with the highest ownership rate at 97.8%. It is followed by China, Romania, Slovakia, and Russia with 96%, 95.6%,

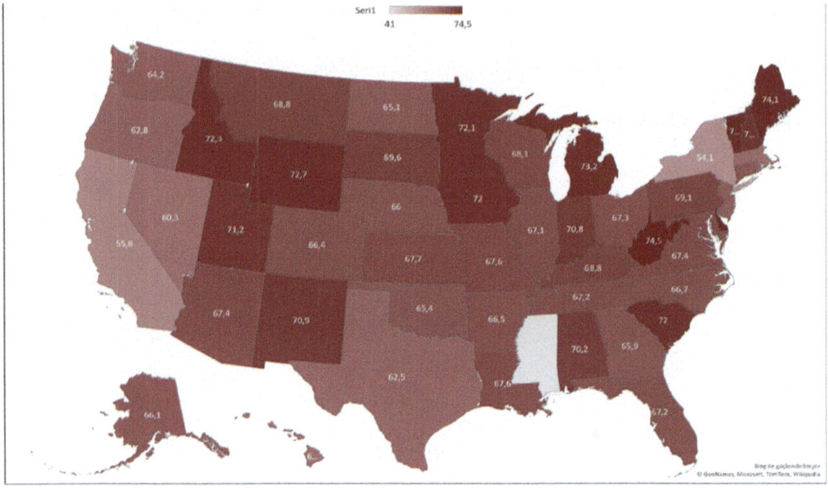

Fig. 3.3 Homeownership by state (PropertyShark, 2024)

93.6%, and 91.7% homeownership rates respectively. While the average rate in the EU is 69.1%, in Türkiye, 56,2% of the population owns a house, a similar decline in the US, as the homeownership rate was 61.1% in 2013 in Türkiye. Austria, Germany, and Switzerland have a stronger tradition of renting; thus, their homeownership rates are the lowest at 51.4%, 47.8%, and 36%, respectively (Trading Economics, 2024a). On the other hand, in most African countries, households live in rental houses. While the rental house rate in Johannesburg is 42%, 63% of people in Cairo and 80% of the population of Nairobi are tenants (Bah et al., 2018).

The population of Kosovo is around 1.8 million (Worldbank, 2024), so 97.8% of home ownership may not be a reference for the rest of the world. For a better understanding of the dynamics of homeownership, it is essential to analyze the reason behind the high ownership rates in countries like China and Russia or vice versa in Switzerland and Germany.

Despite its current housing crisis and excess supply, China has made its citizens homeowners within the last three decades through the housing reform anchored on privatizing previously public rental housing units of the communism period. The high homeownership rate was achieved by promoting homeownership, providing financial support for housing sales, and producing mass housing. It is also important to note that China is

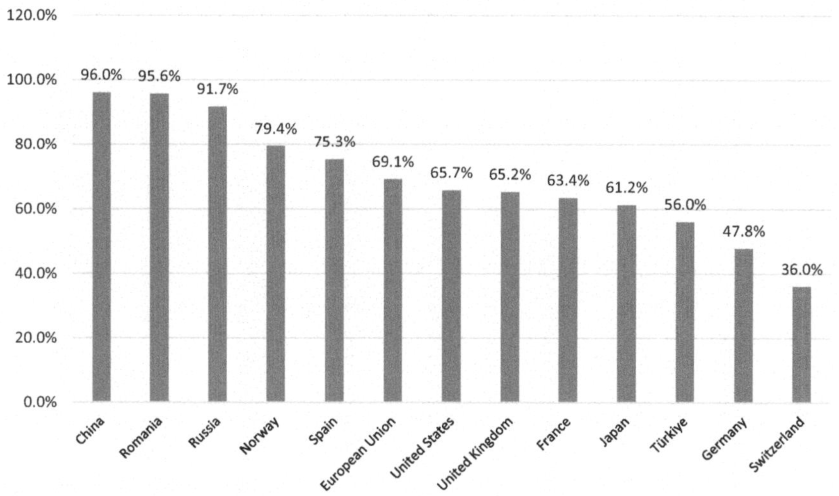

Fig. 3.4 Homeownership rates in selected countries (Trading Economics, 2024a)

the top country in which households own a second house. Families, who receive housing subsidies, have kids attending essential schools, and experience demolition and resettlement tend to purchase multiple houses in China (Huang et al., 2020).

The homeownership rates in Russia have been increasing since the global financial crisis. In 2010, the rate was 82%, and now it stands at around 92%, as exhibited in Fig. 3.5 (Statista, 2024d). The situation in Russia is similar to that in China. Until the 1990s, the state owned the houses. Then, state-sponsored development declined while the housing sector experienced rapid privatization. Many tenants were given free title to their apartments, but many elderly Russians preferred to continue renting rather than completing the required documentation. However, by the middle of the 1990s, most of the housing in Russia was privately held, with the municipal government managing the remaining parts. While conditions in owner-occupied housing significantly improved because building owners could enforce maintenance regulations, public housing continued to weaken due to a lack of funding from local authorities (Keenan & Lieven, 2024).

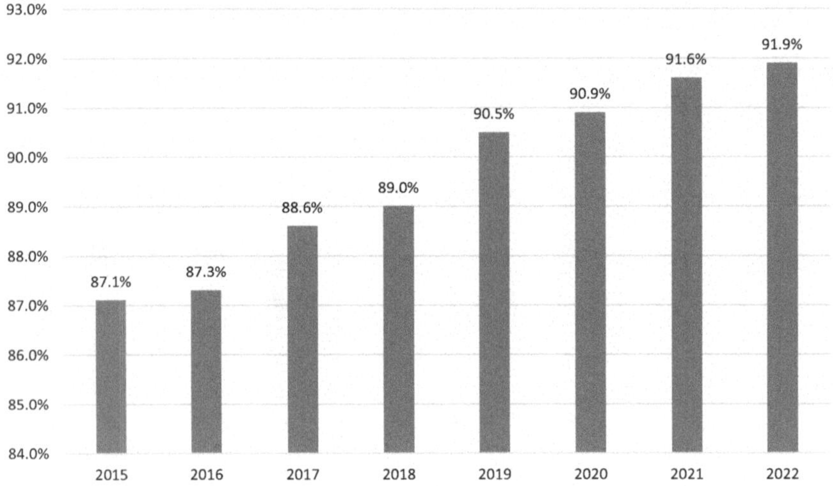

Fig. 3.5 Homeownership rates in Russia (Statista, 2024d)

On the other hand, in countries like Switzerland, Germany, and Austria, high property prices, the flexibility of renting, strict mortgage regulations such as requiring high down payments and limiting the duration of the loans, the regulated rental market that protects lessees, and investing in other financial instruments rather than housing are listed as the most critical factors of lower homeownership rates (Fuller, 2023; Kaas et al., 2020).

Housing Quality

While homeownership rates are important for the housing sector, the quality of the houses is also a significant indicator of the well-being of the occupants.

People's ability to live in a good quality house is one of the most critical components of their lives. Basic requirements like shelter must be met by housing, but housing is more than just a set of four walls and a roof. A place to sleep, rest, feel comfortable, have privacy, and personal space—somewhere they may grow a family—should be provided by housing. All these components make a house more of a home. The United Nations (UN) reports that approximately 1.6 billion people live in shelters lacking

Table 3.1 Housing quality rankings by countries (OECD, 2024b)

1	United States	15	Portugal	29	Italy
2	Australia	16	New Zealand	30	Czechia
3	Norway	17	France	31	Greece
4	Canada	18	Spain	32	Türkiye
5	Belgium	19	Chile	33	Israel
6	Netherlands	20	United Kingdom	34	Poland
7	Korea	21	Iceland	35	Brazil
8	Ireland	22	Finland	36	Russia
9	Luxembourg	23	Denmark	37	Latvia
10	Germany	24	Austria	38	Colombia
11	Estonia	25	Costa Rica	39	Mexico
12	Slovenia	26	Japan	40	Slovak Republic
13	Switzerland	27	Lithuania	41	South Africa
14	Sweden	28	Hungary		

minimum housing requirements globally. An average home has 1.7 rooms per person in OECD countries, where 97% of dwellings have private indoor flushing toilets (OECD, 2024b). Table 3.1 exhibits the ranking based on the quality of housing in OECD countries in terms of housing expenditure, dwelling with basic facilities, and rooms per person. The US is ranked as the top country in terms of housing quality, followed by Australia, Norway, and Canada. Mexico, the Slovak Republic, and South Africa were listed as the countries where the quality of the housing units is low.

Living in a better-quality house costs the homeowner more, so comparing the housing prices and wages from an affordability perspective is essential.

Wages, Housing Sales & Rental Prices and Affordability

Wages

Housing affordability used to be perceived as a problem only in low-income countries. Now, it has become a global issue as housing prices have been booming globally, and the income of nations is not increasing proportionally. Thus, the affordability declined globally.

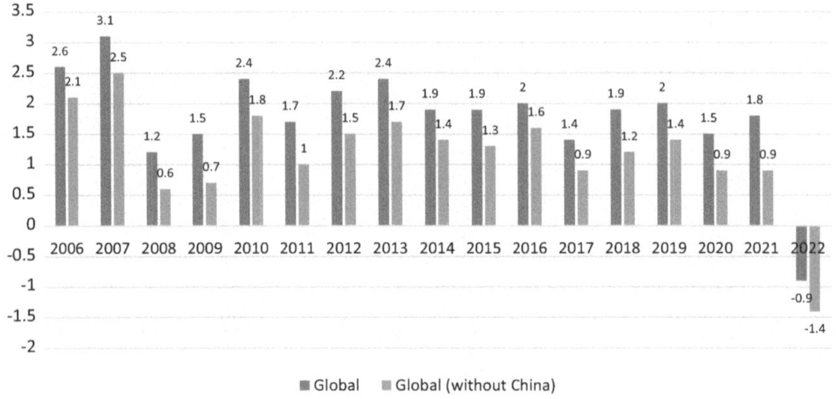

Fig. 3.6 Average annual global real monthly wage growth (%) (2006–2022) (ILO, 2023)

According to the 2023 Global Wealth Report published by the International Labor Organization (ILO), monthly wages declined in real terms to −0.9% in the first half of 2022. That was the first contracted global wage growth among G-20 countries recorded since 2008. Figure 3.6 shows the average annual global real monthly wage growth rates between 2006 and 2022 (ILO, 2022).

It is a big question mark on how we can resolve the affordability problem while housing prices are increasing, wages are declining, and access to financing is becoming more difficult.

Housing Sales & Rental Prices

Housing prices indicate the housing market's conditions and significantly affect the economy. As it impacted the global economy in many ways, including the decline in production, global trade, and mobility, the COVID-19 pandemic affected global housing prices. The limited supply and easy access to financing accelerated the rise in property prices. The average global residential real estate value has increased from USD 205,500 to USD 234,700 within four years since the beginning of the COVID-19 pandemic in 2020.

Despite a decline in some countries, the global average housing prices are still rising. Figure 3.7 shows the current and projected average global

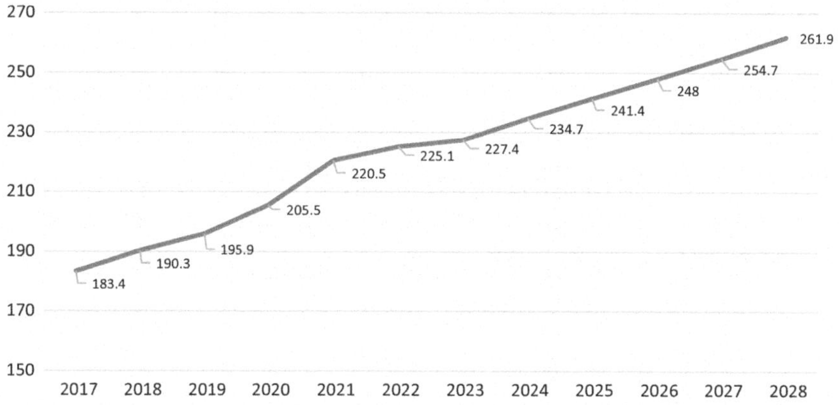

Fig. 3.7 Average global value per residential real estate (Statista, 2024e)

residential real estate values. An annual growth rate of 3.64% is projected for the next few years (CAGR 2024–2028) (Statista, 2024e). This rate is above the 2% target inflation rates of the US and the EU.

As shown in Table 3.2, Hong Kong, Zurich, Seoul, and Singapore are the cities where housing prices are the highest globally (Herring & Barber, 2023). Like many other countries, the value of the US housing market increased, and the rate of this rise was measured as 49% within the last four years. Interestingly, New York is the only US city ranked in the top 10 most expensive cities globally in terms of housing prices. Los Angeles, San Francisco, Boston, and Miami are also the most valuable housing markets in the US (PR Newswire, 2023).

In 2023, the total value of the US housing market reached almost USD 52 trillion, USD 1.1 trillion higher than the previous peak recorded last June. Table 3.3 shows the most valuable states in the US.

The median-priced single-family home prices in the US went up to USD 415,700 in June 2023, as shown in Table 3.4. Figure 3.8 also exhibits the historical movement of housing prices in the US since 1963 (Realtors, 2024). The similar rise and decline before and during the global financial crisis and during and post-COVID-19 pandemic periods (2020–2024) exhibit a potential risk in the housing market in the US.

According to Federal Reserve Economic Data (FRED), after its peak value in October 2022 (USD 552,600), the median housing price in the US is USD 492,300 as of the last quarter of 2023. Before the global

Table 3.2 The cities with the highest housing prices (Herring & Barber, 2023)

Rank	*City*	*Country*	*Average cost of flat in city*	*Compared to the global average*
1	Hong Kong	Hong Kong	USD 1,785,600	718%
2	Zurich	Switzerland	USD 1,484,000	580%
3	Seoul	South Korea	USD 1,248,680	472%
4	Singapore	Singapore	USD 1,222,640	460%
5	Geneva	Switzerland	USD 1,171,800	437%
6	Shanghai	China	USD 1,035,400	374%
7	London	United Kingdom	USD 990,760	354%
8	New York	United States	USD 982,080	350%
9	Tel Aviv	Israel	USD 949,840	335%
10	Beijing	China	USD 942,400	332%

Table 3.3 The 10 most valuable states in the US (PRNewswire, 2023)

Top 10 most valuable states		
State	*Total housing market value (billions)*	*Change since june 2022 "peak" (%)*
California	USD 10,175	−3.3%
Florida	USD 3,846	4.3%
New York	USD 3,689	−0.2%
Texas	USD 3,390	1.5%
New Jersey	USD 1,847	13.1%
Massachusetts	USD 1,733	4.1%
Washington	USD 1,705	−3.9%
Pennsylvania	USD 1,567	6.0%
North Carolina	USD 1,416	3.9%
Virginia	USD 1,382	6.0%

financial crisis, housing prices had increased by around 23% between 2004 and 2007. The sharp increase during and after COVID-19 (2020–2023) has been observed even more than this rise, as shown in Fig. 3.9. This situation, together with the high financing costs, construction costs, and decreased purchasing power, is ringing the alarm bell for the housing sector.

After a decline in the housing market crash in 2008, the median US housing prices kept climbing (a 162% rise between 2000 and 2022). On

Table 3.4 Median housing prices, mortgage rates, and affordability in the US housing market (Realtors, 2024)

Year	*Median priced existing single-family home*	*Mortgage rate (%)*	*Monthly payment*	*Payment as of a % of income*	*Median family income*	*Qualifying income*	*Affordability index*
2021	357.100	3,01	1.206	16,90	85.806	57.888	148,2
2022	392.800	5,40	1.765	23,00	92.148	84.720	108,8
2023	394.100	6,88	2.072	25,40	97.699	99.456	98,2
Feb-23	368.100	6,34	1.830	22,90	95.976	87.840	109,3
Mar-23	379.500	6,62	1.943	24,20	96.508	93.264	103,5
Apr-23	390.200	6,42	1.957	24,3	96.790	93.936	103
May-23	401.500	6,51	2.032	25,10	97.166	97.536	99,6
Jun-23	415.700	6,79	2.166	26,70	97.401	103.968	93,7
Jul-23	411.200	6,92	2.171	26,60	97.865	104.208	93,9
Aug-23	410.200	7,15	2.216	27,10	98.291	106.368	92,4
Sep-23	397.400	7,28	2.175	26,40	98.705	104.400	94,5
Oct-23	396.000	7,70	2.259	27,40	99.109	108.432	91,4
Nov-23	392.200	7,52	2.198	26,50	99.432	105.504	94,2
Dec-23	385.900	6,90	2.033	24,50	99.767	97.584	102,2
Jan-24	382.900	6,72	1.981	23,70	100.472	95.088	105,7
Feb-24	388.700	6,86	2.040	24,30	100.876	97.920	103

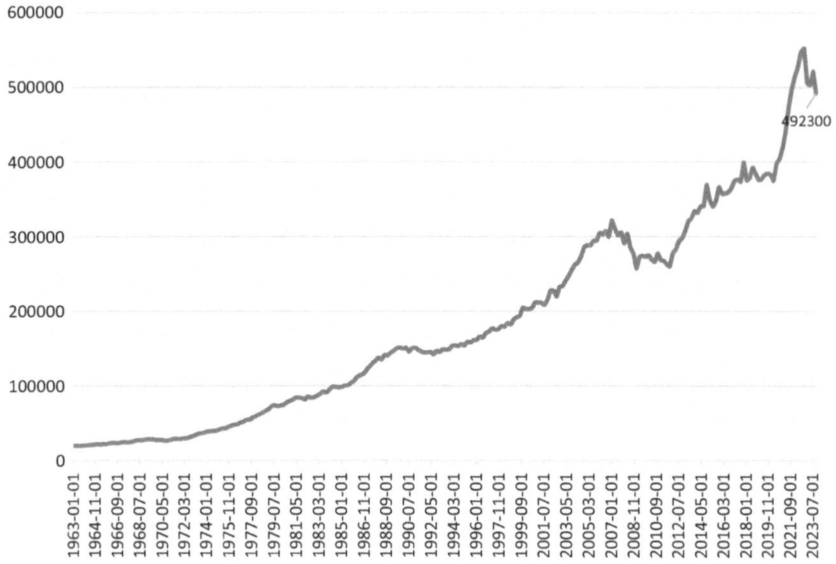

Fig. 3.8 Median housing sales prices in the US (1963–2023) (FRED, 2024)

the other hand, the income of households has increased by only 78% within the same period. House prices have increased more than two times the rise in earnings since 2000.

Another critical index about the housing sector in the US is the Case-Shiller Index, also known as the S&P CoreLogic Case-Shiller U.S. National Home Price NSA Index, which measures the change in value of US single-family homes monthly based on the repeat-sales pricing technique developed in the 1980s by economists Karl Case and Robert Shiller. Figure 3.9 shows the S&P CoreLogic Case-Shiller US National Home Price Index since 1987. The Case-Shiller Index is 321, almost twice its value in 2006.

The US has a well-structured housing rental market. In contrast to the homeowners' age groups, almost half of American renters were under 30 in 2022. Moreover, renters' income level is lower than that of mortgage holders. People prefer to rent a unit in urban areas instead of purchasing one. Living in urban areas is also costly. In November 2023, the median rent for a two-bedroom apartment in California was at least USD 700 higher than the national average. Other states with expensive rentals

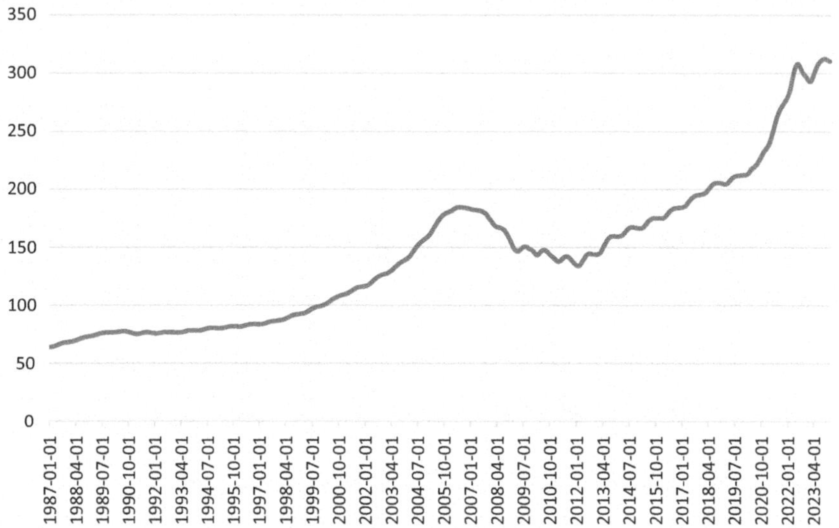

Fig. 3.9 S&P CoreLogic Case-Shiller US National Home Price Index (FRED, 2024)

included Hawaii, New Jersey, and Massachusetts. Despite higher average wages in these states, they often fall short of covering the cost of renting a two-bedroom apartment (Statista, 2023a).

As shown in Fig. 3.10, the median asking rent per month for unfurnished apartments in the US reached USD 1,874 at the end of 2022. Despite a slight decline in the first quarter of 2023, housing rents are still rising in many states.

The case in China is different. According to the International Monetary Fund (IMF) Housing Market Stability and Affordability in Asia–Pacific Report (2022), the housing boom started in the region before the pandemic (Deb et al., 2022). It is noted that many Asian countries are currently experiencing declines in housing prices with the potential to face severe downward risks. According to the IMF report, after a long-term sustainable rise since the 1998 housing reform, housing prices started declining in China in 2022. Between 1998 and 2022, average property prices in China emerged more than 3.8 times, reaching almost 10,000 RMB (USD 5.600) per square meter (Statista, 2023b). China has two

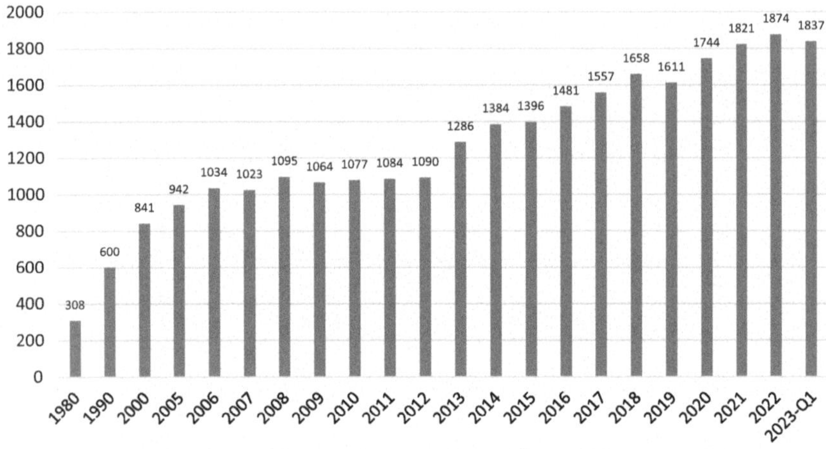

Fig. 3.10 Median asking rental prices in the US (Statista, 2023a)

cities, Shanghai and Beijing, in the top ten highest housing prices list with around RMB 40,000 per square meter.

In addition to the imbalance in supply and demand in the top Chinese, housing affordability is a common problem, considering the country's GDP per capita. Treating housing as an investment created an expectation of a yearly price increase, resulting in a potential property bubble and a debt crisis. The default of China Evergrande and Country Garden, two large Chinese real estate developers, put the banking industry in a vulnerable position due to the increased loans (Zhang, 2023).

Owing to the country's geographical differences, China's fast urbanization caused an enormous flood of internal migrants into its eastern cities, which in turn created a shortage of housing in many areas. However, because of China's distinct land and taxation laws, local administrations frequently rely heavily on the proceeds from land transfers to fund their operations. Consequently, a lot of local governments tend to limit the amount of land that is accessible on the market, which exacerbates the national increase in real estate prices. Figure 3.11 shows the housing price increase in China since 1998.

It is estimated that it may take about two years to clear the existing housing stock and more than ten years to clear the housing inventory under construction in China. Compared to the average price-to-rent

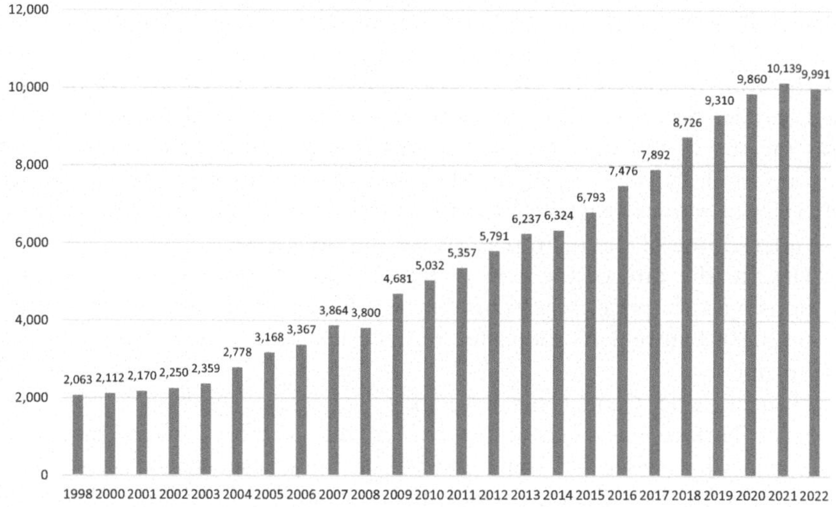

Fig. 3.11 Average housing prices in China (yuan per square meter) (Statista, 2023b)

ratios of global first-tier cities in 2022, excluding China, a decline in property prices in Beijing, Shanghai, Guangzhou, and Shenzhen with 45.66%, 46.19%, 50.51%, and 92.51% rates, respectively, is projected for the normalization of the prices.

The dynamics of the European housing market are similar to those in the US. The COVID-19 pandemic hit the European economy, and the great lockdown, the sudden stance of the economies, and the monetary expansion policies of central banks resulted in high inflation. The ongoing war between Russia and Ukraine kept the inflation higher due to the energy dependency of European countries, especially Germany, on Russian oil and gas. High inflation severely affected the European housing market regarding housing sales and rental prices. The dynamics of supply and balance were broken down. Millions of Ukrainian immigrants and refugees also impacted the balance of supply and demand in Europe.

The housing prices in Europe stabilized after a sharp drop between the second quarter of 2011 and the first quarter of 2013. The rise began in early 2015 and lasted until the third quarter of 2022. In 2022 and 2023, ups and downs were observed, and the last quarter of 2023 indicated a slight decline, as shown in Fig. 3.12. After a rapid rise during and after the pandemic, compared with the previous quarter of 2022, housing prices fell by 1.1% in the euro area and rose by 0.3% in the European Union in the fourth quarter of 2023 (Eurostat, 2024a). Germany, Denmark, and Sweden were the top countries where the decline in housing prices was measured. On the other hand, in the UK, the average house price was up by 3.5% yearly in April 2023, but the development of the house price index shows that the increase has slowed. High financing cost is considered one of the main reasons for the slowdown.

Despite the rate of increase in rental prices being less than the rise in housing sales prices, the rents in the EU region have kept increasing since 2010. Figure 3.13 shows the rental price index of selected countries in Europe.

Housing prices and rents have indeed increased globally in the last decade. Türkiye has been at the top of the countries where rent and sales prices have risen 4.5 times and 12,33 times, respectively, since 2015 (Eurostat, 2024b). Poland, which hosts around 1.5 million Ukrainian refugees, also had a 59% increase in rents and an 89% rise in sales prices within the last decade, as exhibited in Table 3.5. The rise both in Türkiye and Poland sharpened after 2021. Greece was listed as the only country

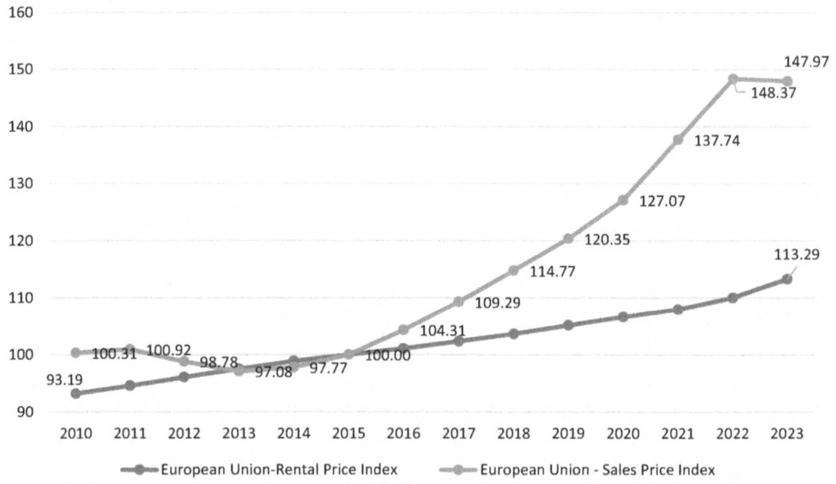

Fig. 3.12 House prices and rents in the EU (Eurostat, 2024a)

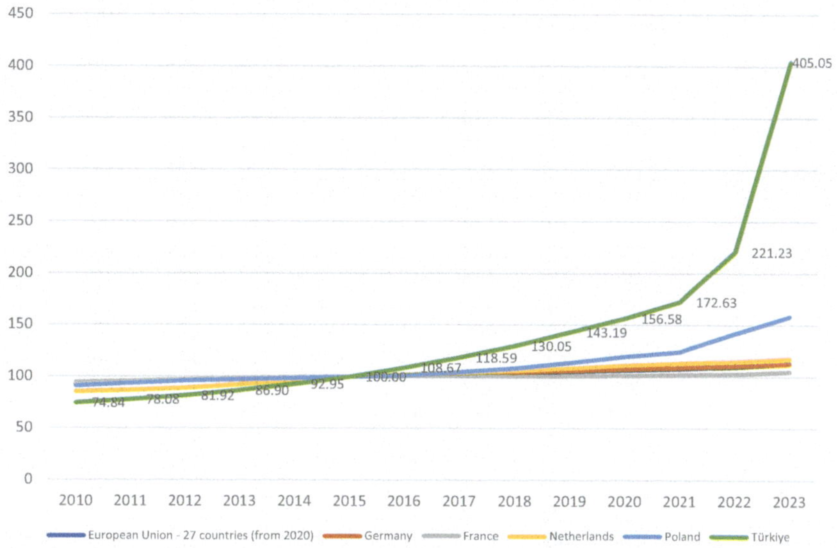

Fig. 3.13 Rental index in selected European countries (Eurostat, 2024b)

where a decline in rents was observed compared to 2015, but there was a rise during and after the pandemic (Table 3.6).

The housing prices in Russia also increased rapidly after the COVID-19 pandemic. The rise speeded up in 2022 after the war against Ukraine started in 2022. From 2019 Q4 to 2022 Q2, the prices rose 56.57%, more than double the inflation rate of the same period. The construction costs of new apartments are 40% more than existing ones (Mohamed, 2023).

In summary, low affordability slows the growth of housing prices, which is expected to remain resilient over the next two years. That may deepen the housing affordability problem if the mortgage rates do not decrease and access to finance does not ease.

Affordability

Housing affordability is widely acknowledged as one of households' most significant issues today. An affordability index, which gives an idea of the standard of living, compares the price of a good or the general cost of

Table 3.5 The housing rental price index in Europe (Eurostat, 2024b)

Countries	*2015*	*2016*	*2017*	*2018*	*2019*	*2020*	*2021*	*2022*	*2023*
Türkiye	100	109	119	130	143	157	173	221	405
Lithuania	100	110	111	117	126	129	132	153	168
Hungary	100	105	108	114	125	130	132	146	166
Slovenia	100	102	107	114	119	116	120	143	160
Estonia	100	106	114	122	131	125	130	159	159
Poland	100	101	104	108	114	120	124	142	158
Ireland	100	109	116	123	130	130	134	147	158
Serbia	100	102	100	101	106	108	110	131	154
Iceland	100	104	108	114	120	125	128	135	146
Malta	100	104	105	107	111	116	114	120	138
Austria	100	103	107	111	115	119	122	123	132
Czechia	100	101	103	106	110	114	117	122	131
Romania	100	101	102	105	108	110	113	118	130
Bulgaria	100	101	102	104	107	110	111	118	128
Portugal	100	102	103	105	108	111	113	116	121
Belgium	100	101	102	103	104	107	109	113	120
Croatia	100	99	99	101	106	108	109	112	119
Cyprus	100	100	100	103	106	109	111	114	119
Netherlands	100	102	104	106	109	112	114	116	119
Norway	100	102	104	106	108	109	111	113	118
Finland	100	102	104	106	108	110	111	112	114
Slovakia	100	100	101	101	101	103	104	108	114
Sweden	100	101	102	103	105	107	108	110	114
European Union	100	101	102	104	105	107	108	110	113
Germany	100	101	103	105	106	108	109	111	113
Latvia	100	99	98	102	107	105	106	110	113
Denmark	100	101	103	104	105	106	108	110	113
Luxembourg	100	101	102	103	105	106	107	109	111
Spain	100	100	100	102	103	104	105	106	109
Switzerland	100	100	101	102	103	103	104	106	108
Italy	100	100	101	101	101	101	101	103	105
France	100	100	101	100	101	101	102	103	105
North Macedonia	100	100	100	100	100	100	101	102	105
Greece	100	97	95	92	92	92	92	93	98

living in a region to that of other areas, or provides some baseline measure of personal income. Housing affordability indexes compare the price of purchasing a home in different locations. Housing is mainly one of the family's most significant expenditures, so a housing affordability index indicates the cost of living in that area (Kenton, 2024).

Table 3.6 The housing sales price index in Europe (Eurostat, 2024b)

Countries	*2015*	*2016*	*2017*	*2018*	*2019*	*2020*	*2021*	*2022*	*2023*
Türkiye	100	113	125	133	141	176	245	637	1233
Hungary	100	113	127	146	170	179	208	255	269
Iceland	100	110	131	142	148	158	178	215	232
Lithuania	100	105	115	123	132	141	164	195	214
Czechia	100	107	120	130	142	154	184	215	212
Portugal	100	107	117	129	142	154	169	190	206
Estonia	100	105	111	117	125	133	153	187	198
Latvia	100	108	118	129	141	146	162	184	191
Bulgaria	100	107	116	124	131	137	149	170	187
Slovenia	100	103	112	122	130	136	151	174	186
Netherlands	100	105	114	124	133	144	165	187	183
Croatia	100	101	105	111	121	130	140	161	180
Poland	100	102	106	113	123	135	148	165	180
Slovakia	100	107	113	121	132	145	154	175	176
Luxembourg	100	106	112	120	132	151	172	189	172
Ireland	100	107	119	131	134	135	146	164	169
Austria	100	107	112	119	126	136	151	168	164
Malta	100	105	111	117	125	129	135	144	152
Germany	100	108	114	122	129	139	155	163	149
Romania	100	106	112	119	123	128	134	144	148
European Union	100	104	109	115	120	127	138	148	148
Spain	100	105	111	119	125	128	132	142	148
Norway	100	108	114	116	120	126	138	146	148
Belgium	100	102	106	109	113	118	126	133	136
Denmark	100	105	110	115	118	123	138	137	132
Sweden	100	108	115	114	117	122	134	139	132
France	100	101	104	107	111	117	124	132	131
Cyprus	100	100	103	104	108	108	104	107	110
Italy	100	100	99	99	99	100	103	107	108
Finland	100	101	102	103	104	106	110	112	106

The composite Housing Affordability Index, published by the National Association of Realtors (NAR), is one of the most watched affordability indices closely monitored in the US. This index measures median household income relative to the income necessary to purchase a median-priced house (Gyourko & Tracy, 1999). An index above 100 indicates better affordability, while below 100 is a bad sign for affordability. According to the NAR Housing Affordability Index, the index declined from 148 in 2021 to 103 in 2024. The index fell to as low as 91.4 in October 2023,

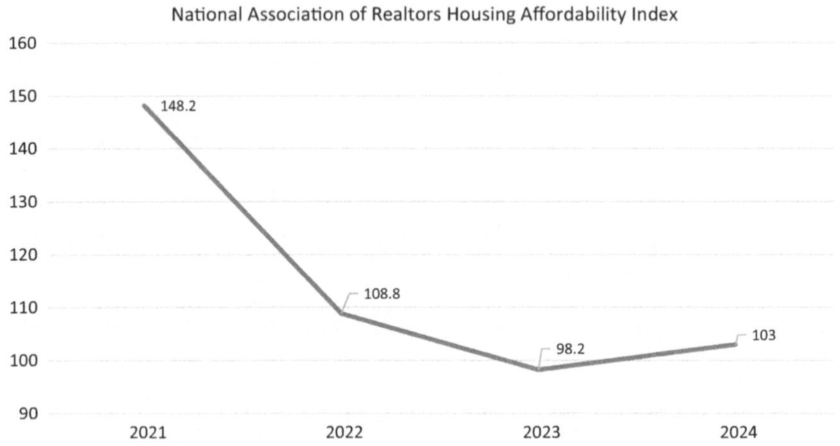

Fig. 3.14 US national association of realtors housing affordability index (Realtors, 2024)

as shown in Table 3.4. Figure 3.14 also exhibits the housing affordability in the US after the pandemic.

Mortgage as a Percentage of Income & Loan Affordability Index

Another measure of affordability is the mortgage as a percentage of income ratio, which is obtained by dividing the actual monthly cost of the mortgage by the take-home family income. The lower this ratio, the more affordable. The Loan Affordability Index is an inverse of the mortgage as a percentage of earnings. In contrast, higher values in the loan affordability index indicate better affordability.

According to the World Population Review 2024 data, Saudi Arabia is the most affordable country regarding mortgages as a percentage of income. United Arab Emirates, Oman, South Africa, and Qatar follow Saudi Arabia in terms of higher affordability. On the other hand, Syria, Argentina, and Cameroon are the least affordable countries with the lowest affordability indices. Although Türkiye has relatively the cheapest unit average sales price (USD 1,131 per square meter), it is the 10th least affordable country due to its high mortgage as a percentage income ratio of 308. Table 3.7 shows the most and the least affordable countries in terms of housing affordability index and mortgage as a percent of income ratio (Worldpopulationreview.com, 2024a).

Analyzing the cities in detail, Houston, with a 5.4 Loan Affordability Index, is the most affordable city in the world. Based on the Numbeo 2024 data, as shown in Table 3.8, among the 10 top cities, the US has five cities (Phoenix, Dallas, Jacksonville, and Orlando) in the most affordable cities list.

In Europe, Aalborg of Denmark is the most affordable city, with a value of Loan Affordability Index of 3. In the top ten list of Europe, there are three cities (Eindhoven, Rotterdam, and Den Haag) from the Netherlands. Turku of Finland, Antwerp of Belgium, Coventry and Aberdeen of the UK, Grenoble of France, and Malmo of Sweden are the top cities where housing affordability is the best in Europe, as exhibited in Table 3.9.

Price-to-income ratio, price-to-rent ratio, and mortgage payments as a percentage of income are the other main measures of affordability or buy or rent decisions in specific locations. Let's take a closer look at these ratios.

Table 3.7 The most & least affordable countries (Worldpopulationreview.com, 2024a)

The most affordable countries				*The least affordable countries*		
No	*Country*	*Housing affordability index*	*Mortgage as a percent of income*	*Country*	*Housing affordability index*	*Mortgage as a percent of income*
1	Saudi Arabia	4,6	22	Syria	0,1	1307
2	United Arab Emirates	4,3	23	Argentina	0,1	1135
3	Oman	4	25	Cameroon	0,1	748
4	South Africa	2,7	37	Sri Lanka	0,2	603
5	Qatar	2,7	37	Nepal	0,2	498
6	United States	2,6	38	Iran	0,2	479
7	Puerto Rico	2,6	39	Ethiopia	0,2	472
8	Belgium	2,3	43	Venezuela	0,2	412
9	Netherlands	2,2	46	Cambodia	0,3	338
10	Denmark	2,2	46	Türkiye	0,3	308

Table 3.8 The most affordable cities in the world based on the loan affordability index (Numbeo, 2024)

Rank	*City*	*Loan affordability index*
1	Houston, TX, United States	5,4
2	Phoenix, AZ, United States	5,2
3	Dallas, TX, United States	4,9
4	Pretoria, South Africa	4,8
5	Ad Dammam, Saudi Arabia	4,6
6	Jacksonville, FL, United States	4,4
7	Riyadh, Saudi Arabia	4,2
8	Orlando, FL, United States	4,2
9	Edmonton, Canada	4
10	Dubai, United Arab Emirates	3,9

Table 3.9 Top ten most affordable cities in Europe (Numbeo, 2024)

Rank	*City*	*Loan affordability index*
1	Aalborg, Denmark	3,0
2	Eindhoven, Netherlands	2,9
3	Rotterdam, Netherlands	2,9
4	Turku, Finland	2,8
5	Antwerp, Belgium	2,8
6	Coventry, United Kingdom	2,8
7	Grenoble, France	2,7
8	Malmo, Sweden	2,7
9	The Hague (Den Haag), Netherlands	2,7
10	Aberdeen, United Kingdom	2,7

Price-to-Income Ratio

The house price-to-income ratio (HPI ratio) is a ratio that divides the median house price with the median household income in a specific location (Abd. Rahim, 2015). While it gives insight into the affordability of a house in that area, it also indicates the housing market's overall health. The lower the HPI ratio, the more affordable houses are.

In terms of price-to-income ratios, Syria, Hong Kong, and Cameroon are listed as the worst-performing countries regardless of their income level and economic development status, as listed in Table 3.10. On the other hand, Saudi Arabia, Oman, and South Africa are the top three countries with the lowest price-to-income ratios, meaning the affordability in these countries performs better than others (World Population Review, 2024).

In the US, roughly USD 166,600 yearly income is needed to afford a home, but the median household income is just USD 74,580. The median housing price-to-income ratio in the US is 5.8. While Pittsburgh, Buffalo, and Cleveland have the lowest home-price-to-income ratio of 3.2, 3.5, and 3.5, respectively, San Jose (12.1), San Francisco (10.4), San Diego (9.5), and Los Angeles (9) are the cities where the price-income-ratio is the highest in the US. Shanghai, with a 46.6 price-to-income ratio, is the least affordable city in the world. Beijing and Hong Kong follow Shanghai with 45.8 and 44.9 price-to-income ratios, respectively. As Table 3.11 exhibits, Colombo, Beirut, Shenzhen, Guangzhou, Manila, Mumbai, and Ho Chi Minh City are the other least affordable cities from a price-to-income ratio perspective (Numbeo, 2024).

In Europe, Moscow and Saint Petersburg are ranked at the top of the list, with the highest price-to-income ratio. Paris, Lisbon, and Belgrade followed these cities with 20.2, 19.6, and 19.6 price-to-rent ratios respectively. Table 3.12 exhibits the price-to-income ratios in Europe (Numbeo, 2024).

Table 3.10 Price-to-income ratios (World Population Review, 2024)

No	*Worst performing*		*Best performing*	
	Country	*Price-to-income ratio*	*Country*	*Price-to-income ratio*
1	Syria	99,5	Saudi Arabia	2,9
2	Hong Kong	42,1	Oman	3,2
3	Cameroon	41,7	South Africa	3,3
4	Nepal	36	United Arab Emirates	3,3
5	Sri Lanka	35,3	United States	4,2
6	China	33	Puerto Rico	4,9
7	Philippines	31	Qatar	5,1
8	Cambodia	29,2	Iceland	5,9
9	Ethiopia	28,9	Palestine	6,3
10	Thailand	25,8	Belgium	6,4

Table 3.11 The least affordable cities in terms of price-to-income ratio (Numbeo, 2024)

Rank	*City*	*Price-to-income ratio*
1	Shanghai, China	46.6
2	Beijing, China	45.8
3	Hong Kong, Hong Kong (China)	44.9
4	Colombo, Sri Lanka	43.7
5	Beirut, Lebanon	41.3
6	Shenzhen, China	40.1
7	Manila, Philippines	37.6
8	Guangzhou, China	37.3
9	Mumbai, India	36.6
10	Ho Chi Minh City, Vietnam	34.5

Table 3.12 Price-to-income ratios in Europe (Numbeo, 2024)

Rank	*City*	*Price to income ratio*
1	Moscow, Russia	21,6
2	Saint Petersburg, Russia	20,3
3	Paris, France	20,2
4	Lisbon, Portugal	19,6
5	Belgrade, Serbia	19,6
6	Dubrovnik, Croatia	19,3
7	Prague, Czech Republic	19,3
8	Milan, Italy	19,0
9	Kazan, Russia	17,8
10	Tirana, Albania	17,5

Price-to-Rent Ratio

The price-to-rent ratio indicates how attractive a location might be for renting a property. The nominal house price index is divided by the housing rent price index to calculate the price-to-rent ratio. If the price-to-rent ratio is high, the home prices are higher relative to the annual rent price, so renting an apartment is more reasonable than buying it (Hargrave, 2021). A high price-to-rent ratio may also be evaluated as an indicator of a strong demand for rental properties. The price-to-rent ratio only gives an insight into how economical it is to buy or rent but does not indicate how affordable it is.

The house price to rent ratio rose in the US until the second quarter of 2022 and hit 141 (2015 = 100). After a few quarters of decline during 2022 Q2 and 2023 Q1 due to the slowed down of housing prices compared to rental growth, the ratio started increasing again, as shown in Fig. 3.15 (Statista, 2024f).

After its lowest value in the first quarter of 2015 (99), the price-to-rent ratio in the Euro area increased and hit 127.84 in the second quarter of 2023, and after a slight decline, it stood at 126.81 in the third quarter of 2023 (Tradingeconomics, 2024b).

The house price-to-rent ratio in the UK continued to rise until the second half of 2022, but growth slowed as the housing market cooled due to financing difficulties. On the other hand, the index in Germany and France dropped significantly between 2022 Q2 and 2023 Q3.

As shown in Fig. 3.16, Türkiye, with a 276 price-to-rent ratio, is also the global leader in this measure. Russia, Portugal, and Latvia follow Türkiye with 174, 172, and 164 price-to-rent ratios, respectively. Finland, with a 91 price-to-rent ratio (the lowest among other countries), is where buying is more economical than renting a unit (Trading Economics, 2023) (Table 3.13).

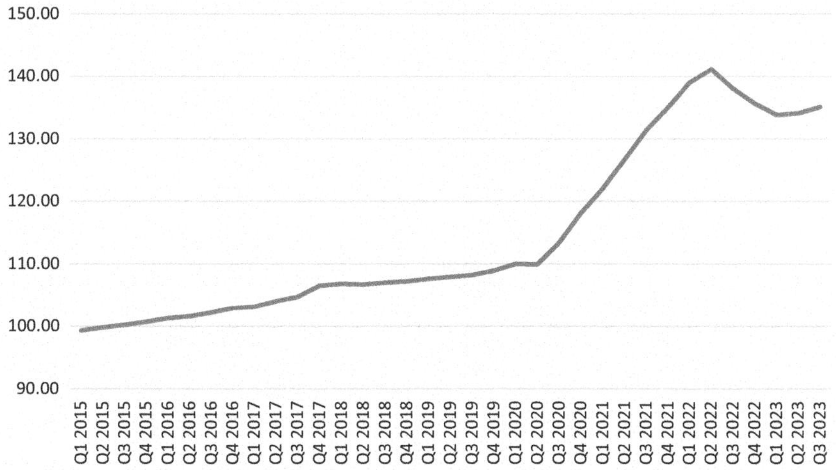

Fig. 3.15 House price-to-rent ratio index in the US (2015–2023 Q3) (Statista, 2024f)

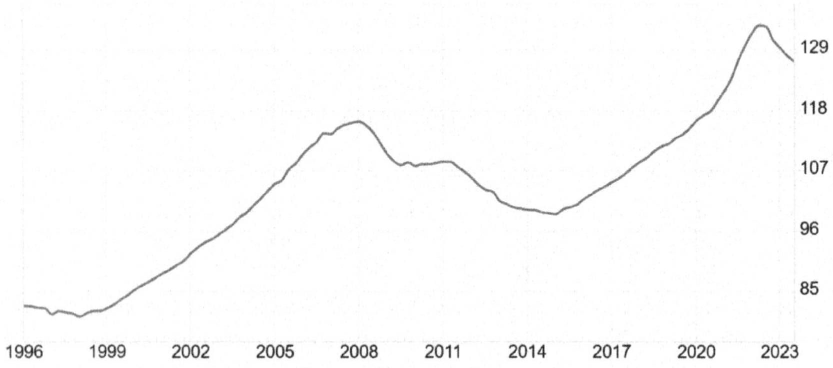

Fig. 3.16 Price-to-rent ratio in the Euro area (Trading Economics, 2024b)

Table 3.13 Price-to-rent ratios (Trading Economics, 2023)

Price-to-rent ratio (Trading Economics, 2023)			
Türkiye	276	Israel	127
Russia	174	Euro Area	127
Portugal	172	Colombia	127
Latvia	164	Switzerland	126
Czech Republic	158	France	122
Greece	157	Austria	120
Hungary	157	Denmark	120
Iceland	157	United Kingdom	119
Mexico	157	Norway	118
Netherlands	153	Sweden	116
Slovakia	150	Slovenia	116
Luxembourg	145	Poland	114
Canada	141	Lithuania	114
Spain	137	Belgium	114
United States	135	Ireland	108
New Zealand	134	Italy	103
Japan	130	South Korea	103
Estonia	129	South Africa	102
Germany	128	Finland	91

From the city perspective, seven cities in China (Guangzhou, Shenzhen, Hangzhou, Beijing, Shanghai, and Macao) are listed globally as the top cities in price-to-rent ratio (city center). South Korea and Taiwan also have two cities on that list. Quebec City, Canada; Buenos Aires,

Argentina; and Curitiba, Brazil, are the top cities with high price-to-rent ratios on the American continent. Vienna, Innsbruck, and Munich are also the top three European cities where price-to-rent ratios are high in Europe (Numbeo, 2024).

Access to Financing, Interest Rates, and Outstanding Mortgage Loans

When it is easy to access financing, people tend to spend more. Decreasing interest rates stimulates spending and increases inflation, skyrocketing housing prices. Investing in housing is considered a safe haven during the high inflation periods. The COVID-19 pandemic led to monetary expansion policies being implemented by several central banks, such as the FED and ECB, resulting in a high inflation environment that continues to challenge the global economy. Insisting on the "*inflation is temporary*" approach of the ECB and FED made inflation *more permanent* and increased its prolonged negative impact.

The situation is different now. Despite a recession risk, central banks raised the interest rates to decrease inflation. The interest rates rose to 5.5% in the US and Europe. In addition to the extremely high housing prices, affordability became even more difficult due to high financing costs caused by the increased interest rates. After the partial success of the ECB and FED in their battle with inflation, there is no declared victory yet to start decreasing the interest rates. The presidents of central banks are more prudent now. That negatively affects mortgage sales and the total number of sales due to the high cost of mortgage loans.

In the early 1990s, the US rate on a 15-year fixed-rate mortgage was between 6 and 9%. Before the global financial crisis, the rate increased to 6,07% in 2006. The rate on 15-year fixed-rate mortgages decreased after the post-COVID-19 pandemic (the Great Recession) and reached its lowest level, 2.27% in 2021. Then, a steep increase in the next two years moved the mortgage rate to 6.11% in 2023 (Statista, 2024g). Figure 3.17 shows the historical mortgage rates in the US.

As exhibited in Fig. 3.18, from 2001 to 2008, the outstanding mortgage loans in the US skyrocketed from USD 7.48 trillion to USD 14.72 trillion, which resulted in a mortgage crisis. After a relatively small decline after the global financial crisis, outstanding mortgage loans rose again, exceeding USD 20 trillion in 2023 (Statista, 2024h). The increase in home sales positively impacts the size of mortgage loans as banks are

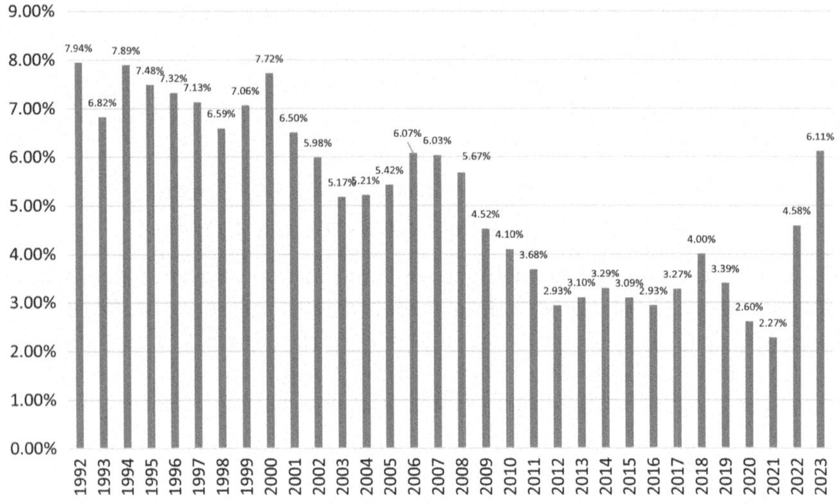

Fig. 3.17 Rates on 15-year fixed-rate mortgages in the US (1992–2023) (Statista, 2024g)

the primary source of home financing. The increase in sales prices also enlarges the outstanding mortgage loan values. Conversely, an increase in housing foreclosures, restructuring of mortgage debt, and short sales can lead to a decrease in mortgage debt, similar to what occurred after the global financial crisis.

In 2005, the percentage of housing units facing foreclosure was 0.46%, but it surged to 2.23% within the next five years. Following the Global Financial Crisis, there was a decline, reaching a low of 0.11% in 2021. Despite a recent increase, the foreclosure rate for 2023 stands at 0.26%, which is lower than the long-term historical average. Throughout the COVID-19 pandemic, the government implemented measures such as a foreclosure moratorium, a mortgage forbearance program, and mortgage servicing guidelines, resulting in the lowest rates seen in 2020 and 2021 (Statista, 2024i). Figure 3.19 shows the evolution of foreclosure rates since 2005.

Before the GFC, the number of US home sales peaked in 2005 and hit 7.08 million sales. A sharp decline in 2007 and 2008 decreased the yearly 4.12 million in 2008. Since then, the number of sales has climbed and reached 6.12 million in 2021, with the impact of the pandemic. In

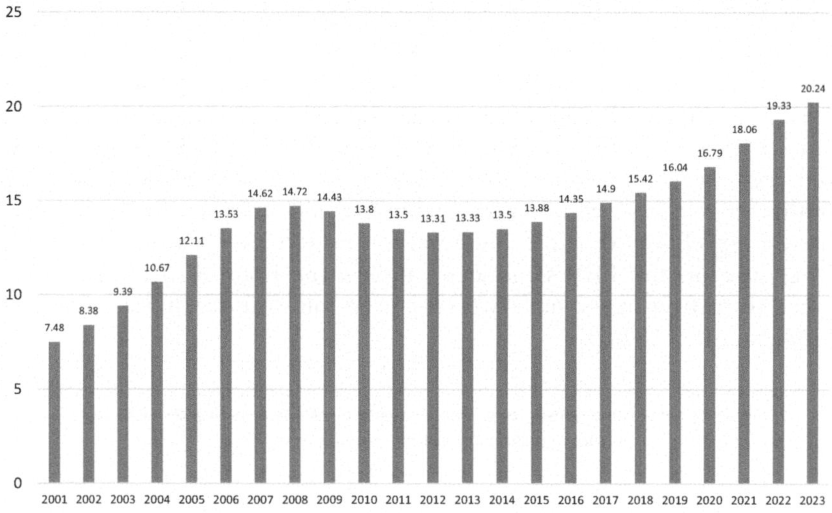

Fig. 3.18 Value of mortgage debt outstanding in the US (2001–2023) (in trillion USD) (Statista, 2024h)

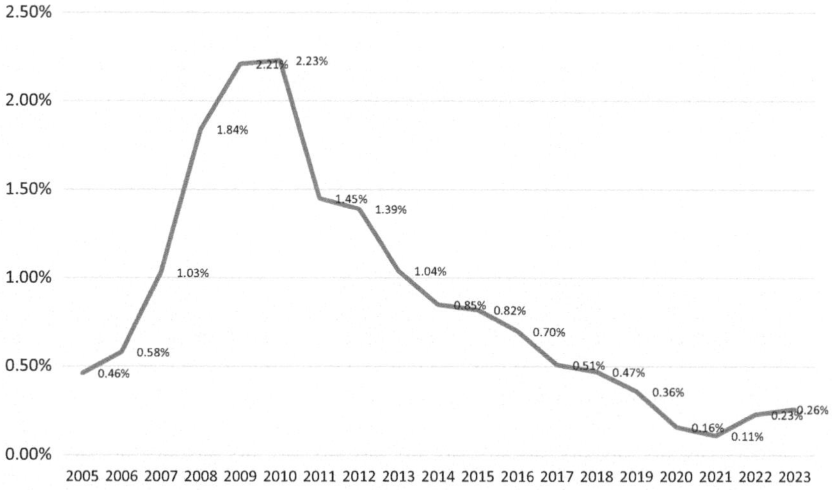

Fig. 3.19 Foreclosure rate in the US (2005–2023) (Statista, 2024i)

2023, there was a decrease in home sales due to high prices and affordability issues, resulting in a total of 4.09 million transactions, which was lower than the sales in 2008. To qualify for a mortgage loan, having sufficient savings for a down payment, a good credit score, and a stable and adequate income is essential. The year 2022 saw the most significant increase in mortgage rates in history, leading to a substantial rise in the overall cost of homeownership. Home sales are stuck because interest rates have not made any significant moves. As shown in Fig. 3.20, depending on the FED's monetary policy, the housing market is forecasted to recover in the next two years, and sales will reach 5.4 million in 2025 (Statista, 2024j).

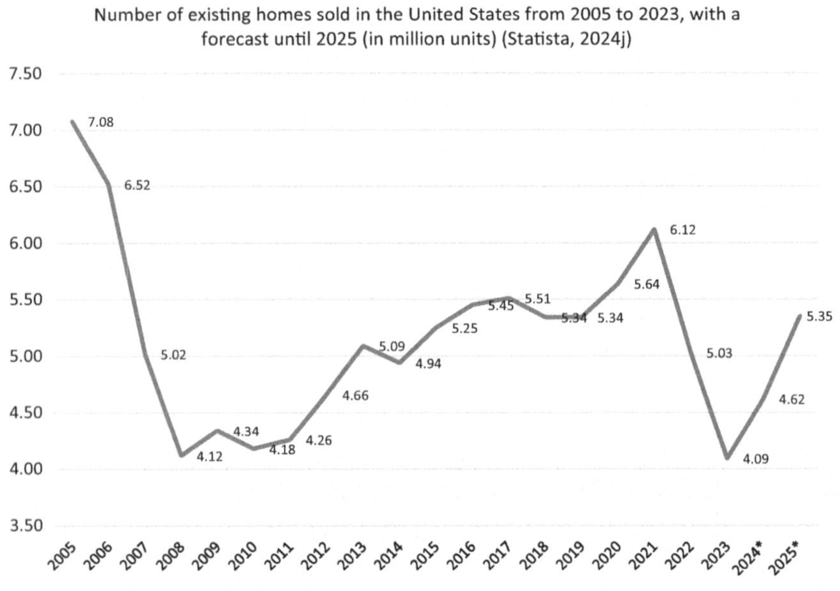

Fig. 3.20 The number of home sales in the US (in millions) (Statista, 2024j)

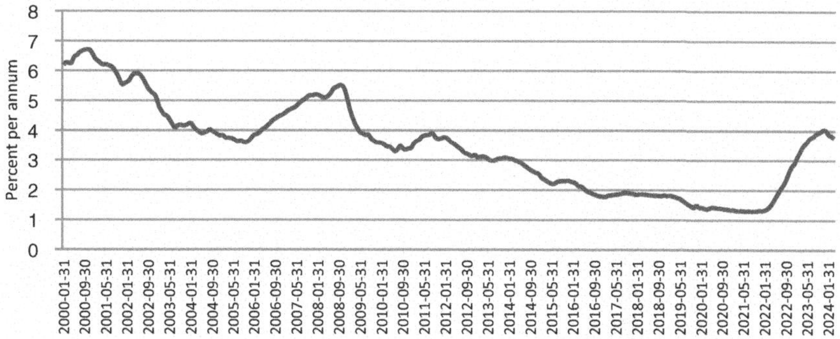

Fig. 3.21 Mortgage interest rates in the Euro area (ECB, 2024)

Mortgage Interest Rates and Outstanding Mortgage Lending in Europe

Mortgage Interest Rates

Mortgage interest rates are important indicators for determining the purchasing trends of homebuyers and the direction of housing prices. After the COVID-19 pandemic, many central banks started increasing interest rates to fight against inflation. That increase was observed in mortgage rates in many countries. Since 2022, mortgage rates have risen significantly in Europe, increasing financing costs and decreasing affordability. During the period from 2022 to 2023, there was a more than twofold increase in mortgage rates in several countries. Figures 3.21 and 3.22 show the Euro area and Europe mortgage interest rates, respectively.

While the average mortgage interest rate in the Euro area is 3.77%, the cheapest cost of borrowing is in Malta, with a 1.99% yearly interest rate. On the other hand, Estonia and Latvia are the most expensive countries in terms of financing costs, with 5.79 and 5.96% interest rates, respectively.

Outstanding Mortgage Loans

The UK, with close to 1.9 billion Euros worth of outstanding mortgage value, has the largest mortgage market in Europe in 2023. Germany and France follow the UK, with 1.8 and 1.3 billion Euros value of loans outstanding, respectively. In the UK, there was a decline of around 34% in the value of new mortgage loans in the first quarter of 2023 compared

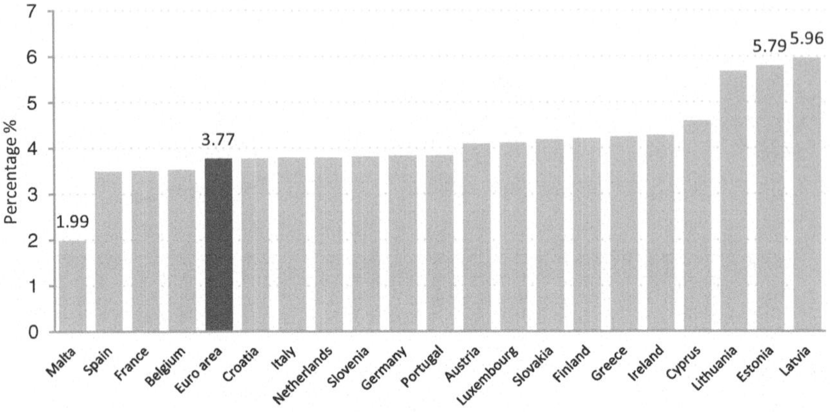

Fig. 3.22 Mortgage interest rates in Europe (ECB, 2024)

to the same period in 2022. In Germany, mortgage lending decreased by over 50% between March 2022 and October 2023. (Statista, 2024k). As shown in Table 3.14, the Netherlands, Spain, Sweden, and Italy—all exceeding 400 billion Euros—are the other top countries with high outstanding mortgage loans.

While the size of total outstanding mortgage loans reached around Euros 7 trillion in 2023, non-performing loans (NPLs), which are generally defined as loans whose repayment has been past due for a certain period (i.e., 90 days according to the European Banking Authority), are also important criteria to see the big picture of the housing industry. As Fig. 3.23 exhibits, the NPL rates have fallen dramatically from 7.48% of its value in the second quarter of 2015 to 1.85% as of Q2 of 2023 in the Euro area (Statista, 2024l). Comparing the NPL rates from a country perspective, Sweden had the lowest NPL ratios in Europe in 2022 (0.2%), and Greece had the highest one (8.6%) (Statista, 2024m).

The total value of loans with non-performing exposures in the EU is Euro 344.1 billion as of 2023. From a mortgage loan perspective, Spain, France, and Italy were identified as the top three countries with the highest value of non-performing mortgage loans in the second quarter of 2023. Non-performing mortgages to households in Spain amounted to around Euro 21.7 billion, while France had approximately Euro 11.7 billion in NPL. Italy, the Netherlands, and Germany followed France with 6.3, 6.30, and 2.80 billion Euros, respectively. Compared with its

Table 3.14 Total outstanding residential mortgage loans in Europe (Statista, 2024k)

Total outstanding residential mortgage lending in Europe, by country in 2nd quarter 2023 (in billion euro)	
United Kingdom	1.895,79
Germany	1.824,50
France	1.291,64
Netherlands	816,64
Spain	481,5
Sweden	452,77
Italy	425,25
Belgium	312,12
Denmark	247,13
Poland	107,96
Finland	107,89
Portugal	100,89
Ireland	83,14
Czechia	68,24
Greece	28,9
Romania	21,07
Hungary	15,27

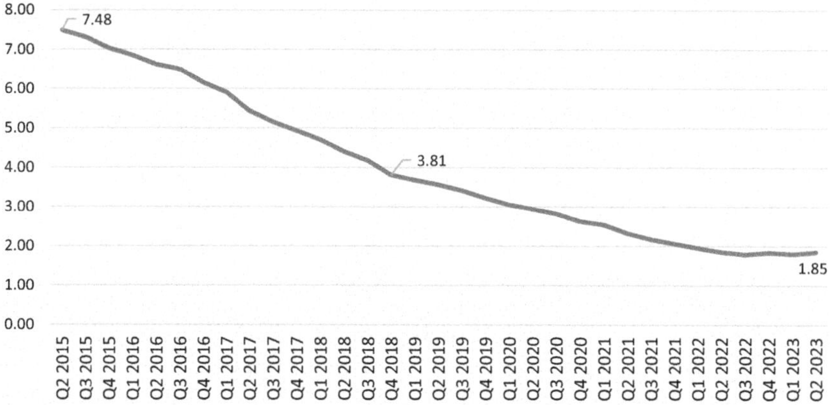

Fig. 3.23 NPL rates in Europe (Statista, 2024l)

economic size, the NPL volume of Greece (ranked 6th with Euros 2.70

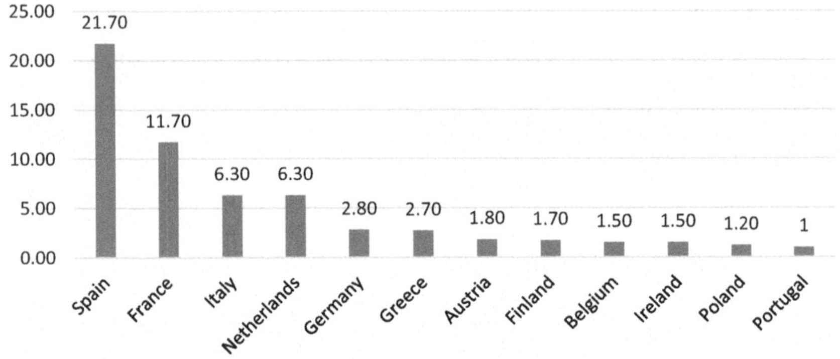

Fig. 3.24 Total non-performing mortgage loans in Europe 2023 (Billion Euros), (Statista, 2024n)

billion) is remarkable. The housing industry of Greece needs to be monitored cautiously. Figure 3.24 exhibits the volume of NPLs in Europe (Statista, 2024n).

The east side of the world has different dynamics and problems. The economy in China is facing persistent deflationary pressure. In 2023, the inflation fell as low as 0.23% and is projected to stand around 1% in 2024 (Statista, 2024o) (Fig. 3.25).

The decline in prices was also observed in the housing industry. In June 2024, new home prices in 70 Chinese cities fell by 4.5% year-on-year, marking the 12th consecutive month of decline and the most rapid pace since June 2015, despite Beijing's various attempts to alleviate the impact of a prolonged property downturn and sluggish economic recovery. Prices decreased further in most cities, with Beijing experiencing a drop of −2.4% compared to −1.8% in May, Guangzhou seeing a decline of −9.3% versus −8.3%, Shenzhen experiencing a −7.3% decrease compared to −7.4%, Tianjin reporting a −1.2% drop as opposed to −0.7%, and Chongqing's prices falling by −3.4% versus −2.7%. In contrast, Shanghai saw an increase in prices of 4.4% compared to 4.5%. Additionally, new home prices shrunk by 0.7% monthly for the second consecutive month in June, marking the steepest fall since October 2014 (Trading Economics, (2024c), Trading Economics, 2024d).

Since real estate loans make up a sizable portion of China's non-performing debt, the number of property owners compelled to sell due

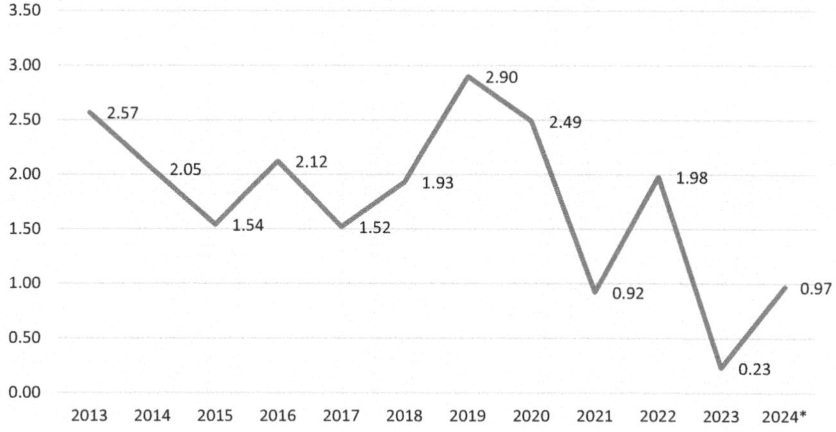

Fig. 3.25 Inflation rate in China (Statista, 2024o)

to debt is rising due to the country's economic downturn. Due to distressed prices, firms and homebuyers have been able to purchase affordable homes, warehouses, and land within the last two years. China Index Holdings reports that in January 2024, residential foreclosures sold for an average of 23% less than their asking prices. On the other hand, China's outstanding mortgage loans, which sharply increased from Yuan 25 trillion to Yuan 40 trillion (USD 5.5 trillion) within the last five years, declined 1.6% in 2023, marking the first annual drop in nearly two decades (Statista, 2024p) (Fig. 3.26).

The share of the total mortgage and real estate developer loans in total outstanding peaked in 2019 at 29%. This rate went down as low as 22.2% in the last quarter of 2023 compared to its value of 24.8% in the same period of 2022.

As shown in Fig. 3.27, China decreased the interest rates to stimulate consumption. They also announced the biggest-ever reduction in the benchmark mortgage rate with a 25-basis point cut in February 2024 to facilitate the housing market and lower mortgage costs. While the 1-year loan prime rate (LPR) was maintained at 3.45%, for household loans, the 5-year rate, a reference for property mortgages, was retained at 3.95%. Five-Year Loan Prime Rate in China was 4.85% in September 2019 and averaged 4.49% from 2019 until 2024. The 3.95% rate was the lowest rate recorded ever (Tradingeconomics, 2024d). In addition, the

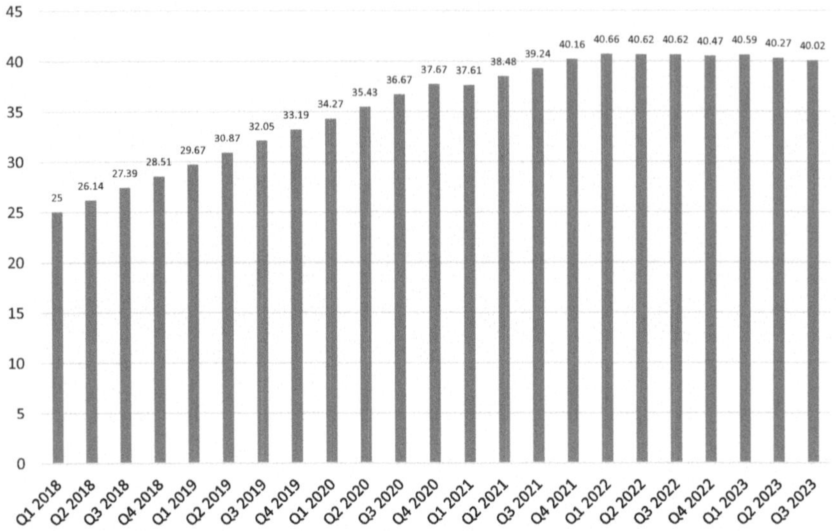

Fig. 3.26 Quarterly value of real estate housing mortgages in China 2018–2023 (Statista, 2024p).

minimum down payment ratios for housing mortgages lowered to 15% for first-home purchases and 25% for second-home purchases in May 2024. Despite the actions taken, China's housing market still suffers, which may take time to recover.

The Russian economy is experiencing a different story, especially after the war with Ukraine started in February 2022. Despite the problems it struggled with due to the sanctions applied, the Russian GDP expanded by 5.4% annually in the first quarter of 2024. As shown in Fig. 3.28, although the inflation rose to 17.8% in April 2022 and a decline was observed until April 2023, it stood at around 7.7% compared to the same month of the previous year (Statista, 2024q).

Russia is also discussing the potential housing bubble within the country. The Central Bank of Russia asked the government to cut mortgage subsidies to cool down the housing market and decrease demand. In response, the Russian authorities increased the down payment from 20 to 30%. Russia also ended its mortgage program after granting loans to millions of people at interest rates of up to 8%, half the Central Bank's existing base rate (The Bell, 2024).

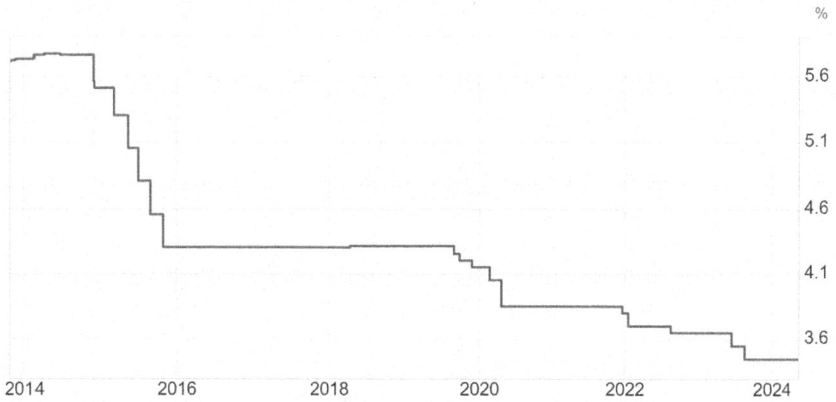

Fig. 3.27 China loan prime rate (Trading Economics, 2024d)

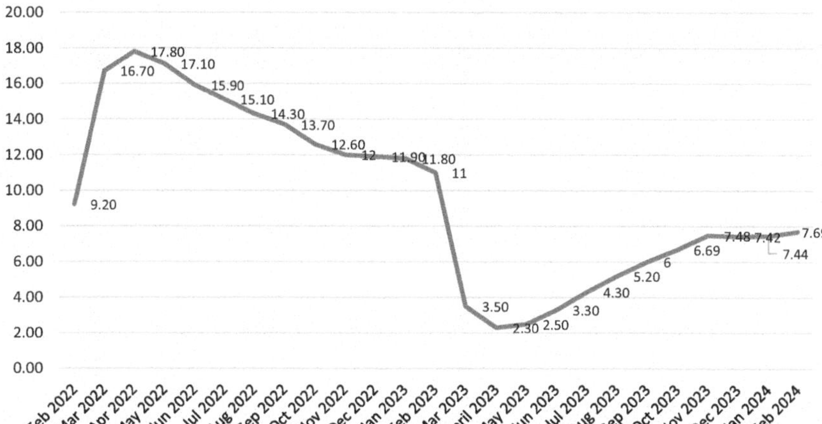

Fig. 3.28 Monthly inflation rate in Russia 2022–2024 (Statista, 2024q)

Before the COVID-19 pandemic, Russia's yearly mortgage interest rates were more than 10%. After a long-term decline, the average weighted mortgage loan interest rate was below 7% in May 2022. The mortgage interest rate is 7.92% as of September 2023. As of April 2024, the outstanding mortgage loan is Ruble 18,5 trillion (approximately USD 206 billion), and the overdue mortgage debt size is Ruble 64,4 billion (around USD 718 million) as of the same date (Bank of Russia, 2024). The share of overdue mortgage credits in Russia is 0.5%, which fell from 1.7%, its peak value in 2016, but slightly rose from 0.4%, its lowest point in January 2023 (Statista, 2024r). Figure 3.29 shows Russia's monthly mortgage interest rates (Statista, 2024q).

The case in Türkiye is unique. In contrast to many central banks, CBRT decreased interest rates to as low as 8.5% during and after COVID-19. After a steep rise in inflation, the CBRT had to change its policy in 2023 and started increasing the interest rates sharply (Fig. 3.30).

The yearly interest rates in Türkiye hit 50%, the second highest rate among G-20 countries after Argentina, in April 2024 (Central Bank Republic of Türkiye [CBRT], 2024). The high inflationary period in Türkiye resulted in high construction costs, skyrocketing housing sales and rent prices, difficulties with access to finance, high financing costs, and affordability problems. As exhibited in Fig. 3.29, parallel to the CBRT interest rates, the mortgage interest rates rose to 43% in March 2024. According to Turkstats (2024), the rate of mortgaged housing sales fell to as low as 9,4% of the total sales. This rate was 39.8% in 2013. As of May 2024, the total outstanding mortgage loans in Türkiye was TL

Fig. 3.29 Mortgage loan interest rate in Russia monthly 2019–2023 (Statista, 2024r)

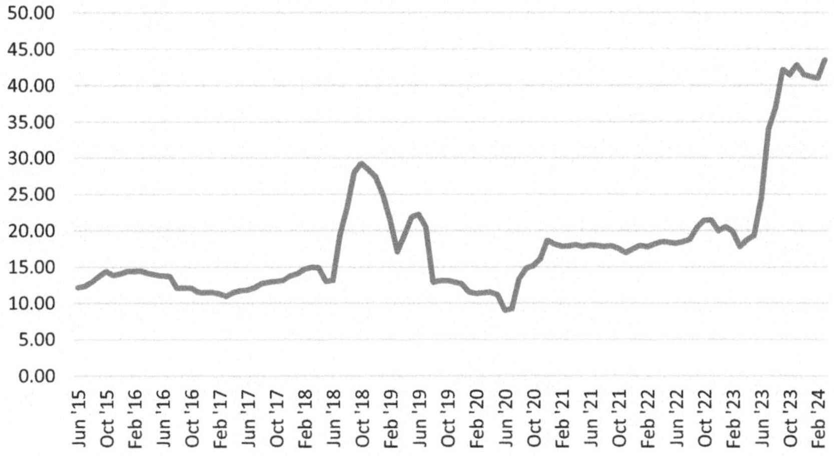

Fig. 3.30 The average interest rate for housing bank loans in Türkiye from June 2015 to March 2024 (CBRT, 2024)

445,6 billion (USD 13.8 billion). Despite the decrease in the purchasing power of Turks due to high inflation rates, the non-performing mortgage loan was TL 490 million, which is 0,11% of the total outstanding mortgage loans (BDDK, 2024). This low NPL rate is a good indicator of the stability of the Turkish mortgage market. A detailed analysis of the Turkish housing market is made in Chapter 5.

Overall, a significant decline in the affordability of new mortgages will not improve much in 2024, with mortgage rates remaining high globally. A decrease in inflation may improve affordability in 2024, but homebuyers whose savings have been diminished may only qualify for smaller mortgage loan amounts (Fitch Ratings, 2023).

Construction Costs

One of the main determinants of housing sales price is the construction cost. Inflation, costs of materials and workmanship, energy prices, and more all affect the cost. The construction cost index is a tool to measure the statistics behind those changes (World Population Review, 2024b).

With a 5.451 USD/m^2 unit construction cost, New York is listed as the most expensive city in which to build a residential unit in the world.

Tokyo and Geneva, ranked second and third most expensive cities, had 4.691 USD/m^2 and 4.662 USD/m^2 unit construction costs, respectively. In Geneva, construction costs of industrial data centers and logistics projects are expected to increase above 150% of the average in 2023. Table 3.15 exhibits the unit cost of construction in different countries.

Table 3.15 Construction costs per square meter (World Population Review, 2024b)

Country	*City*	*Construction cost (USD/m^2)*
United States	New York	5.451
Japan	Tokyo	4.691
Switzerland	Geneva	4.662
Hong Kong	Hong Kong	4.292
Thailand	Bangkok	3.980
United Kingdom	London	3.879
Germany	Munich	3.787
Ireland	Dublin	3.708
Austria	Vienna	3.594
Netherlands	Amsterdam	3.338
Singapore	Singapore	3.307
Belgium	Brussels	3.169
France	Paris	3.149
Sweden	Stockholm	3.127
Malaysia	Kuala Lumpur	2.938
South Africa	Cape Town	2.829
Italy	Milan	2.689
Chile	Santiago	2.668
Uruguay	Montevideo	2.641
Taiwan	Taipei	2.632
Spain	Madrid	2.159
Mexico	Mexico City	2.028
Poland	Warsaw	1.916
Brazil	Rio de Janeiro	1.895
Vietnam	Hanoi	1.853
Peru	Lima	1.828
Argentina	Buenos Aires	1.790
Colombia	Medellín	1.560
Philippines	Manila	1.300
Georgia	Tbilisi	1.170
Indonesia	Jakarta	812

According to the data from the Census Bureau (2024), in the US, as of the end of 2022, the construction cost index is 186, 86% more than its value in 2005. After the global financial crisis, the index fell to as low as 97.4 but rose continuously. After the COVID-19 pandemic, due to high inflation rates, the rate of increase speeded up and peaked at 186. In Fig. 3.31, the Laspeyres Price Index illustrates the calculation method, which involves determining the cost of a set of goods at current prices, dividing it by the cost of the same set of goods at base period prices, and multiplying the result by 100. This pertains to new single-family houses under construction in the US.

Table 3.16 shows the cost of residential construction in the US cities. New York, Honolulu, and San Francisco are the cities that the construction cost of housing for low- and high-end quality, single, and multi-family houses. The cost of constructing multi-family homes in Phoenix was among the lowest, at USD 218 per square foot. Meanwhile, the construction cost for single-family homes in Las Vegas and Portland ranged from USD 180 to USD 275 per square foot (Statista, 2024s).

Prices and expenses for constructing residential buildings in the EU experienced a relatively consistent increase and reached their highest point

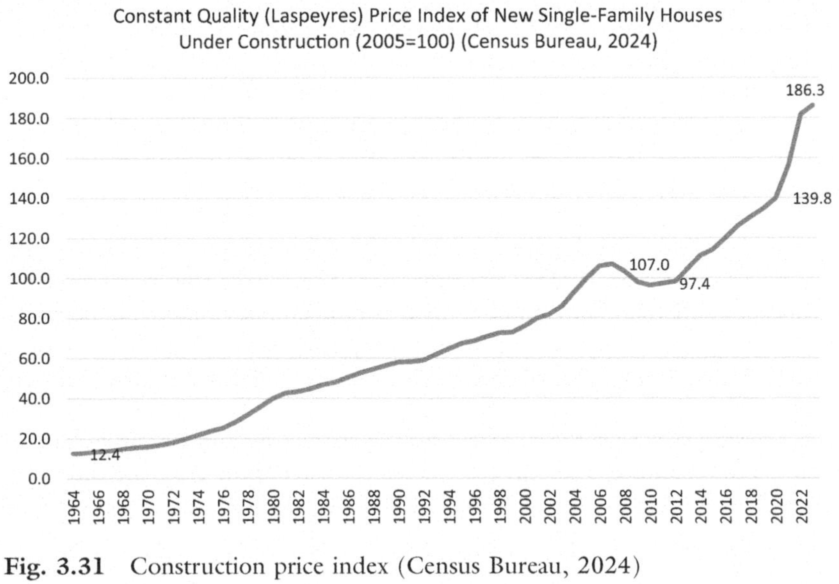

Fig. 3.31 Construction price index (Census Bureau, 2024)

Table 3.16 Residential construction costs in the US Q1, 2024 (USD per square foot) (Statista, 2024s)

Cities	*Low-end single-family*	*High-end single-family*	*Low-end multi-family*	*High-end multi-family*
New York	340	675	235	460
Honolulu	310	580	275	470
Chicago	275	550	200	460
San Francisco	310	520	400	625
Phoenix	190	515	180	275
Denver	230	465	185	355
Las Vegas	230	460	195	465
Portland	275	420	275	385
Boston	295	410	260	360
Washington	265	390	210	355
Los Angeles	220	390	250	410
Seattle	250	380	270	455

in the third quarter of 2008. Following a decrease during the global financial crisis, the indices for prices and costs saw a resurgence in 2010. The impact of COVID-19 on construction costs was minimal during the first and second quarters of 2020. However, from 2020 to 2023, disruptions in the supply chain due to the COVID-19 pandemic, escalating energy costs stemming from the conflict between Russia and Ukraine, high inflation, and the unstable nature of the construction industry all contributed to a rise in building material prices, thereby elevating overall construction costs (Fig. 3.32).

As shown in Fig. 3.33, between the first quarter of 2021 and the last quarter of 2020, construction prices and costs increased by around 23% in Europe (Eurostat, 2024c). Türkiye is at the top of the list where the annual growth rates and construction producer prices for new residential buildings went up the most in Europe, according to the Eurostat (2024c) data. Türkiye is followed by Germany and Poland, as exhibited in Fig. 3.34.

It is estimated that the construction costs will keep growing in 2024. Figure 3.34 exhibits the forecast of the construction costs in different cities. Lagos, Mexico, and Tokyo are listed as the top cities where construction costs will go up the most, with 15%, 8%, and 7.5% growth

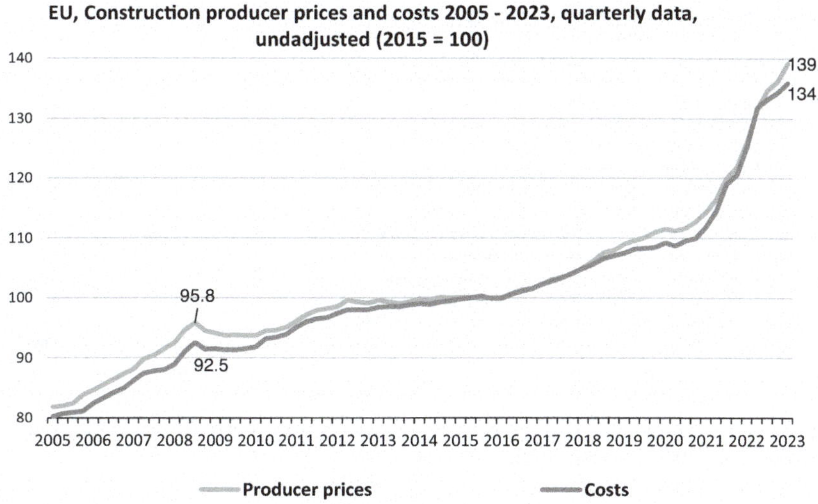

Fig. 3.32 Construction producer prices and costs in the EU (Eurostat, 2024c)

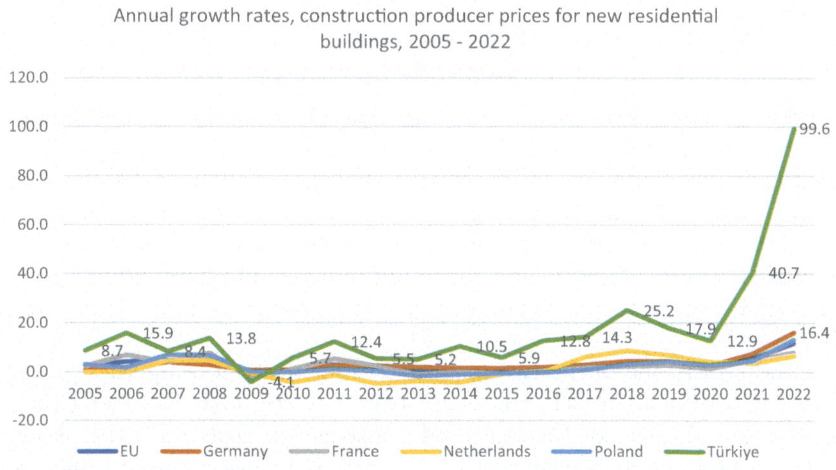

Fig. 3.33 Annual growth rates, construction producer prices for new residential buildings (Eurostat, 2024c)

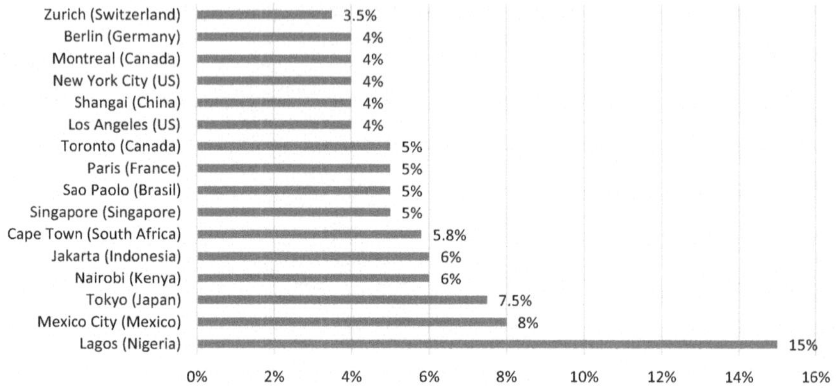

Fig. 3.34 Forecast of the growth of construction costs in selected cities worldwide in 2024 (Statista, 2024t)

rates, respectively. Considering all other cities, the rise in construction costs may keep the housing prices increasing in 2024 (Statista, 2024t).

Land Costs

Land speculation is buying and holding vacant land until the area becomes attractive for real estate development. For many centuries, people have used land speculation as an investment strategy. In the mid-1960s, Walt Disney discreetly started acquiring farmland in central Florida. Land investors need patience and a long-term perspective instead of seeking immediate profits. Conducting thorough research and developing a solid strategy is crucial to maximizing returns on land investments (Retipster, 2024).

Land cost is one of the two main determinants of housing sales prices. When it is difficult to sell, the developers may consider decreasing their profits, but the rise of the land and construction costs limit the ability of home builders to determine the sales prices. In many cities in the US, land prices make up over two-thirds of the value of those properties in 2021. San Jose, Los Angeles, and San Francisco are the top three cities where land costs constitute 78%, 74%, and 72% of the property value, respectively (Statista, 2024u).

Land prices are on the rise in many countries. In 2024, the land prices in Tokyo, Osaka, and Nagoya in Japan exhibited the highest increase in the last decade, with a 3.5% annual growth rate (Statista, 2024v). Land prices are higher in metropolitan areas. For instance, in cities with at least half a million residents in Germany, the residential land area prices are Euro 1,644 per square meter (Statista, 2024w).

The rise in land prices may increase housing prices or vice versa, as some scholars claim the rise in land prices results from high housing prices (Ball et al., 2022; Kok et al., 2014). High land prices due to high future price expectations may also impact the rental price of housing upward. Indeed, homeowners who rent their apartments expect higher rental income if they purchase them for high prices.

Price Projections and Bubble Risk

Compared to 2023, a modest nominal home price growth is expected in 2024. China, which experienced a 7% decline over the past two years, France, due to affordability constraints and strict financing conditions, and Japan may experience a decrease in prices. On the other hand, the prices in 2024 and 2025 may moderately increase in Mexico, Colombia, Brazil, Australia, Canada, and the Netherlands. The lagged impact of inflation is expected to be observed in Latin America, and the prices in the US and the UK will be mostly flat. Figure 3.35 shows the home price cycle of selected countries (Fitch Ratings, 2023).

Holzey et al. (2023) report that Zurich and Tokyo are the two countries that may face a bubble with 1.71 and 1.65 bubble index scores, respectively. The index score is calculated as the weighted average of price-to-income and price-to-rent ratios, change in mortgage-to-GDP ratio and change in construction-to-GDP ratio, and city-to-country price ratio. While the above 1.5 score indicates a risk of a bubble, a 0.5 to 1.5 score means an overvalue of the prices. In that context, property prices in the report are considered overvalued in Miami, Munich, Frankfurt, Hong Kong, Toronto, Geneva, Los Angeles, London, Tel Aviv, Vancouver, Amsterdam, Stockholm, and Paris. Figure 3.36 shows the UBS Global Real Estate Bubble Index.

Overall, high land and construction costs, the current extreme level of housing prices, the expensive cost of borrowing money from banks both for home purchasers and developers, the size of the outstanding mortgage loans, the levels of affordability indices, the mortgage payments

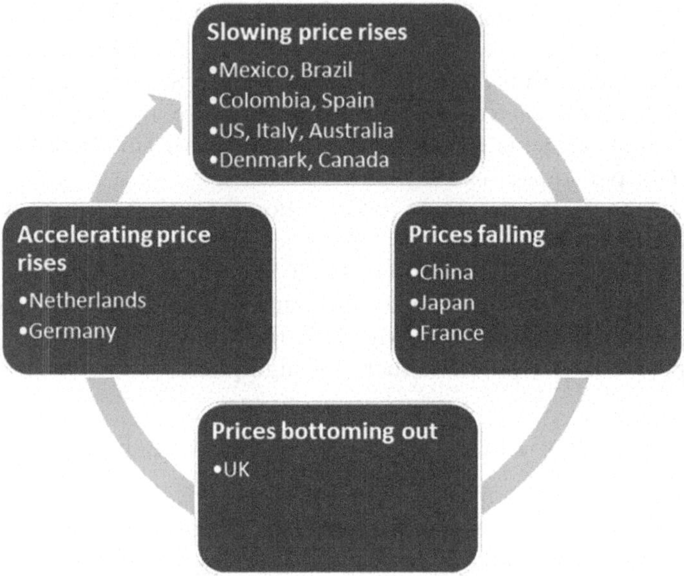

Fig. 3.35 Position in housing price cycle (Fitch Ratings, 2023)

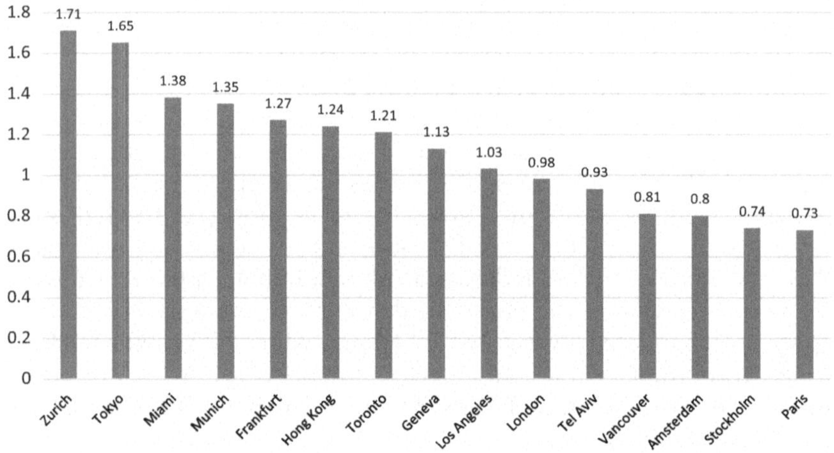

Fig. 3.36 UBS global real estate bubble index (Holzey et al., 2023)

as a percentage of income, the price to rent and price-to-income ratios indicate that the housing industry is running to a housing crisis under high inflationary period.

We must find urgent, sustainable solutions and develop concrete policies to overcome the housing crisis. To achieve that, we need to analyze the reasons behind the past housing bubbles and crises, their consequences, and potential lessons (not) learned. The following chapter focuses on that.

References

Abd. Rahim, N. M. S. (2015). Price to income ratio approach in housing affordability. *Journal of Economics, Business and Management, 3*(12), 1190–1193.https://doi.org/10.7763/JOEBM.2015.V3.357

Bah, E. M., Faye, I., & Geh, Z. F. (2018). Housing market dynamics in Africa. Palgrave Macmillan. https://doi.org/10.1057/978-1-137-59792-2

Ball, M., Shepherd, E., & Wyatt, P. (2022). The relationship between residential development land prices and house prices. *Town Planning Review, 93*(4), 402–421. https://doi.org/10.3828/tpr.2021.2

BDDK. (2024). *Weekly banking sector data*. https://www.bddk.org.tr/BultenHaftalik/en. Last Accessed on July 21, 2024.

Betterdwelling.com. (2021). *The world has millions of vacant homes, and 1.3 million are In Canada: OECD*. https://betterdwelling.com/the-world-has-millions-of-vacant-homes-and-1-3-million-are-in-canada-oecd/. Last Accessed on July 21, 2024.

Çağlar, İ., & Aslan, A. (2019). *Biz Ne Seçimler Gördük, Ne Vaatler Duyduk*. https://www.setav.org/yorum/biz-ne-secimler-gorduk-ne-vaatler-duyduk. Last Accessed on July 21, 2024.

CBRT. (2024). *Weighted average interest rates for banks' loans*. https://www.tcmb.gov.tr/wps/wcm/connect/EN/TCMB+EN/Main+Menu/Statistics/Interest+Rate+Statistics/Weighted+Average+Interest+Rates+For+Banks+Loans/. Last Accessed on July 21, 2024.

Census Bureau. (2024). *Construction price indexes*. https://www.census.gov/construction/cpi/current.html. Last Accessed on July 21, 2024.

Congressional Research Service. (2023). *Introduction to U.S. economy: Housing market*. https://crsreports.congress.gov/product/pdf/IF/IF11327. Last Accessed on July 21, 2024.

De Sousa, T., Andrichik, A., Cuellar, M., Marson, M., Prestera, E., & Rush, K. (2022). *The 2022 Annual Homelessness Assessment Report (AHAR) to Congress. The U.S. Department of Housing and Urban Development Office of Community Planning and Development*. https://www.huduser.gov/por

tal/sites/default/files/pdf/2022-ahar-part-1.pdf. Last Accessed on July 21, 2024.

Deb, P., Finger, H., Kashiwase, K., Kido, Y., Kothari, S., Papageorgiou, E., Hoyle, H., & Oeking, E. (2022). *Housing market stability and affordability in Asia-Pacific*. https://www.elibrary.imf.org/view/journals/087/2022/020/article-A001-en.xml. Last Accessed on July 21, 2024.

Duboust, O. (2023). *Housing crisis: Are you prepared to wait 6 months to rent a studio in Paris?* https://www.euronews.com/business/2023/11/04/housing-crisis-are-you-prepared-to-wait-6-months-to-rent-a-studio-in-paris. Last Accessed on July 21, 2024.

ECB. (2024). *Loans*. https://data.ecb.europa.eu/main-figures/bank-interest-rates/loans. Last Accessed on July 21, 2024.

Eurostat.com. (2024a). *House prices down, rents up between Q3 and Q4 2023*. https://ec.europa.eu/eurostat/web/products-eurostat-news/w/ddn-20240404-1. Last Accessed on July 21, 2024.

Eurostat.com. (2024b). *Housing price statistics—House price index*. https://ec.europa.eu/eurostat/statistics-explained/index.php?title=Housing_price_statistics_-_house_price_index. Last Accessed on July 21, 2024.

Eurostat. (2024c). *Construction producer price and construction cost indices overview*. https://ec.europa.eu/eurostat/statistics-explained/index.php?title=Construction_producer_price_and_construction_cost_indices_overview. Last Accessed on July 21, 2024.

FEANTSA. (2022). *Urban challenges, housing solutions understanding cities vacant housing potential to provide adequate affordable housing solutions*. https://www.feantsa.org/public/user/Resources/reports/2023/Urban_challenges_housing_solutions_REPORT.pdf. Last Accessed on July 21, 2024.

Filipenco, D. (2023). *Homelessness statistics in the world: causes and facts*. https://www.developmentaid.org/news-stream/post/157797/homelessness-statistics-in-the-world. Last Accessed on July 21, 2024.

Fitch Ratings. (2023). *Global housing and mortgage outlook 2024*. https://www.fitchratings.com/research/structured-finance/global-housing-mortgage-outlook-2024-11-12-2023. Last Accessed on July 21, 2024.

FRED (2024). *Median sales price of houses sold for the United States*. https://fred.stlouisfed.org/series/MSPUS. Last Accessed on July 21, 2024.

Fuller, T. (2023). *In this country, most people rent for life. Is that really what they want?* https://www.nytimes.com/2023/11/06/realestate/zurich-switzerland-renting-homes.html. Last Accessed on July 21, 2024.

Gyourko, J. E., & Tracy, J. (1999). A look at real housing prices and incomes: Some implications for housing affordability and quality. *Economic Policy Review*.https://doi.org/10.2139/ssrn.1007465

Hargrave, M. (2021). *Price-to-rent ratio: Determining if It's better to buy or rent*. https://www.investopedia.com/terms/p/price-to-rent-ratio.asp. Last Accessed on July 21, 2024.

Herring, E., & Barber, S. (2023). *Average property price by country around the world*. https://www.finder.com/uk/mortgages/world-cost-of-a-flat. Last Accessed on July 21, 2024.

Holzhey, M., Skoczek, M., Saputelli, C., & Hofer, K. (2023). *UBS global real estate bubble index*. https://www.ubs.com/global/en/wealth-management/insights/2023/global-real-estate-bubble-index.html. Last Accessed on July 21, 2024.

Huang, Y., Yi, D., & Clark, W. A. V. (2020). Multiple home ownership in Chinese cities: An institutional and cultural perspective. *Cities, 97*, 102518.

Huduser.gov. (1994). *Homeownership-past, present, and future*. https://www.huduser.gov/periodicals/ushmc/summer94/summer94.html. Last Accessed on July 21, 2024.

ILO.com. (2022). *Global Wage Report 2022–23: The impact of inflation and COVID-19 on wages and purchasing power*. https://webapps.ilo.org/digitalguides/en-gb/story/globalwagereport2022-23. Last Accessed on July 21, 2024.

Kaas, L., Kocharkov, G., Preugschat, E., & Siassi, N. (2020). *Reasons for the low homeownership rate in Germany*. https://www.bundesbank.de/resource/blob/822176/e2eaf8a360c5b8f908e55b635885fed3/mL/2020-30-research-brief-data.pdf. Last Accessed on July 21, 2024.

Keenan, E. L., & Lieven, D. (2024). *Housing of Russia*. https://www.britannica.com/place/Russia/Housing. Last Accessed on July 21, 2024.

Kenton, W. (2024). *Affordability index: Overview and examples*. https://www.investopedia.com/terms/a/affordability-index.asp. Last Accessed on July 21, 2024.

Kok, N., Monkkonen, P., & Quigley, J. M. (2014). Land use regulations and the value of land and housing: An intra-metropolitan analysis. *Journal of Urban Economics, 81*.https://doi.org/10.1016/j.jue.2014.03.004

Massink, W. (2023). *Amid soaring housing costs, İstanbul is packed with vacant, newly-built homes*. https://www.turkeyrecap.com/p/amid-soaring-housing-costs-istanbul. Last Accessed on July 21, 2024.

Mohamed, T. (2023). *Russia's latest headache is a housing bubble*. https://www.businessinsider.com/russia-ukraine-war-economy-housing-bubble-mortgages-rates-inflation-debt-2023-12. Last Accessed on July 21, 2024.

Numbeo.com. (2024). *Property prices index by country 2024 mid-year*. https://www.numbeo.com/property-investment/rankings_by_country.jsp?title=2024-mid. Last Accessed on July 21, 2024.

Obasi, C.O., & Anierobi, C. M. (2021). The homeless-poor and the covid-19 stay-at-home policy of government: Rethinking the plight of homelessness in Nigeria. *Sage Open*, 1–10. https://doi.org/10.1177/21582440211045078

OECD. (2024a). *Housing prices*. https://www.oecd.org/en/data/indicators/housing-prices.html. Last Accessed on July 21, 2024.

OECD. (2024b). *Housing*. https://www.oecdbetterlifeindex.org/topics/housing/. Last Accessed on July 21, 2024.

PR Newswire.com. (2023). *U.S. housing value has surged, gaining more than $2.6 trillion in the past year*. https://www.prnewswire.com/news-releases/us-housing-value-has-surged-gaining-more-than-2-6-trillion-in-the-past-year-301938414.html. Last Accessed on July 21, 2024.

PropertyShark.com. (2024). *2024 homeownership rates in the U.S. by state and city*. https://www.propertyshark.com/info/us-homeownership-rates-by-state-and-city/. Last Accessed on July 21, 2024.

Realtors. (2024). *Housing affordability index*. https://www.nar.realtor/research-and-statistics/housing-statistics/housing-affordability-index. Last Accessed on July 21, 2024.

Retipster.com. (2024). *Land speculation*. https://retipster.com/terms/land-speculation/. Last Accessed on July 21, 2024.

Statista.com. (2023a). *Monthly median asking rent for unfurnished apartments in the United States from 1980 to 2023*. https://www.statista.com/statistics/200223/median-apartment-rent-in-the-us-since-1980/. Last Accessed on July 21, 2024.

Statista.com. (2023b). *Average real estate sale price in China between 1998 and 2022*. https://www.statista.com/statistics/242851/average-real-estate-sale-price-in-china/. Last Accessed on July 21, 2024.

Statista.com. (2024a). *Real estate*. https://www.statista.com/outlook/fmo/real-estate/worldwide. https://www.statista.com/outlook/fmo/real-estate/worldwide. Last Accessed on July 21, 2024.

Statista.com. (2024b). *Apartment vacancy rates in the United States from January 2017 to May 2024*. https://www.statista.com/statistics/1375114/monthly-apartment-vacancy-usa/. Last Accessed on July 21, 2024.

Statista.com. (2024c). *Homeownership rate in the United States from 1990 to 2023*. https://www.statista.com/statistics/184902/homeownership-rate-in-the-us-since-2003/. Last Accessed on July 21, 2024.

Statista.com. (2024d). *Share of housing stock owned by the population in Russia from 2015 to 2022*. https://www.statista.com/statistics/1139285/russia-home-ownership-rate/. Last Accessed on July 21, 2024.

Statista.com. (2024e). *Residential real estate*. https://www.statista.com/outlook/fmo/real-estate/residential-real-estate/worldwide. Last Accessed on July 21, 2024.

Statista.com. (2024f). *House price to rent ratio index in the United States from 1st quarter 2015 to 3rd quarter 2023*. https://www.statista.com/statistics/591978/house-price-to-rent-ratio-usa/. Last Accessed on July 21, 2024.

Statista.com. (2024g). *Rates on 15-year fixed rate mortgage in the United States from 1992 to 2023*. https://www.statista.com/statistics/187656/rates-on-conventional-15-year-fixed-mortgages-in-the-us/. Last Accessed on July 21, 2024.

Statista.com. (2024h). *Value of mortgage debt outstanding in the United States from 2001 to 2023*. https://www.statista.com/statistics/1193742/combined-sum-of-all-holders-of-mortgage-debt-outstanding-in-the-us/. Last Accessed on July 21, 2024.

Statista.com. (2024i). *Foreclosure rate in the United States from 2005 to 2023*. https://www.statista.com/statistics/798766/foreclosure-rate-usa/. Last Accessed on July 21, 2024.

Statista.com. (2024j). *Number of existing homes sold in the United States from 2005 to 2023, with a forecast until 2025*. https://www.statista.com/statistics/226144/us-existing-home-sales/. Last Accessed on July 21, 2024.

Statista.com. (2024k). *Total outstanding residential mortgage lending in Europe, by country in 2nd quarter 2023*. https://www.statista.com/statistics/614792/outstanding-residential-mortgage-lending-europe-by-country/. Last Accessed on July 21, 2024.

Statista.com. (2024l). *Non-performing loans and advances in the euro area from 2nd quarter of 2015 to 4th quarter 2023*. https://www.statista.com/statistics/1364408/loans-with-non-performing-exposures-in-the-eu/. Last Accessed on July 21, 2024.

Statista.com. (2024m). *Share of non-performing mortgage loans in Europe in 2nd quarter 2023, by country*. https://www.statista.com/statistics/1331856/share-of-non-performing-loans-mortgages-europe/. Last Accessed on July 21, 2024.

Statista.com. (2024n). *Value of total non-performing mortgage loans in Europe in 2nd quarter 2023, by country*. https://www.statista.com/statistics/1331831/total-non-performing-loans-mortgages-europe/. Last Accessed on July 21, 2024.

Statista.com. (2024o). *Inflation rate in China from 2013 to 2024*. https://www.statista.com/statistics/270338/inflation-rate-in-china/. Last Accessed on July 21, 2024.

Statista.com. (2024p). *Value of residential real estate mortgages in China from Q1 2018 to Q3 2023*. https://www.statista.com/statistics/1214346/china-value-of-real-estate-housing-mortgages/. Last Accessed on July 21, 2024.

Statista.com. (2024q). *Russia: Inflation rate from April 2022 to April 2024*. https://www.statista.com/statistics/276323/monthly-inflation-rate-in-russia/. Last Accessed on July 21, 2024.

Statista.com. (2024r). *Average weighted mortgage loan interest rate in Russia from January 2019 to September 2023.* https://www.statista.com/statistics/1330970/russia-mortgage-loan-interest-rate/. Last Accessed on July 21, 2024.

Statista.com. (2024s). *Average construction costs of single-family and multi-family residential buildings in the United States in the 1st quarter 2024, by city.* https://www.statista.com/statistics/830432/construction-costs-of-residential-buildings-in-us-cities/. Last Accessed on July 21, 2024.

Statista.com. (2024t). *Forecast of the growth of construction costs in selected cities worldwide in 2024.* https://www.statista.com/statistics/868616/global-construction-cost-growth-by-country/. Last Accessed on July 21, 2024.

Statista.com. (2024u). *Land price as a share of property value in selected cities in the United States in 2021.* https://www.statista.com/statistics/1376634/land-price-as-a-share-of-property-value-in-selected-cities-in-the-us/. Last Accessed on July 21, 2024.

Statista.com. (2024v). *Annual growth rate of the official land prices in the metropolitan areas of Tokyo, Osaka and Nagoya in Japan from 2015 to 2024.* https://www.statista.com/statistics/666313/japan-land-price-change-major-metropolitan-areas/. Last Accessed on July 21, 2024.

Statista.com. (2024w). *Price of construction-ready land in Germany in 2022, by end use and population size.* https://www.statista.com/statistics/1294099/price-of-land-in-germany-by-end-use-and-population-size/. Last Accessed on July 21, 2024.

The Bell.com (2024). *Russia ends subsidized mortgages, leaving a housing bubble and inequality behind.* https://en.thebell.io/russia-ends-subsidized-mortgages-leaving-a-housing-bubble-and-inequality-behind/. Last Accessed on July 21, 2024.

Trading Economics. (2023). *Price to rent ratio by country.* https://tradingeconomics.com/country-list/price-to-rent-ratio. Last Accessed on July 21, 2024.

TradingEconomics.com. (2024a). *Home ownership rate—by country.* https://tradingeconomics.com/country-list/home-ownership%20rate. Last Accessed on July 21, 2024.

Trading Economics. (2024b). *Euro zone price to rent ratio.* https://tradingeconomics.com/euro-area/price-to-rent-ratio. Last Accessed on July 21, 2024.

Trading Economics. (2024c). *China newly built house prices YoY change.* https://tradingeconomics.com/china/housing-index. Last Accessed on July 21, 2024.

Trading Economics. (2024d). *China loan prime rate.* https://tradingeconomics.com/china/interest-rate. Last Accessed on July 21, 2024.

Turkstat. (2024). *Konut Satış İstatistikleri.* https://data.tuik.gov.tr/Kategori/GetKategori?p=insaat-ve-konut-116&dil=1. Last Accessed on July 21, 2024.

Worldpopulationreview.com. (2024a). *Affordable housing by country 2024*. https://worldpopulationreview.com/country-rankings/affordable-housing-by-country. Last Accessed on July 21, 2024.

World Population Review. (2024b). *Construction cost index by country 2024*. https://worldpopulationreview.com/country-rankings/construction-cost-index-by-country. Last Accessed on July 21, 2024.

Worldbank. (2024). *Population total, Kosovo*. https://data.worldbank.org/indicator/SP.POP.TOTL?locations=XK. Last Accessed on July 24, 2024.

Zhang, J. (2023). *What Evergrande's collapse means for China's economy, consumers and luxury*. https://jingdaily.com/posts/evergrande-collapse-china-economy-and-consumer-sentiment. Last Accessed on July 21, 2024.

Zhu, M. (2014). *Housing markets, financial stability and the economy*. https://www.imf.org/en/News/Articles/2015/09/28/04/53/sp060514. Last Accessed on July 21, 2024.

CHAPTER 4

Lessons (Not) Learned from Past Housing Bubbles and Crises

> The Western economies exhibit an average 18.6-year real estate/credit cycle. Generally, this averages 14 years up and 4 years down. (Anderson, 2009)

Anderson (2009), in his book "The Secret Life of Real Estate and Banking," emphasizes the average cycle (18.6 years) in US real estate prices, measured from peak to peak. He states the shortest cycle is 17 years, whereas the longest is 21 years. He also underlines that understanding this cycle may help people forecast the future, protect their capital, and make money. A peak in land prices followed by a construction peak and bank loan policies, which also impact land prices, are the main determinants of this cycle.

On the other hand, housing cycles can have significant consequences for the economies. Housing bubble busts may result in spillover of financial stability and severe economic recessions, mostly starting with the construction and related industries. Declines in wealth, employment, and consumption also impact housing busts (Deb et al., 2022).

The dynamics of the real estate industry are very interrelated to the local and global economic conditions. The sector is exposed to the consequences of central bank policies and is subject to internal and external shocks. Many economic developments in macro and micro levels, monetary expansion and tightening policies, the interest rates, inflation rates,

L. Sümer, *The Global Housing Crisis*,
https://doi.org/10.1007/978-3-031-72604-0_4

growth rates, the levels of wages and the unemployment rates, the hedging abilities and return rates of other investment tools such as stocks, gold, bonds, etc. are also critical for the housing industry.

The housing industry, which covers around 80% of the total size of the real estate sector, has experienced many crises in history. Some of the housing crises initiated a financial crisis, as the mortgage crisis was the main reason for the global financial crisis in 2008, and some were the consequences of financial or economic crises. Indeed, housing is considered a capitalist commodity directly linked to international economic and political moves, crises, and shocks (Çelik, 2024).

Political conflicts, wars, refugees, and immigrants also impact the housing industry in terms of the supply–demand balance and the rise and fall of housing prices. The extreme rise in the prices may cause a housing bubble, and after that, the bubble burst may end up a housing crisis or, in a larger context, an economic or financial crisis. Although the housing crisis generally affects the whole country, past studies indicated that metropolitan regions typically experience longer and deeper housing recessions (Dong & Hansz, 2016).

A housing bubble is a sharp and unsustainable rise in property prices far above market prices in a particular region. This increase is not driven by underlying economic fundamentals but by vigorous market behavior and *speculative demand* (Samuel, 2024; Stiglitz, 1990). On the other hand, Lind (2009) criticizes the definition of Stiglitz and shifts the focus from the reason for the price developments to the specific development of the prices and defines the housing bubble as an immediate and sharp decline of the prices after rising dramatically over several months or years.

Oust and Hrafnkelsson (2017) extend the definition of the housing bubble with numbers. Their research, which analyzed quarterly housing price data from 20 OECD countries over 45 years, reveals that a large housing bubble can be identified if prices increase by 50% in five years or 35% in three years, followed by a dramatic 35% decrease. Conversely, a small bubble is characterized by a significant price increase of at least 35% over five years or 20% over three years, followed by an immediate 20% decrease. The outcome of the study of Claessens et al. (2008), who analyzed the housing price dynamics of OECD countries from 1970 to 2007, is similar to Oust and Hrafnkelsson (2017). Their research exhibits an average 30% price decline over 4 to 5 years.

When the housing prices hedge the high inflation rates, which means the rise in prices is more than the increase in the inflation rates, and the rate of the rise in wages is slower than the growth of the housing prices, a housing bubble is a term that we need to discuss. Future expectations are that rising housing prices will make people consider homes as investment tools. Moving away from the actual worth of the property creates affordability problems. Until a peak, the housing prices increase, but when the demand starts falling or access to finance becomes difficult due to a rise in interest rates or economic turbulence, the prices start dropping even as fast as they rose, and the bubble bursts with social and financial consequences.

Depending on the size and location of the bubble, the global economy may also be impacted, as we all experienced the global financial crisis initiated by the US mortgage crisis in 2008. In such crises, when the housing prices decline sharply, the homeowners may have to repay more outstanding loans than the value of the house itself, the foreclosures may increase, the wealth of consumers may shrink, the consumption may decrease, the unemployment rates may rise rapidly, and the economies may go into recession. From the perspective of financial institutions, due to defaults in mortgage repayments, banks may go bankrupt, as Lehman Brothers collapsed in 2008.

One of the leading indicators of a housing bubble is the overpricing. A property may be overpriced, but this does not necessarily mean that there is a bubble. Price-to-rent ratio, comparison of the cost of new construction with the actual housing price (price to construction cost ratio), price-to-income ratio, price-to-wage ratio, price-to-household income ratio, and cost of mortgage to income ratio are significant indicators to name the overpricing as a bubble or not.

According to Shiller (2010), sharp increases in asset prices which involve the majority of the public alongside media turmoil, rise in income inequality, increase in properties among the society, accepting the price increases as the "*new normal*," and a decline in borrowing standards are the signs of a housing bubble. The rate of the financing cost over the income of homebuyers, supply–demand balance, buyer expectations about the prices, bank behaviors and their willingness to provide loans, occupancy rates of the houses, and high loan-to-value ratio are also considered other vital indicators of a housing bubble (Geltner et al., 2007; Lind, 2009). Speculative buying, low-interest rate policies that enable more people to buy homes, increasing demand, and loose loan conditions also help the housing prices go upward.

Minsky (2008) defines the cyclical stages of a bubble under 5 phases: *displacement, boom, euphoria, profit-taking, and panic*.

The start point is the displacement when investors are attracted by a new paradigm, such as historically low-interest rates, as experienced at the beginning of the 2000s and 2020s.

Then, the boom period starts, when the prices increase slowly at first, but it gets faster as more participants enter the market. The initial increase attracts people, and the media starts discussing the boom in housing prices. The rumors and stories of significant gains made in short periods make people rush to invest in properties and start perceiving the situation as a once-in-a-lifetime opportunity. This irrational behavior urges more speculation, and more investors are involved in this boom stage.

Next, the euphoria stage, the phase in which the prices skyrocket, starts. The link between the fundamentals of the economic indicators and the prices is cut. No matter how prices go, buyers in the market will always be willing to pay more, not for living but for investment purposes. The 1992 Japanese real estate bubble is an excellent example of this *greater fool theory*, where the square foot prime office prices went as high as 139,000 USD in Tokyo.

Although it is difficult to predict the peak point, the profit-taking phase follows the euphoria stage; when the bubble nears a burst, the investors start selling the assets and getting profits.

The final stage is the panic stage. The bubble burst, and the asset prices go down as fast as they rise. The burst is the turning point, which may be triggered by many factors, such as a rise in interest rates, a decline in purchasing power, difficulties in accessing financing, an economic recession, or market saturation. When the number of properties for sale suddenly exceeds the demand, the prices start declining and crashing rapidly. Many investors who dreamed of profiting from the assets they bought are in a risky position, resulting in foreclosures or distress sales. This situation increases the speed of the price decline. Figure 4.1 shows the five phases of a housing bubble.

The cyclical problem of the housing bubbles is not a new issue in the twentieth century. The history of the bubble goes back to Ancient Rome, where land speculation existed. The 1630s Dutch tulip bulb bubble was a different kind of bubble compared to the housing bubble. It is one of history's most well-known instances of asset bubbles and subsequent crashes. During its highest point, the value of tulips reached around 10,000 guilders, equivalent to the price of a mansion on the Amsterdam

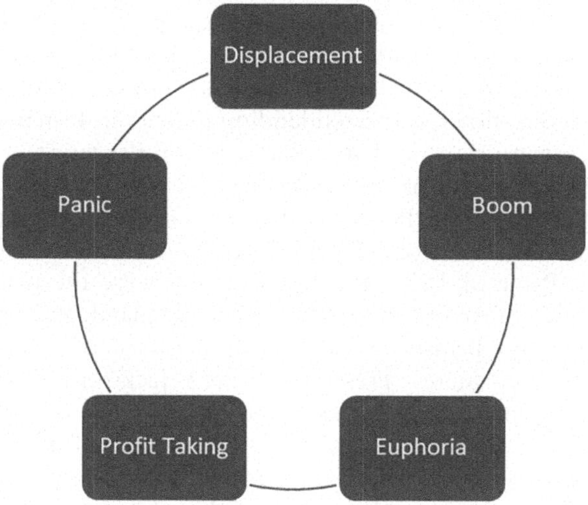

Fig. 4.1 Five phases of a Bubble (Minsky, 2008)

Grand Canal. In the sixteenth and seventeenth centuries, Spain rapidly urbanized thanks to the rise of wealth from its colonies, but it then experienced a building boom. This boom increased the demand for properties. Indeed, the rise in wealth stimulated the construction activities within the country.

The housing bubble and subsequent crises were observed in the 1800s and, more often thereafter. Let's start with the Panic of 1837.

The Panic of 1837

The Panic of 1837, also referred to as "*hard times*," was a significant recession in the US economy that took seven years to recover from the date it started at the beginning of the spring of 1837. The main reasons for the crisis were the real estate bubble and inconsistent American banking policy (Hammond, 1957). The crisis resulted in the collapse of hundreds of banks, value loss in currency due to a decrease in prices, a rise in unemployment rates, a decline in wages, and financial losses or ruins of farmers, merchants, and business owners across the country.

After the Indian removals, western land opened for settlement, and the northeastern forests were overvalued. The speculation in Maine timber lands was one of the examples of the overvaluation of the lands, which caused the collapse of Nahant Bank and Boston's Oriental Bank. Several causes contributed to the collapse of the land bubble, including international specie (coin) flows, restricted lending policies in Britain, a dramatic decrease in cotton prices, and speculative lending practices in the West. Another critical factor was the absence of a central bank to oversee financial problems, which President Andrew Jackson had guaranteed by refusing to extend the Second Bank of the United States' charter.

Before the Panic of 1837, the British banks were the main determinants of the trade of American merchants with England, and the US banks were dependent on British banks. In 1832, instead of rechartering the Bank of the United States, President Andrew Jackson redistributed the federal funds to smaller state banks in the country. The lack of a national bank resulted in a lack of standardization. Hundreds of new small banks across the country printed paper currency without considering the value of gold and silver coinage in their vaults. Taking advantage of the current banking conditions, state governments, land speculators, and business owners borrowed money to finance infrastructure development, launch new ventures, and purchase newly evacuated Indian and federal lands in the West using paper currencies.

The withdrawal of British banks on lending to the US in 1836 and the Specie Circular that President Jackson issued that the purchase of federal lands to be made with specie ended up with the depreciation of the paper money and the burst of the bubble in the spring of 1837. Cashing paper money by thousands of people made the banks close their doors and left the customers with worthless currency. Despite a brief recovery in 1838 when Dutch and England banks raised the interest rates, the recession lasted around seven years, and over 40% of all banks failed. 343 banks closed entirely, and 62 failed partially. The recovery from the hard years occurred after the discovery of gold in California in 1848, which increased the money supply and boomed the US economy by 1850 again. Still, after a decade, in April 1861, the Civil War started in the US, lasting 15 years.

The 1873 Stock Market Crisis

The economy of the South Side had nearly collapsed after the Civil War in the US. Before the American Civil War, the South Side's economy relied heavily on the unpaid labor of enslaved people to cultivate and harvest cash crops. Private banks issued paper money (banknotes), and there was limited road, canal, and railroad infrastructure on the west side of the Mississippi River. On the other hand, a quarter of all Northerners lived in cities due to the mass migration and industrialization, which created job opportunities. Following the Civil War, government-issued money became popular, military expenditures significantly increased the infrastructure and industry, and the government provided financial support for the settlement of the West.

In the following years after the Civil War, one of the worst banking crises in the US occurred in 1873. The panic was initiated by the stock market crash in Europe (Musson, 1950). On May 9, 1873, the Vienna Stock Exchange crashed, and many banks in Vienna failed. International investors who invested in bonds of railroad projects in the US began to sell off their investments, resulting in many railroad companies' bankruptcy. The bankruptcy of the firms also ended up with the solvency of one of the biggest banks in New York City, Jay Cooke & Company, which also had invested vast amounts in railroads. Jay Cooke & Co. had raised millions of dollars by selling bonds to finance construction after the authorization of President Lincoln printing paper money, called "*Greenbacks*," to pay expanding expenses. Withdrawal of the funds of thousands of people from banks made at least 100 banks go bankrupt in Washington, DC, Pennsylvania, New York, Virginia, Georgia, Indiana, Illinois, and Ohio. Inflation in the US, demonetization of silver in Germany and the US, political developments in Europe, and many property losses in the 1871 Great Chicago Fire and 1872 Great Boston Fire, which negatively impacted the bank reserves, were also other factors of the crisis (HBS, 2024).

Even though Britain greatly benefited politically and economically from the Suez Canal, its opening in 1869 is recognized as a contributing factor to the Panic of 1873 in Britain. Merchandise from the Far East used to be transported in sailing ships around the Cape of Good Hope and then stored in British warehouses. The Suez Canal was unsuitable for these ships due to the direction of the prevailing winds in the Mediterranean Sea, resulting in the decline of British entrepôt trade.

The Panic of 1873 significantly affected various sectors, including the US housing market. The decline in income resulted in a decrease in housing demand, which ended with a drop in housing prices and an increase in foreclosures (US Treasury, 2024). The panic lasted until 1879 in France and Britain and was named the *Long Depression* after the collapse of stock markets in 1929. This crisis weakened the economy of

Britain due to the two decades of stagnation that had started within the country.

Due to the crisis, the railroad building programs were canceled or postponed across the South, and deep debt and heavy taxes were left behind in many states. The South commonly responded to state debts during the Depression by implementing retrenchment measures. The local political landscape and power dynamics were also influenced by the Panic of 1873.

Great Depression

The 1929 Great Depression is one of the two most significant global crises of the last century. The superfluous consumption trend, oversupply and overproduction in the Roaring Twenties, the collapse of the stock markets in 1929, a decline in demand and rise in unemployment rates, monetary tightening policies of Federal Reserve, ill-tariffs resulted in a decrease in trade volume, and inadequate governmental response were the main reasons for the Great Depression which lasted a decade (Sümer, 2023).

When urban settlements first emerged in America, providing housing services was not the obligation of the government but the individual's responsibility to choose, build, and buy a place to live. Starting in the mid-1800s, social reformers called for improvements as urban housing was inadequate. With the onset of the Great Depression, the housing problems worsened. The construction of new housing units was almost entirely suspended, repairs were left unfinished, and slums expanded. The common idea was that focusing on construction activities could stimulate economic recovery.

The housing industry boomed in the mid-1920s, increasing homeownership rates alongside the rise in housing prices, construction prices, and the volume of mortgage loans (Brocker & Hanes, 2013). The crash of the stock market in 1929 resulted in a 67% decline in housing prices in 1932 from the peak value in the third quarter of 1929, as there was a strong correlation between the housing prices and the stock market prices between 1929 and 1932 (Nicholas & Scherbina, 2011). By 1933, 25% of the Americans (more than 15 million) were unemployed. In contrast to President Herbert C. Hoover's approach, which let people struggle with the crisis and unemployment on their own, his successor, President

Franklin D. Roosevelt, who won the elections in 1933, initiated a government program known as the New Deal that helped people get jobs and reduced the unemployment rates.

As the crisis got worse, many Americans became homeless and started building shantytowns (named *Hoovervilles*) in many cities within the country. In 1926, 68,000 individuals were affected by the loss of their homes, but in 1932, this number increased to 273,000 homeowners, and the subsequent year saw a daily foreclosure rate of one thousand mortgages. Many homeowners faced defaults and struggled to meet their mortgage payments. During the early 1930s, homeowners spent more on their mortgages than the reduced value of their properties. By 1933, 40 to 50% of all home mortgages in the US were in default, bringing the home financing system to the brink of complete collapse. The early 1930s banking crisis was caused mainly by the mortgage default and subsequent foreclosure.

The Great Depression led to a surge in foreclosures, allowing federal and local officials to implement their vision of developing a contemporary living space centered around owning a home and a single-family residence (Taylor Jr., 2011).

The housing investments declined during and after the Great Depression. The extended decrease in residential investment from 1928 to 1933 can be attributed to various factors such as housing prices, construction expenses, credit limitations, reduced demand, and financing expenses. A significant impact was observed from stricter monetary policies during 1928–1929, while the influence of financial disintermediation was prominent during 1933–1934 (Greasley & Madsen, 2013).

In the early 1930s, the US federal government intervened in the housing problem to relieve the distressed homeowners and banks and start new construction. They were providing long-term loans with low-interest rates, reducing construction costs, and providing government financial support to private efforts to build housing for low-income groups. The Emergency Relief and Reconstruction Act addressed the problems of low-income housing. In 1932, during President Hoover's era, the Home Loan Bank Act of 1932 was passed. When President Roosevelt took the presidency from his predecessor, the Home Owners' Refinancing Act of 1933 was passed, and the Home Owners' Loan Corporation (HOLC), which aimed to stop homeowners' defaults, was established. The HOLC refinanced risky mortgages by applying long-term low-interest policies alongside regulating the appraisal standards.

Then, the National Housing Act of 1934 was issued, creating the Federal Housing Authority (FHA), which established national standards for housing construction. With the National Housing Act (Wagner-Steagall Housing Act) signed in 1937, the United States Housing Authority (USHA) was established. 1938, the Federal National Mortgage Association (Fannie Mae) under the Reconstruction Finance Corporation (RFC) was established. By purchasing mortgages from banks and other lenders, Fannie Mae expanded the pool of funds available for additional mortgages and construction loans. The FHA and Fannie Mae did not directly engage in house construction or loan provision, but their support gave lenders the confidence that government funds would cover the repayment of construction and home loans in case of default. As a result, banks extended more loans to builders and homeowners, thus stimulating construction and laying the groundwork for the housing boom after World War II.

The federal government also started initiatives for lower-income groups to build shantytowns nationwide. By using public tax income, dwellings were built for those who could not afford a house. The federal government accepted housing as a social need, first mentioned in the New Deal's Wagner-Steagall Housing Act of 1937. Despite such efforts, public housing initiatives became partially successful in the late 1930s, but by the early 1940s, many Hoovervilles were demolished as the recovery of the economy during World War II. (History.com, 2023).

1992 Japanese Asset Bubble

Another severe real estate crisis occurred in Japan, lasting a decade to recover. Monetary expansion policies and uncontrolled money supply sometimes result in serious economic problems that are hard to recover. After a brilliant economic rise in the 1980s, the 1990s were named the *Lost Decade* in Japan due to wrong or late decisions of the Bank of Japan. Krugman (1998) defines the situation faced by Japan as a liquidity trap. From 1986 to 1991, Japan experienced a real estate and stock market bubble due to excessive monetary easing policies. The bubble burst and resulted in long-term stagnation in the Japanese economy (Sümer, 2023). While residential land prices increased by 180.5%, Japan's total real estate value quadrupled the size of the real estate in the US (Al Rifai, 2015). In the early 1990s, the Japanese Financial Ministry raised interest rates, the bubble burst, the stock market crashed, and a debt crisis began

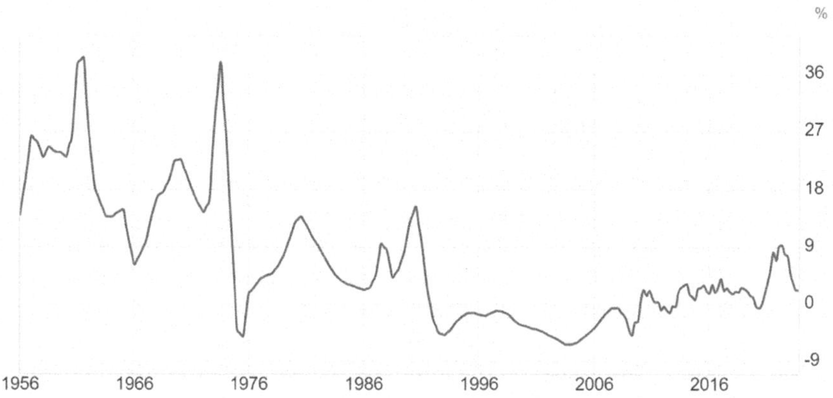

Fig. 4.2 Japan residential property prices (Trading Economics, 2024)

(Yoshino & Taghizadeh-Hesary, 2015). By 2001, the land values declined by 70% (Makin, 2008). Figure 4.2 shows the Japanese residential price change over the years (Trading Economics, 2024).

2008 Global Financial Crisis

The global economy experienced the most severe financial crisis of its history, triggered by the 2008 secondary mortgage crisis (Grant & Wilson, 2012). Consumption is one of the prominent veins of the current capitalist economic system. More consumption requires more money, and the consumers access financing primarily via banks. While high financing costs decrease spending and slow economic activities, low funding costs stimulate more borrowing and increase demand. The interest rate policies of central banks are one of the main determinants of such market trends and consumer behaviors. The 2008 Global Financial Crisis (GFC) is a remarkable outcome of such policies.

In 2001, the Federal Reserve (FED) started decreasing the interest rates to surge the US economy, struggling after the dot-com bubble. Such rate declines resulted in the rapid rise in the volume of mortgage borrowing by US households, and the number of housing sales and prices skyrocketed. Before the GFC, US houses were typically financed using variable interest rate mortgages (negotiable each year), short durations of less than five years, and one-time large payments due at the end of the loan term (Garriga & Hedlund, 2019). Figure 4.3 shows the number of housing units sold in the last two decades (Statista, 2024a). In 2005, the number of home sales peaked at 7.08 million units. The following year, the homebuyers purchased an additional 6.52 million units. A sharp rise in mortgage debt of US households was observed, and the rate rose from 61% of GDP in 1998 to 97% in 2006. However, 2008 and thereafter were the years that the number of housing sales declined sharply. Housing sales have never reached the same level as in the pre-crisis period since then.

From 1998 to 2006, the US housing industry experienced the sharpest rise in American history as the prices doubled on average. As shown in Fig. 4.4, the US Case-Shiller housing price index peaked at 183 in 2006 (2000 = 100). The share of the residential investment in the US GDP rose from 4.5% to 6.5% over the same period. After its peak value, the housing prices fell steeply, and the index was calculated to its lowest value of 135 in 2011. The housing prices started increasing after 2011 and reached in 2016 to its pre-crisis level (Statista, 2024b).

Before the crisis, the perception of people about buying a house shifted from seeing the property they live in to an investment tool that they profit over its price increase. Mortgage-backed securities (MBS) and collateralized debt obligations (CDOs), which bundled home loans and sold

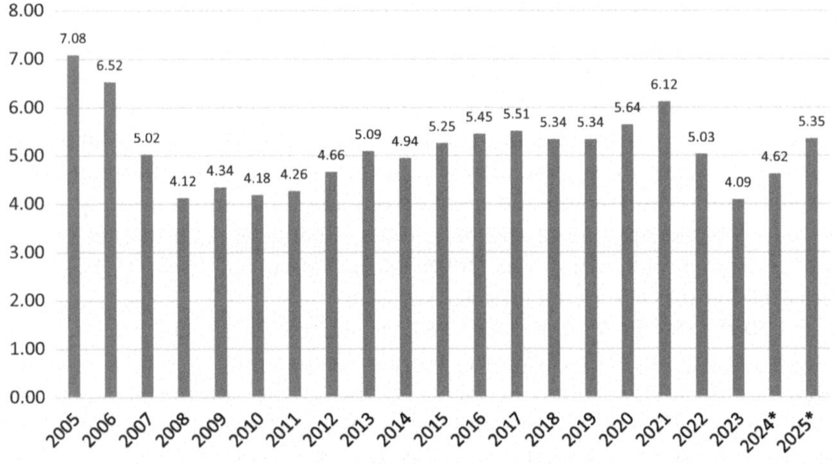

Fig. 4.3 Number of existing homes sold in the US from 2005 to 2023 (in million units) (Statista, 2024a)

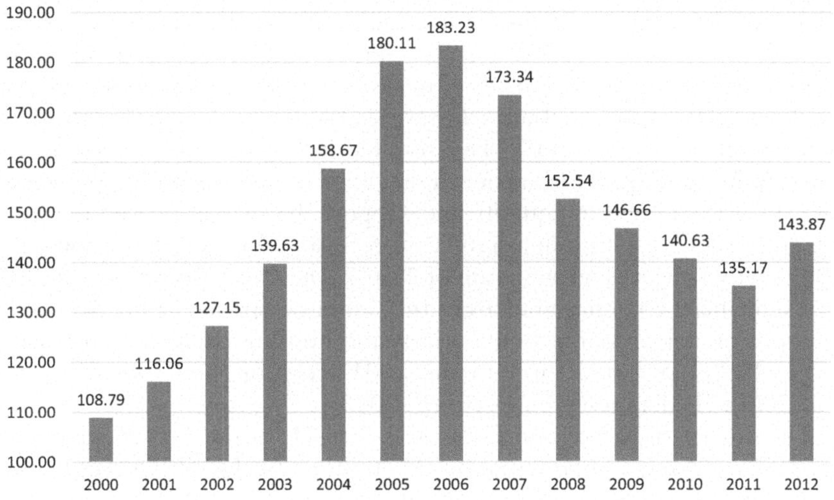

Fig. 4.4 The US Case-Shiller national home price index 2000–2012 (Statista, 2024b)

them as financial products, increased the appetite for housing investments. In 2005 and 2006, 90% of the new homes were financed by conventional mortgage loans. The loose lending standards and loans granted to individuals without seeking good credit scores increased the risks of the housing sector as the prices kept rising and the outstanding mortgage loans surged.

From 2001 to 2004, employment in the housing-related sector reached 40% of net private sector job creation. From 2000 to 2007, America's household debt rose from 104% of household income to 144%. Housing prices increased by 50% in real terms. In 2006, the prices started declining, and the bubble began to burst. Millions of foreclosures and defaults in mortgage loans resulted in significant losses for financial institutions that invested in mortgage securities. The collapse of Lehman Brothers, a giant investment bank, in 2008, alongside many global banks, was the consequence of the GFC. As shown in Fig. 4.5, in 2000, the unemployment rate in the US was as low as 4%. During the GFC, the unemployment rate increased to 9.6%, and 8.7 million jobs were lost (Statista, 2024c). Further, the US households lost roughly USD 19 trillion in net worth as the stock market crashed. The American dream was about to come true as the homeownership rates peaked from 64% of its value in 1994 to 69% in 2004, but the GFC ruined the dreams of millions.

In 2007, the global financial markets were adversely affected by mortgage-related financial asset losses, leading to a recession in the US economy in December 2007. This resulted in financial distress for many institutions, leading to turbulence in the financial markets during the same year. Efforts to provide liquidity and support the market proved ineffective, ultimately resulting in a significant recession for the US economy in 2009, with a negative growth rate of 2.60%. The Great Recession and the global financial crisis stemmed from the prolonged period of expansion in US housing construction, home prices, and housing credit, which began in the 1990s, persisted through the 2001 recession, and surged in the mid-2000s (Federalreservehistory.org, 2013).

The impact of the housing crisis was first felt in the US, triggering a financial crisis and a great recession. Main Street banks, Wall Street banks in the US, and many global banks went bankrupt due to their investments in mortgage-backed securities (MBS) (Aalbers, 2015) (Fig. 4.6).

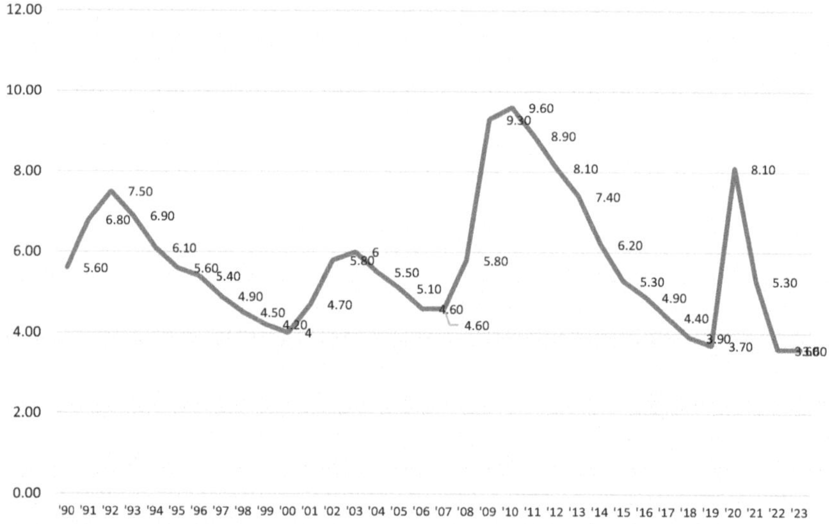

Fig. 4.5 Annual unemployment rate (%) in the US (1990–2023) (Statista, 2024c)

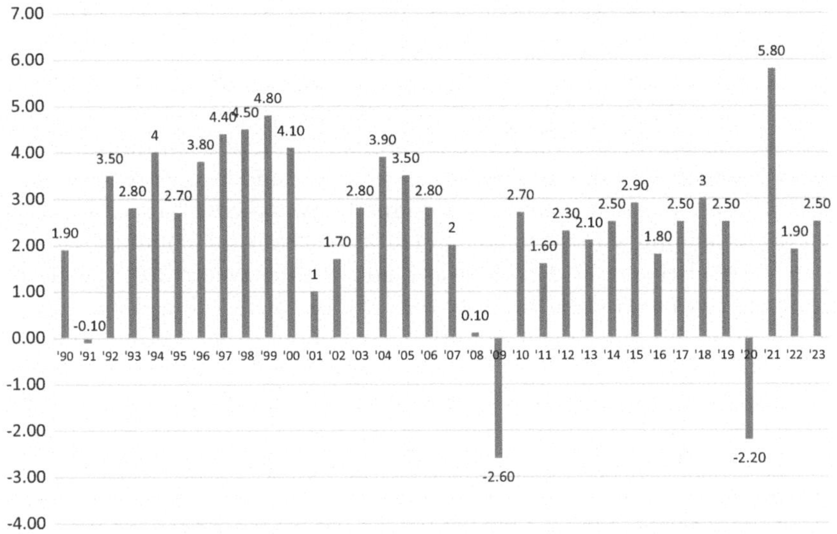

Fig. 4.6 The US real GDP growth rate 1990–2023 (Statista, 2024d)

In the aftermath of the crisis, the US had 2.8 million and 2.9 foreclosed properties in 2009 and 2010, respectively. That was a 21% increase from 2008 and a 120% increase from 2007. California was ranked number 1, with 632,573 foreclosed properties. Florida and Arizona followed that with 516,711 and 163,210 foreclosures, respectively (Indiviglio, 2010). The rate of foreclosures also rose to 2.21% in 2009 and peaked at 2.23% in 2010. The crisis also hit the landlords, who owned more than half of the housing stock, due to the decline in housing values and decreased rental income as the tenants had to evict the houses (Harris, 2024).

To reduce the risks in the US financial system, the Dodd-Frank Wall Street Reform and Consumer Protection Act, which made significant changes affecting all federal financial regulatory agencies and almost every part of the nation's financial services industry, was enacted in 2010. According to Dodd-Frank Act, the banks were required to have more capital on hand which means they took the risk of their resources, risky lending activities were restricted, and large institutions in advanced economies were subject to stress tests to measure their stability in a case they face a sales shock similar to 2008 crisis (Frick, 2017).

The Financial Crisis Inquiry Commission (FCIC) report in January 2011 emphasized that financial regulation and supervision deficiencies caused the financial crisis. These deficiencies included the FED's inability to monitor and avoid problematic assets, failures in corporate governance and risk management by many irresponsible financial institutions, excessive borrowing, lack of transparency, unprepared and inconsistent government actions, a systemic failure in accountability and ethics, the collapse of mortgage-lending standards, deregulation of "over-the-counter" derivatives, particularly credit default swaps, and mismanagement of the credit rating agencies regarding the price risk. (FCIC, 2011) (Fig. 4.7).

The GFC impacted many countries, including Spain, Ireland, and the UK, with a less conservative mortgage system, a limited rental market, and a generous fiscal system. Even Switzerland had the fear of a housing bubble due to the housing prices surging by low-interest rate policy. Conversely, Germany and Austria are distinguished by a conservative mortgage credit system, a substantial rental market, and a less liberal fiscal system. Unlike the first group, these countries have experienced a decline in house prices (Martins et al., 2021; Stalder, 2016).

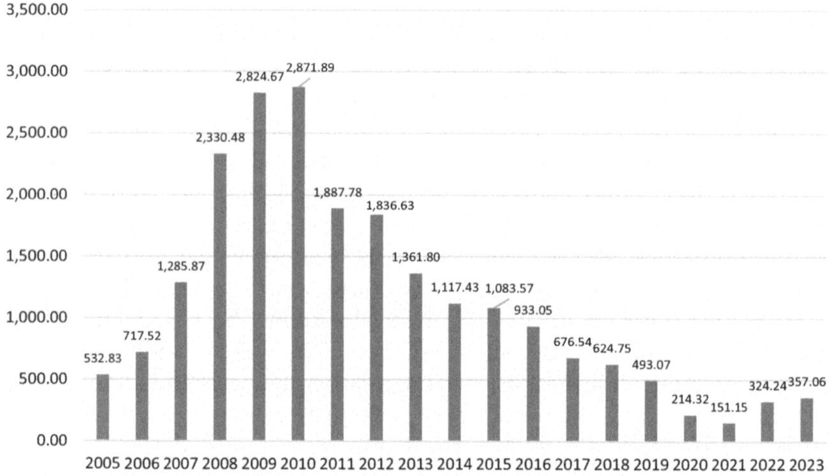

Fig. 4.7 Number of properties with foreclosure filings in the US (in thousands) 2005–2023 (Statista, 2024e)

In contrast to the situation in the US, the housing market crisis in post-socialist states was not primarily due to their mortgage markets failing, particularly from an increase in the offering of high-risk subprime mortgages. Initially, the crisis stemmed from an unforeseen external shock, a worldwide loss of trust in the financial sector. Additionally, the economic downturn in the West impacted exports from small, open post-socialist economies. Decreased international demand reduced economic growth and increased unemployment in numerous post-socialist states. As a result, the global credit crunch and reduced international demand thrust many Central and East European states into an economic recession (Hegedüs et al., 2011).

The Spanish Housing Bubble of the 2000s

Similar to the US housing market, Spain experienced a massive housing boom, which tripled the housing prices by a factor of three from the mid-1990s to 2007. The skyrocketing housing prices peaked in 2004, slowed down until the US subprime crisis in 2007, and then crashed parallel to the global financial crisis. Spain entered the Euro area in 1999, and the consumers had access to cheaper financing due to the sharp reduction in real interest rates of around 4%. The borrowing was fostered, the construction activities boomed, and the maturity periods became longer. The demand also increased due to the rise in population caused by 4 million immigrants within the last ten years, corresponding to 10% of the population. Between 1999 and 2007, many people purchased houses in Spain as a second home investment, mainly on the Mediterranean coasts. Between 2000 and 2007, 600,000 units on average were constructed. The rise in housing units skyrocketed mortgage loans. By 2007, the construction industry was a major player in driving Spain's economy, making up 12% of the country's GDP (Samuel, 2024).

The global financial crisis 2008 became a breaking point for the Spanish housing sector. Spain's over-leveraged banks faced crises due to the contracting of the worldwide credit market. The crash in property prices led to numerous newly constructed units sitting empty. Unemployment rates rose in 2009, primarily due to the construction sector. The Spanish government implemented significant measures to stabilize the economy, resulting in protests and significant socio-political issues. Spain's economy started to rebound by the mid-2010s (Samuel, 2024). Before the Spanish property bubble burst in 2007, the unit price of the

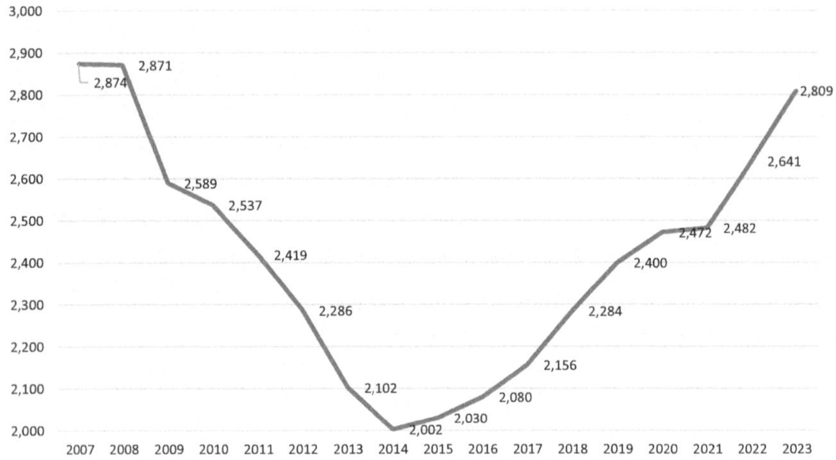

Fig. 4.8 Average square meter house price of newly built homes Spain 2007–2023 (in Euros) (Statista, 2024f)

houses peaked at Euros 2,874 per square meter. After the collapse of the prices, the unit prices went down to as low as Euros 2,002, a 30% decline within seven years. As shown in Fig. 4.8, after the lowest point, the prices started rising again in 2015 and reached Euros 2,809, just slightly below 2008 levels (Statista, 2024f).

Ireland's Property Bubble

Another property bubble burst in 2008 during the global financial crisis in Ireland, in which its economy surged in the 1990s and late 2000s due to low-interest rate policies, rapid rise in the size of loans, and inflow of foreign capital investments. This period is called the *Tiger Years*. Ireland experienced an average real gross domestic product growth of over 7% in the 1990s. Household lending expanded from 2003 to 2007 as the welfare of Irish citizens improved. Between May 2000 and May 2001, house prices saw a 17% increase. In August 2000, the International Monetary Fund (IMF) cautioned about the potential collapse of property prices, noting that no industrial country in the past 20 years had seen price increases of the scale of Ireland without subsequently experiencing a fall (Donovan, 2016). The development of new housing units continued, and housing prices more than doubled between 2000 and 2006. The demand started declining in 2007. Dublin, one of the most expensive cities, experienced a sharp increase in housing prices, which lost more than 50% of their value from 2007 to 2010. The 2008 financial crisis led many Irish banks to collapse, and the Irish government took severe steps with the EU and the International Monetary Fund in 2010 to recover the economy. As of 2012, house prices were still below the 2001 prices, and the gains of the *Celtic Tiger* years were wiped out; in other words, the housing crisis killed the Celtic Tiger (Elliott, 2009; Norris & Coates, 2014).

Aftermath of Housing Crises

Oust and Hrafnkelsson (2017) classified the past housing bubbles between 1970 and 2015 in terms of the periods of price increase and decrease, their peaks, the duration, and the price change before/after the peak. The most extended cycle in price increases was observed in Ireland, with 56 quarters, lasting until the first quarter of 2007. That was followed by a 41 quarter and 38 quarter price rise in Spain and the US respectively. In 1978, the Netherlands also experienced 33 quarters of price surge followed by 29 quarters of drop. Long periods of price decline were also seen in Ireland, Spain, and the US after the prices reached the peak values. Table 4.1 shows how the prices are increasing, peaking, and descending, or, to name it better, crushing. The housing bubbles are not only creating volatility in the market and affecting affordability but also resulting in economic and social disruptions.

Past housing bubbles and crises revealed similar mistakes made by policymakers, regulators, and central banks in different periods and countries. Sometimes, the crisis occurred with a housing bubble that impacted the local economy only, and sometimes, it had a global effect that included the collapse of stock markets, recession, and prolonged stagnation. Sometimes, a housing crisis initiated a global crisis, and sometimes, the housing sector was affected by a financial crisis.

The crises also have political consequences. At the end of 2016, during Donald Trump's presidential election, over 5.4 million US properties with a mortgage (9.6% of all US properties) were significantly submerged. The total loan amount linked to the property exceeded the property's estimated market value by at least 25%. Only 35% of the people who lost their houses in GFC could purchase another house by 2018. The election

Table 4.1 Large housing bubbles between 1970 and 2015 (Oust & Hrafnkelsson, 2017)

Country	*Price*	*Peaks/ troughs*	*Duration (quarters)*	*Aggregated (%)*	*Price change before/after peak*				
					Aggregated 5 year (%)	*An. 5Y average (%)*	*Aggregated 3 year (%)*	*An. 3Y average (%)*	*1 year (%)*
Finland	Increase	1989-Q2	15	68.3	63.3	12.7	65.8	21.9	24.1
Finland	Fall	1995-Q4	26	−50.5	−46.0	−9.2	41.0	−13.7	−11.9
Ireland	Increase	2007-Q1	56	235.6	52.9	10.6	30.5	10.2	10.1
Ireland	Fall	2013-Q1	24	−53.6	−51.6	−10.3	−31.8	−10.6	−7.1
Netherlands	Increase	1978-Q2	33	138.9	94.4	18.9	69.0	23.0	6.5
Netherlands	Fall	1985-Q3	29	−52.6	−47.9	−9.6	−35.5	−11.8	−11.8
New Zealand	Increase	1974-Q3	18	66.2	66.2	14.7	64.4	21.5	29.9
New Zealand	Fall	1980-Q4	25	−39.4	−34.7	−6.9	−22.7	−7.6	−9.2
Norway	Increase	1987-Q1	8	44.0	37.8	7.6	39.8	13.3	25.0
Norway	Fall	1993-Q1	24	−45.5	−41.2	−8.2	−28.6	−9.5	−2.3
South Africa	Increase	1984-Q1	21	55.1	54.9	11.0	25.5	8.5	9.2
South Africa	Fall	1987-Q1	12	−44.1	−42.8	−8.6	−44.1	−14.7	−18.1
Spain	Increase	2007-Q2	41	138.8	69.2	13.8	30.1	10.0	9.0
Spain	Fall	2014-Q1	27	−45.5	−36.0	−7.2	−14.1	−4.7	−4.5
UK	Increase	1973-Q3	14	67.4	67.4	19.3	66.2	22.1	23.5
UK	Fall	1977-Q3	16	−35.6	−29.3	−5.9	−28.9	−9.6	−11.2
US	Increase	2006-Q1	38	92.9	54.1	10.8	35.4	11.8	7.8
US	Fall	2011-Q4	23	−39.6	−37.1	−7.4	−33.0	−11.0	−4.3

of Donald Trump is considered the political choice of angered Americans due to the consequences of the housing crisis (Henry, 2022).

Wrong monetary policies (expansion or tightening), timing problems of such decisions, wrong market interventions, lack of or inadequate land and zoning regulations, poor credit granting and monitoring, banking-dependent financing solutions, insufficient supply, political impacts, and inflation were the leading causes of such crises.

If policymakers learn from the outcomes of these crises, we can develop sustainable solutions and resolve the problems. Otherwise, we will face new crises almost every decade. In that context, the next chapter covers a case study of how Turkish monetary and economic policies deeply impacted the housing industry and created housing affordability problems.

References

Aalbers, M. B. (2015). The Great Moderation, the Great Excess and the global housing crisis. *International Journal of Housing Policy, 15*(1), 43–60. https://doi.org/10.1080/14616718.2014.997431

Al Rifai, T. (2015). *Islamic finance and the new financial system: An ethical approach to preventing future financial crises*. Wiley. ISBN: 978-1-118-99063-6.

Anderson, P. J. (2009). *The secret life of real estate and banking*. Shepheard-Walwyn. 978-0856832635.

Brocker, M., & Hanes, C. (2013). *The 1920s American real estate boom and the downturn of the great depression: Evidence from city cross sections* (NBER Working Paper No. 18852).

Çelik, Ö. (2024). Cracking the housing crisis: Financialization, the state, struggles, and rights. *Housing Studies, 39*(6), 1385–1394. https://doi.org/10.1080/02673037.2024.2333569

Claessens, S., Kose, M. A., & Terrones, M.E. (2008). *When crises collide*. https://www.imf.org/external/pubs/ft/fandd/2008/12/pdf/claessens.pdf. Last Accessed on July 21, 2024.

Deb, P., Finger, H., Kashiwase, K., Kido, Y., Kothari, S., Papageorgiou, E., Hoyle, H., & Oeking, E. (2022). *Housing market stability and affordability in Asia-Pacific*. https://www.elibrary.imf.org/view/journals/087/2022/020/article-A001-en.xml. Last Accessed on July 21, 2024.

Dong, H., & Hansz, J. A. (2016). The geography of the recent housing crisis: The role of urban form. *Housing Policy Debate, 26*(1), 150–171. https://doi.org/10.1080/10511482.2015.1038575

Donovan, D. (2016). *The IMF's role in Ireland*. https://ieo.imf.org/-/media/IEO/Files/evaluations/completed/07-28-2016-the-imf-and-the-crises-in-greece-ireland-and-portugal/eac-bp-16-02-04-the-imf-s-role-in-ireland-v5.ashx. Last Accessed on July 21, 2024.

Elliot, L. (2009). *Mr Austerity tending Celtic Tiger's wounds*. https://www.theguardian.com/business/2009/may/28/irish-finance-minister-profile. Last Accessed on July 21, 2024.

FCIC. (2011). *The financial crisis inquiry report*. https://www.govinfo.gov/content/pkg/GPO-FCIC/pdf/GPO-FCIC.pdf. Last Accessed on July 21, 2024.

Federalreservehistory.org. (2013). *The great recession and its aftermath*. https://www.federalreservehistory.org/essays/great-recession-and-its-aftermath. Last Accessed on July 21, 2024.

Frick, W. (2017). *What you should know about Dodd-Frank and what happens if it's rolled back*. https://hbr.org/2017/03/what-you-should-know-about-dodd-frank-and-what-happens-if-its-rolled-back. Last Accessed on July 21, 2024.

Garriga, C., & Hedlund, A. (2019). *Crises in the housing market: Causes, consequences, and policy lessons* (The Center for Growth and Opportunity at Utah State University Working Paper 2019.006).

Geltner, D. M., Miller, N. G., Clayton, J., & Eichholtz, P. (2007). *Commercial real estate analyses and investments*. Thomson Higher Education.

Grant, W., Wilson G. K., (2012). The Consequences of the Global Financial Crisis: The Rhetoric of Reform and Regulation. Oxford University Press.ISBN 978-0-19-964198-7

Greasley, D., & Madsen, J. B. (2013). The housing slump and the great depression in the USA. *Cliometrica, 7*, 15–35. https://doi.org/10.1007/s11698-012-0078-7

Hammond, B. (1957). *Banks and politics in America from the revolution to the Civil War*. Princeton University Press.

Harris, R. (2024). A local housing market in the great depression. *Social Science History, 48*(1), 93–119. https://doi.org/10.1017/ssh.2023.29

HBS. (2024). *1873: Off the rails*. https://www.library.hbs.edu/hc/crises/1873.html. Last Accessed on July 21, 2024.

Hegedüs, J., Lux, M., & Sunega, P. (2011). Decline and depression: The impact of the global economic crisis on housing markets in two post-socialist states. *Journal of Housing and the Built Environment, 26*, 315–333. https://doi.org/10.1007/s10901-011-9228-7

Henry, N. (2022). How public administrators inadvertently helped get Donald J. Trump elected president: The great recession, the housing crisis, and the failure of public policy. *Public Organizational Review, 22*, 1325–1342. https://doi.org/10.1007/s11115-021-00519-3

History.com. (2023). *Stock market crash of 1929*. https://www.history.com/topics/great-depression/1929-stock-market-crash. Last Accessed on July 21, 2024.

Indiviglio, D. (2010). *Which states had the most foreclosures in 2009?* https://www.theatlantic.com/business/archive/2010/01/which-states-had-the-most-foreclosures-in-2009/33538/. Last Accessed on July 21, 2024.

Krugman, P. (1998). *Japan's trap*. https://www.princeton.edu/~pkrugman/japans_trap.pdf. Last Accessed on July 21, 2024.

Lind, H. (2009). Price bubbles in housing markets: Concept, theory and indicators. *International Journal of Housing Markets and Analysis, 2*, 78–90. https://doi.org/10.1108/17538270910939574

Makin, J.H. (2008). *Japan's lost decade: Lessons for the United States in 2008*. https://www.aei.org/wp-content/uploads/2011/10/20080225_22772EOMarch_g.pdf. Last Accessed on July 21, 2024.

Martins, A. M., Serra, A. P., Martins, F. V., & Stevenson, S. (2021). EU housing markets before financial crisis of 2008: The role of institutional factors and structural breaks. *Journal of Housing and the Built Environment, 36*, 867–899. https://doi.org/10.1007/s10901-021-09848-7

Minsky, H. P. (2008). *Stabilizing the unstable economy*. McGraw Hill.

Musson, A. E. (1950). The great depression in Britain, 1873–1896: A reappraisal. *The Journal of Economic History, 19*(2), 199–228. https://doi.org/10.1017/S0022050700109994

Nicholas, T., & Scherbina, A. D. (2011). *Real estate prices during the roaring twenties and the great depression* (UC Davis Graduate School of Management Research Paper No. 18-09). SSRN. https://ssrn.com/abstract=1470448 or https://doi.org/10.2139/ssrn.1470448

Norris, M., & Coates, D. (2014). How housing killed the Celtic tiger: Anatomy and consequences of Ireland's housing boom and bust. *Journal of Housing and the Built Environment, 29*, 299–315. https://doi.org/10.1007/s10901-013-9384-z

Oust, A., & Hrafnkelsson, K. (2017). What is a housing bubble? *Economics Bulletin, 37*(2), 806–836.

Samuel, N. (2024). *The complete history of housing bubbles around the world*. https://pictureperfectportfolios.com/the-complete-history-of-housing-bubbles-around-the-world/. Last Accessed on July 21, 2024.

Shiller, R. J. (2010). *Shiller's list: How to diagnose the next bubble*. The New York Times by Jack Ewing.

Stalder, P. (2016). Exchange rate shocks, monetary policy and boom-bust cycles in the housing market: An econometric analysis for Switzerland. *Journal of Business Cycle Research, 12*, 217–251. https://doi.org/10.1007/s41549-016-0011-4

Statista.com. (2024a). *Number of existing homes sold in the United States from 2005 to 2023, with a forecast until 2025*. https://www.statista.com/statistics/226144/us-existing-home-sales/. Last Accessed on July 21, 2024.

Statista.com. (2024b). *S&P/Case Shiller U.S. National Home Price Index from 2000 to 2023*. https://www.statista.com/statistics/199360/case-shiller-national-home-price-index-for-the-us-since-2000/. Last Accessed on July 21, 2024.

Statista.com. (2024c). *Unemployment rate in the United States from 1990 to 2023*. https://www.statista.com/statistics/193290/unemployment-rate-in-the-usa-since-1990/. Last Accessed on July 21, 2024.

Statista.com. (2024d). *Annual growth of the real gross domestic product of the United States from 1990 to 2023*. https://www.statista.com/statistics/188165/annual-gdp-growth-of-the-united-states-since-1990/. Last Accessed on July 21, 2024.

Statista.com. (2024e). *Number of properties with foreclosure filings in the United States from 2005 to 2023*. https://www.statista.com/statistics/798630/number-of-properties-with-foreclosure-filings-usa/. Last Accessed on July 21, 2024.

Statista.com. (2024f). *Average square meter house price of newly built homes in Spain from 2007 to 2023*. https://www.statista.com/statistics/771735/prices-media-from-the-living-place-spain/. Last Accessed on July 21, 2024.

Stiglitz, J. (1990). Symposium on bubbles. *Journal of Economic Perspectives, 4*, 13–18. https://doi.org/10.1257/jep.4.2.13

Sümer, L. (2023). *The world economy and financial system: A paradigm change offering a sustainable approach*. Palgrave Macmillan.https://doi.org/10.1007/978-3-031-27530-2

Taylor Jr., H. L. (2011). *The historical roots of the crisis in housing affordability: The Case of Buffalo, New York 1920–1950*. https://ppgbuffalo.org/files/documents/housing_neighborhoods/the_historical_roots_of_the_crisis_in_housing_affordability__the_case_of_buffalo__ny.pdf. Last Available on July 21, 2024.

Trading Economics. (2024). *Japan residential property prices*. https://tradingeconomics.com/japan/residential-property-prices. Last Accessed on July 21, 2024.

US Treasury. (2024). *The panic of 1873.* https://home.treasury.gov/about/history/freedmans-bank-building/financial-panic-of-1873. Last Accessed on July 21, 2024.

Yoshino, N., & Taghizadeh-Hesary, F. (2015). *Causes and remedies for Japan's long lasting recession: Lessons for the People's Republic of China* (ADBI Working Paper 554). Tokyo: Asian Development Bank Institute. http://www.adb.org/publications/causes-and-remedies-japan-long-lasting-recession-lessonschina/. Last Accessed on July 21, 2024.

CHAPTER 5

How Do We Create a Housing Affordability Crisis: Türkiye Case

I wish I had named this chapter "How can we avoid or overcome a housing affordability crisis?" but the situation we are experiencing tells us the opposite because the ***numbers do not lie***. Of course, the numbers are not the only determinants of such crises, and many global and local political, economic, social, psychological, demographic, and environmental factors contribute to the crisis's development. It is a fact that the COVID-19 pandemic disrupted many economies, and political conflicts increased the pressures on policymakers. Türkiye, thanks to its rich history and strong ties in the Europe, Middle East, and Africa (EMEA) region and geopolitical location where three continents meet, is a country that is always in the middle of all international issues, including the refugee problems, Middle Eastern and Caucasian conflicts, or ongoing tango between North Atlantic Treaty Organization (NATO) and Russia. Every day, you can wake up with a new issue that has never been listed on your agenda the day before.

Türkiye is an emerging country with a rising population. The second most populated country in Europe is struggling with a housing affordability problem like many other European countries. Despite the decline in the birth rate in the last decades, the population of the country is younger and increasing faster than those in Europe due to the millions of refugees and immigrants it has been hosting for more than a decade. Indeed, Türkiye, with 3.3 million refugees living in the country, is ranked

L. Sümer, *The Global Housing Crisis*,
https://doi.org/10.1007/978-3-031-72604-0_5

second on the list of top refugee hosting countries according to the 2024 report of the United Nations Refugee Agency. The population of Türkiye exceeded 85 million as of the end of 2023 (Turkstat, 2024a). The ongoing civil war in Syria, the war between Russia and Ukraine, the Israeli attacks on Gazza, and the political instability in the Middle East resulted in mass migrations to Türkiye. Around 4.6 million refugees and immigrants live in different cities in Türkiye, where most are settled in Istanbul (Presidency of Migration Management, 2024). This figure does not include the number of people illegally living in the country. The housing sales policy to foreigners granting citizenship and residency permits based on the housing purchase prices also encourages more immigrant inflow to the country. Thousands of foreigners consider Türkiye a second homeland and try settling there.

Market equilibrium provided by the balance of supply and demand is essential for housing price stability. Demographic changes mainly impact the purchase demand (Wang & Kinugasa, 2022), and income and population growth are the fundamental drivers of the long-run price dynamics (Igan & Loungani, 2012).

The current homeownership rate of the country compared to the population and housing supply indicates a dynamic housing market where the demand will surge (Aydın, 2019). Parallel to the population increase, the demand for housing is also rising due to many marriages and divorces. Millions of university students who leave their hometowns and move to the cities where they continue their higher education also raise the demand from the rental market perspective. In the last decade, the housing supply has also declined, as it is hard to estimate construction costs due to economic uncertainty and the never-ending rise of material and labor prices. Families tended to live outside city centers during and after the COVID-19.

People also considered investing in land as a hedging tool against inflation to protect their wealth. These trends increased land prices sharply, and the combined effect of construction costs resulted in a rapid rise in housing sales. In addition, two catastrophic earthquakes that occurred in February 2023 directly affected more than 14 million people living in 11 cities and had a profound impact on the market equilibrium of the Turkish housing industry. Hundreds of thousands of internal migrations and resettlements disrupted the dynamics of the cities, and the demand for rental houses skyrocketed, contributing to the sharp rise in rental prices.

Affording to buy a house for low- and middle-income Turkish citizens has become a ***dream that may not come true soon***. Renting is as difficult as buying, especially in metropolitan cities like Istanbul, İzmir and Ankara. The post-pandemic monetary expansion and the low-interest rate policies of the Central Bank of Türkiye Republic (CBRT) between 2021 and 2023, which devaluated Turkish Lira against other currencies, resulted in high inflation and loss of purchasing power of millions of citizens. This policy lasted until the end of the presidential election in May 2023, and soon after Mehmet Şimşek, who was also on duty in the past years, was assigned by re-elected President Recep Tayyip Erdoğan as the Minister of Treasury, that policy was replaced by monetary tightening and high interest rates policy to fight against the inflation. Although this strict policy has been in effect for over a year, and the interest rates have risen from 8.5% to 50%, the inflation rate is still 71.60% by the end of June (CBRT, 2024a). On the other hand, despite the efforts to balance the rise of prices with increasing wages, the rate of escalation in wages could not reach the speed of the upsurge of housing sales and rental prices. High interest rates made it almost impossible for low and middle-income families to purchase a house.

Thus, the current figures indicate that the Turkish housing market is experiencing a crisis which may deepen in the upcoming months as the inflation rate will still be high (JP Morgan and Barclays expect the inflation rate in Türkiye to fall to 42.5% and 44% at the end of 2024 and 25% and 30.8% by the end of 2025, respectively) (Egeeye.com, 2024).

The housing affordability problem in Türkiye is also very much related to political decisions on the local economy. There are several experiences in Türkiye regarding the impacts of interest rates and political choices on the housing market and affordability. For instance, in early 2013, the mortgage rates were relatively low compared to the historical interest rates of Türkiye, the predictability level in the Turkish economy was high, and the housing market was stable to make investments. That year, I decided to purchase a flat, made a financial analysis, and compared the rental cost of the unit with the financing cost of the potential mortgage payments. Based on the calculations, I determined the maturity period. When I discovered the financing cost would be less than the monthly rent I paid, I decided to purchase the house. The bank approved a mortgage loan for 80% of the total sales price with a 4-year maturity period, and I became a homeowner.

On the other hand, after a few months of my purchase, within the same year, Türkiye had some international disagreements with the US and Russia about bringing permanent solutions to the ongoing Syrian civil war. In addition, in June 2013, the government also faced severe local protests, known as "Gezi Park Events." Thereafter, in December 2013, the "17–25 Corruption Scandal" or, from another aspect, "Judicial Coup Attempt," and the economy was negatively impacted by such political developments (Erikli, 2015; Kanat & Duran, 2022). On November 24, 2015, Türkiye shot down a Russian jet that crossed the border, and despite the good relations between the President of Russia, Vladimir Putin, and the President of Türkiye, Recep Tayyip Erdoğan, a political crisis arose between the two countries. Lastly, on July 15, 2016, the Military Coup Attempt, defeated by the brave civil resistance, made the economy more fragile in many aspects, including tourism, investments, capital inflows, financing, etc.

After several months, the economy started to recover with the help of some government incentives. It was the first half of 2017 when my brother called and told me he wanted to purchase a new house. The mortgage rates were increasing again then, and I wondered how he would finance his purchase. He told me that the real estate developer (seller) offered him an interest rate lower than the market rates, and the real estate developer would subsidize the difference between the bank rate and the offered rate. At first, it sounded like a good deal, but I was also wondering why the developer used such a method instead of making a discount on the sales price. After two years, I got an answer to my question when the real estate developer did not complete the project, even the rough construction. When my brother wanted to terminate the sales agreement and asked for his money back, the real estate developer wanted to charge him the financing cost that they bear, and they did so. He sued the company, won the case, and got his money back. That reputable company survived by getting bank loans and developing new projects.

One year after, another political conflict between Türkiye and the US in 2018 arose regarding the extradition of Pastor Andrew Brunson (who was imprisoned in Türkiye for the crime of being a secret agent) to the US, which resulted in the rapid devaluation of the Turkish Lira over the USD. The tension between Türkiye and the US intensified after the letter of former President Donald Trump to Recep Tayyip Erdoğan threatening Türkiye about destroying the Turkish economy on October 09, 2019. This situation increased the inflation rates, and the CBRT had to increase the interest rates again. The rate of mortgaged housing sales fell to as low as 5% at the end of 2018. Home sales decreased sharply, and while some real estate developers decreased their sales prices to manage their cash flows, others asked government agencies to cut interest rates to increase access to finance.

After a partial recovery in the housing sector in the first quarter of 2020, during the first months of the COVID-19 pandemic in 2020, as many central banks did, the Central Bank of the Republic of Türkiye (CBRT) applied monetary expansion policies. As a result, the mortgage loan rates were decreased, and housing prices started increasing sharply. This policy ended up with unaffordable housing sales prices and rental prices, which created an affordability problem even for renting. The new management of CBRT finally decided to increase the interest rates in the second half of 2023, but in this case, the financing costs skyrocketed. Today, in the second quarter of 2024, if we use a mortgage loan to finance our home, we need to pay a monthly financing cost of at least 4–5 times the monthly rental fee compared to the figures in 2013, despite the highly increased rents within the last few years. Access to financing became difficult due to the sharp increase in interest rates, and financing a home through bank loans is almost impossible for even mid-level income groups.

To better understand whether the current situation in Türkiye can be named as a housing crisis, we can go deep into some significant facts, figures, and ratios about the housing sector in the country.

Inflation Rates

The inflation rate has always been a significant economic problem for Türkiye. While the developed countries consider yearly inflation rates to be more than 2% high, policymakers in Türkiye always target a one-digit annual inflation rate and consider it a success. Unfortunately, as shown in Fig. 5.1, despite success in the early 2010s when the inflation rates fell to as low as 6%, the target of CBRT was never met in the last decade; in contrast, the applied policies created almost hyperinflation after 2021. Many economists and politicians claim that moderate inflation levels positively impact economic growth due to their stimulation of spending and driving consumption. Still, uncontrolled inflation rates result in great disasters, including the psychological, social, and economic failure of societies.

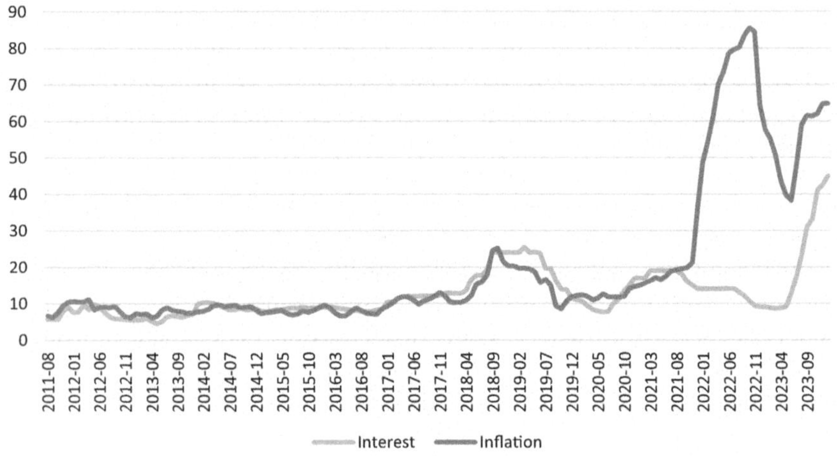

Fig. 5.1 The interest and inflation rates in Türkiye (CBRT, 2024b)

The case in Türkiye is running to that unfortunate consequence. It is true that high inflation stimulated economic growth but put the consumers into a spiral, and they decided to bring their spending forward as they thought the prices would keep rising. They also seek investment tools that could protect their savings, and the rise in housing prices has attracted many people in that context. The policy of CBRT, which created that mindset among customers, prolonged the negative impact of inflation on society.

Interest Rates

"*Interest rate is the cause, and the inflation is the consequence. We need to keep the interest rate as low as possible for a low inflation rate*". This approach was used in 1994 and resulted in hyperinflation and a rapid rise in interest rates (Eğilmez, 2021). It was tried again in 2021 when the inflation and interest rates were close, as shown in Fig. 5.1. The policy change of CBRT in September 2021 devaluated the Turkish Lira rapidly and skyrocketed the inflation rates. CBRT chose not to use the interest rate weapon to control inflation until June 2023. As exhibited in Fig. 5.2, since then, within a year, the rates rapidly went up and stood at a yearly 50% level, still very much behind the inflation rate, which was 71.60%

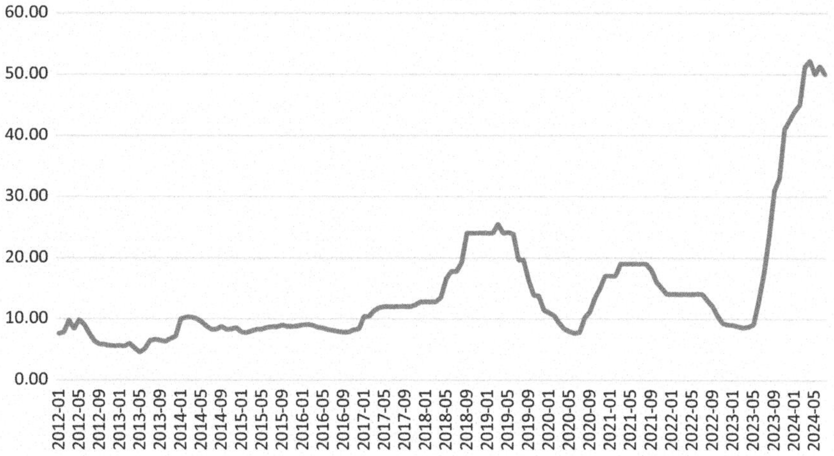

Fig. 5.2 Weighted average cost of CBRT funding (CBRT, 2024a)

at the end of June 2024 (CBRT, 2024b). Being late about using the interest rate tool to battle inflation did not result in an immediate decline in the inflation rate. Still, it is a positive sign for stability and eliminating uncertainty.

As shown in Fig. 5.3, the high weighted cost of CBRT funding was also reflected in mortgage rates, and high mortgage loan interest rates resulted in difficulties accessing finance, and the expensive cost of borrowing negatively impacted homebuyers. While the developers could not find adequate funds to help them finance the construction, the homebuyers could not afford the high financing costs of their current income levels.

Construction Costs

One of the main problems of the housing developers is the difficulty of forecasting the construction costs. Accurately predicting the construction cost of a housing project, which takes a few years to accurately, is essential to determine the housing sales price. Under high inflationary periods, this is almost impossible. The vendors do not provide long-term quotations for the prices and often change their offers due to the increase in raw materials based on the rise in currency and labor prices. As can be analyzed in Fig. 5.4, the construction cost is now almost seven times its

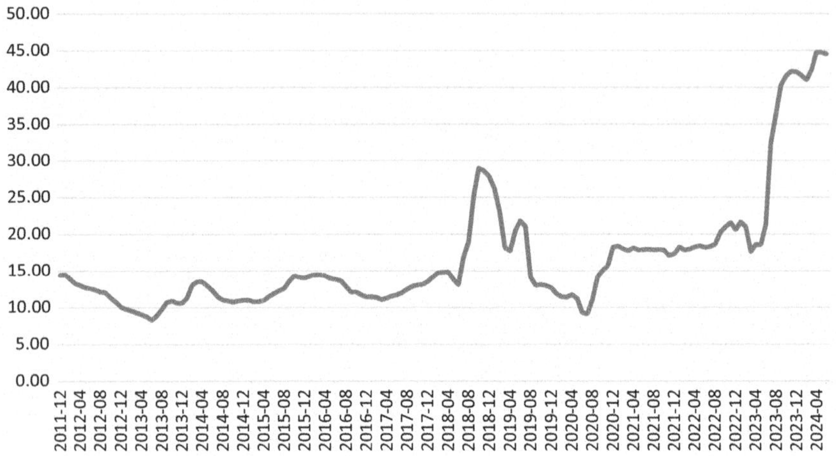

Fig. 5.3 Mortgage loan interest rates (CBRT, 2024c)

value in 2020 (Turkstat, 2024b). This extreme rise is a market disruptor and not sustainable at all. In such circumstances, many developers either decide not to develop new projects until the market finds its balance, which results in the shortage of demand and helps increase the prices, or try to add more contingency to sales prices, another contributing to the rise in housing prices.

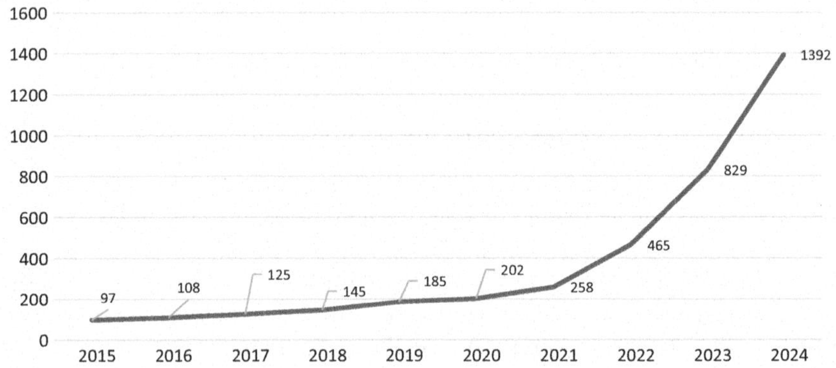

Fig. 5.4 Construction cost index in Türkiye (Turkstat, 2024b)

Table 5.1 The average zoned prices in Türkiye (Endeksa, 2024a)

Years	*Unit Price (USD/m2)*	*USD/TL*	*Unit price TL/m2)*	*Yearly change (%)*
January 2019	92	5,21	479	
January 2020	83	5,95	494	3,03
January 2021	95	7,36	699	41,58
January 2022	85	13,42	1.141	63,14
January 2023	134	18,7	2.506	119,67
January 2024	169	29,67	5.014	100,10
5 years of change				**946,11**

Land Prices

Land investment is considered a safe haven in inflationary periods. According to the data provided by Endeksa (2024a), the average zoned land prices in Türkiye increased almost ten times in TL currency within the last five years. As shown in Table 5.1, the prices also nearly doubled in USD currency measure. The average zoned land price in Istanbul was 139 USD per square meter in January 2019, which is 473 USD/m2 as of June 2024. The land prices in Istanbul are 3.40 times their value in 2019 in USD currency (Endeksa, 2024a). The rise in land prices may seem reasonable for landowners to protect their wealth, but it is a lousy indicator of housing prices. The more the land prices increase, the more housing sales prices surge.

Housing Unit Sales Prices

Adding up the land cost, the construction cost, and the potential profit of the developers, we reach the average sales price of the new housing units. To buy a residential property in Istanbul today, you must pay around TL 46,213 per square meter. This unit price corresponds to 1,417 USD/m2. Izmir and Ankara follow İstanbul with USD 1,166 and USD 785 per square meter, respectively. The average unit sales price in Türkiye is USD 995 (CBRT, 2024d). Figure 5 shows the rise in unit prices in Türkiye. As clearly shown in Fig. 5.5, the monetary policies of CBRT applied after September 2021 skyrocketed the housing prices. Although the unit sales prices in USD currency seem relatively low compared to the European

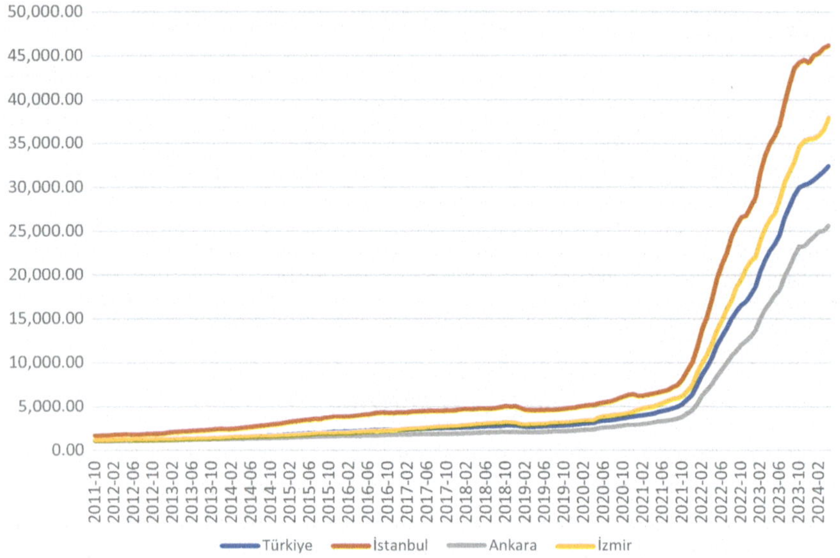

Fig. 5.5 Housing unit sales prices (TL/m^2) (CBRT, 2024d)

market, with the current average income level in Türkiye, the prices are not affordable even for mid-income families.

Rent prices have also risen steeply in Türkiye over the last five years. As shown in Fig. 5.6, while the rental cost of a 100 m2 house was 1,563 TL in 2019, it was 14.835 TL in 2014, 9.5 times its value five years ago (Endeksa, 2024b). Considering the base wage in Türkiye is 17,000 TL, it is almost impossible for an individual earning only the base wage to afford to rent a house alone (Turkstats, 2024b).

Number of Sales

The rise in sales prices and borrowing costs declined the total units sold in 2023. In 2020, housing sales hit a record with almost 1.5 million total sales. In consecutive years, sales were slightly less than in 2020, but sales dropped steeply in 2023, with a 17.5% decline compared to the previous year. This was below the level of 2015, the year that around 1,3 million units were sold (Turkstats, 2024b). The figures for the first five months

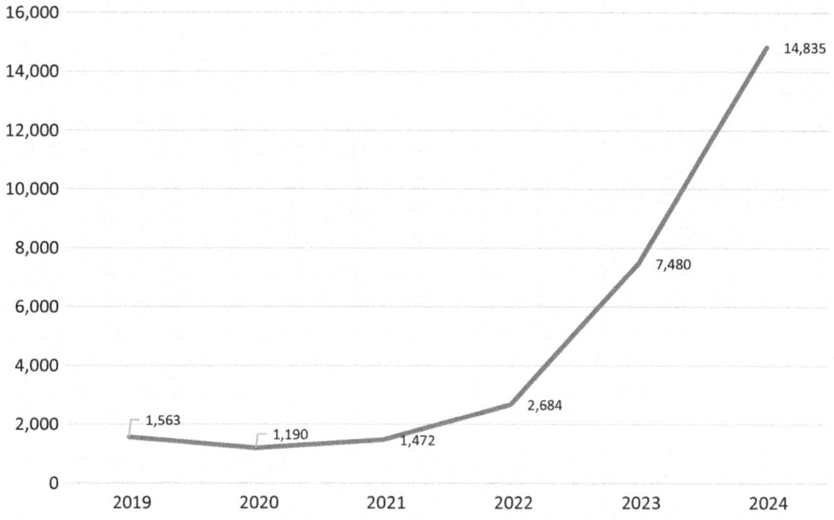

Fig. 5.6 Average rental price of a 100 m^2 house (Endeksa, 2024b)

of 2024 also show that the decline in sales continues. The yearly number of housing sales is shown in Fig. 5.7.

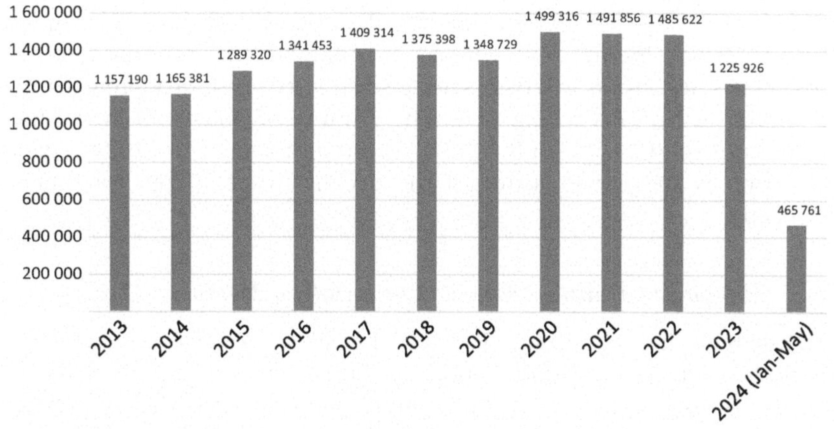

Fig. 5.7 Total housing sales (Turkstat, 2024c)

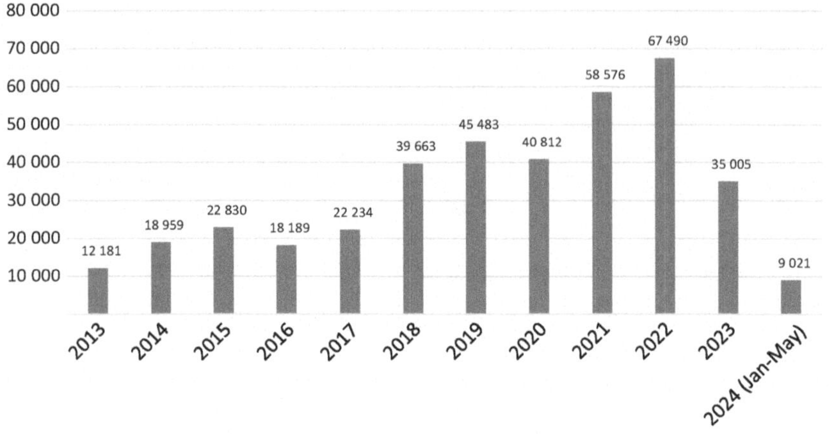

Fig. 5.8 Housing sales to foreigners (Turkstats, 2024c)

Sales to Foreigners

The same decline in total housing sales can be observed in foreigners' sales. Foreigners can purchase a house in Türkiye since the 6302 numbered Reciprocity Law passed in the parliament in May 2012. Those who buy a house of value USD 400.000 are granted citizenship, and the ones who pay USD 200.000 to purchase a house can get a residency permit in Türkiye (Presidency of the Republic of Türkiye Investment Office, 2024). Figure 5.8 exhibits the number of housing sales to foreigners since 2013. In 2022, sales peaked at 67,490, dropping sharply to 35,005 in the succeeding year. The number of units sold in the first five months of 2024 was only 9,021, according to Turkstat (2024c) data. This drop is another indicator of the decline in sales from foreigners' perspective.

Mortgaged Housing Sales & Outstanding Mortgage Loans

Like many other countries, Türkiye also uses conventional financing methods to help individuals purchase houses. According to Turkstat (2024c) statistics, the rate of homebuyers who financed their purchases through mortgage loans was almost 40% in 2013. After a decline to 33.4% in 2014, this rate was stable until 2017. In 2018, the political conflict between the US and Türkiye harmed the economy; the Turkish Lira devaluated against the US Dollar, the inflation rose, and the interest rates increased. This situation increased the financing cost, and homebuyers preferred other financing methods over mortgage loans. The rate of mortgaged housing sales fell to 20.1% in 2018. Since then, the low-interest rate policy applied by the CBRT resulted in a rapid rise in the rate of mortgaged sales, and with 38.2% in 2020, it almost reached its level of 2013. Figure 5.9 exhibits the rate of mortgage housing sales over the years. The high inflation rates and the sharp rise in housing prices hit the market severely. People could not even afford the down payments on their home purchases. This situation resulted in another decline in mortgage sales, and the rate fell to as low as 9.6% in June 2024. Currently, the home financing is in a deadlock in Türkiye.

In 2020, the public banks granted mortgage loans with interest rates below the market rates, and the size of the outstanding mortgages skyrocketed. Within a year, the total outstanding mortgage loans rose from TL 198 billion to TL 278 billion at the end of 2020. The low-interest policy and the high inflation speeded up that increase, and by the end of 2023, this figure had reached TL 438 billion.

2024 was the year that the interest rates were very high, so the growth size of the granted mortgage loans slowed down. As shown in Fig. 5.10, banks approved only TL 9 billion in the first six months of 2024, and as of the end of June 2024, the total outstanding mortgage loan stood

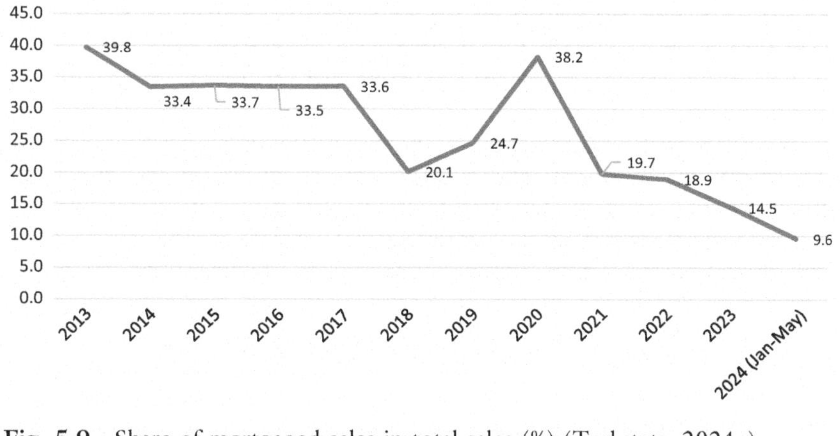

Fig. 5.9 Share of mortgaged sales in total sales (%) (Turkstats, 2024c)

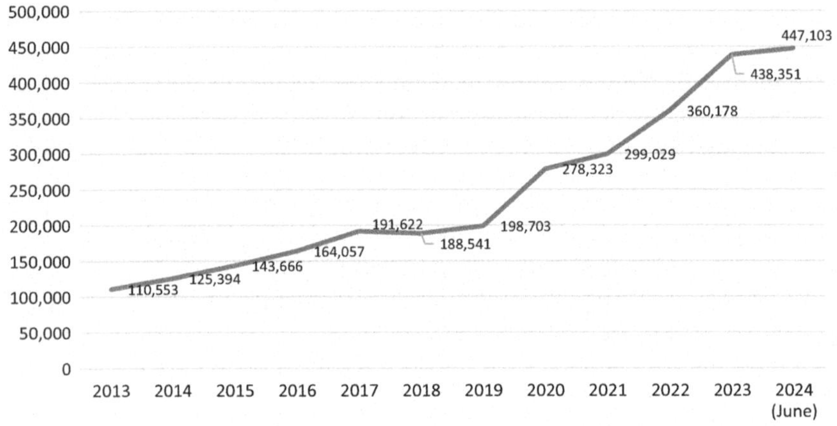

Fig. 5.10 Outstanding mortgage loans (million TL) (BDDK, 2024)

at TL 447 billion. An important data about these loans is that 60% of them were granted by public banks (BDDK, 2024). This rate is a noteworthy indicator of the public bank dependency on home financing in Türkiye. Despite the negative picture of the current situation of the Turkish housing market, the non-performing home loan size and the rates over the total mortgage loans give a positive sign about the banking sector's stability in terms of a non-payment scenario. Indeed, the NPL rate of 0.12% shows that the Turkish housing market does not carry any risk that may trigger a banking risk. Moreover, there is not a deep secondary mortgage market in Türkiye, so even if the non-performing loans increase, this may not have as profound impact as experienced in the US.

The current housing crisis in Türkiye can be named mostly an affordability crisis, which may not be resolved by relying on financing through banks under high interest rates. Sustainable alternative models are required to resolve the problem. Figure 5.11 shows the size and the rates of non-performing mortgage loans over the last decade.

Permits & New and Second-Hand Housing Sales

According to Turkstats (2024c), there has been a 45% to 55% traditional balance between new and second-hand home sales, as shown in Fig. 5.12.

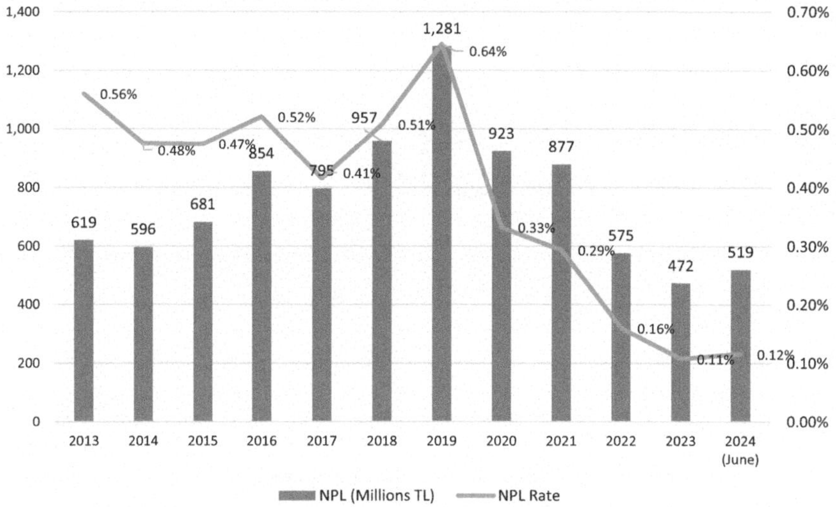

Fig. 5.11 Non-performing mortgage loan (millions TL) and NPL rates (BDDK, 2024)

In 2018, when Türkiye experienced high inflation, primarily due to the devaluation of the Turkish Lira, the construction starts of new homes declined. As shown in Fig. 5.13, the number of new construction permits crashed in 2018. Since then, people have tended to purchase second-hand houses, and the rate of new home sales has dropped to around 30% of the total sales. This decline can be considered an essential factor in the supply and demand imbalance. This imbalance also had an upward impact on housing prices. Considering the construction period of the houses, which may take 2–3 years, the occupancy permits also gradually declined in the following years.

There has been a recent increase in building permits due to the high demand for houses, as investing in housing was accepted as a hedging tool against inflation. Recent figures about the slowed-down rise in housing prices reveal that purchasing a house no longer protects individuals against inflation, so this may be a significant sign for finding a *new price equilibrium* in the housing market.

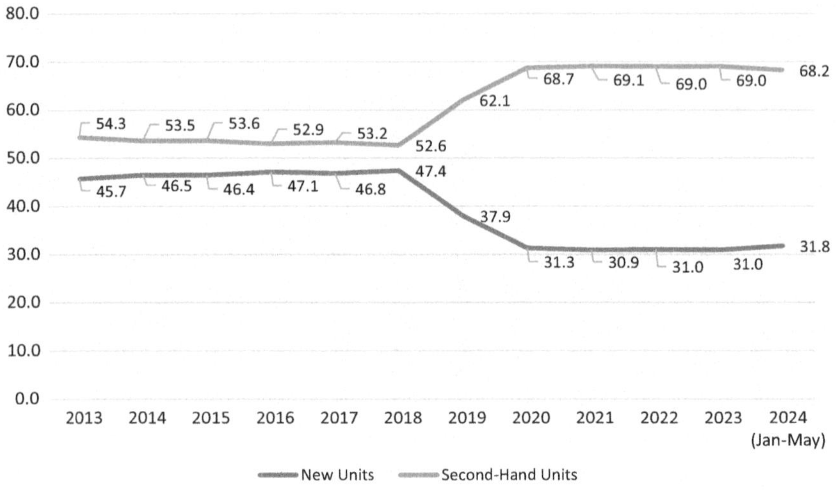

Fig. 5.12 Rates of new vs. second-hand housing sales (Turkstats, 2024c)

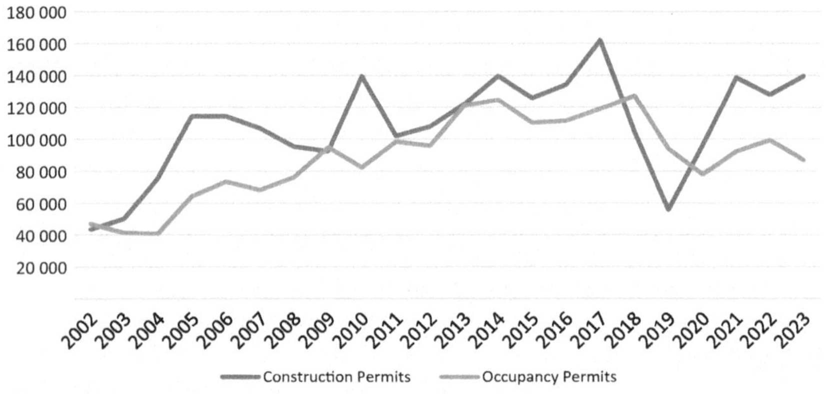

Fig. 5.13 Building permits vs. occupancy permits (Turkstats, 2024c)

Homeownership Rates

Like Americans and many other nations, Turks also consider owning a house a dream. The highest homeownership rate in Türkiye was recorded in 2014 at 61.1%. This record was two years after the last decade's

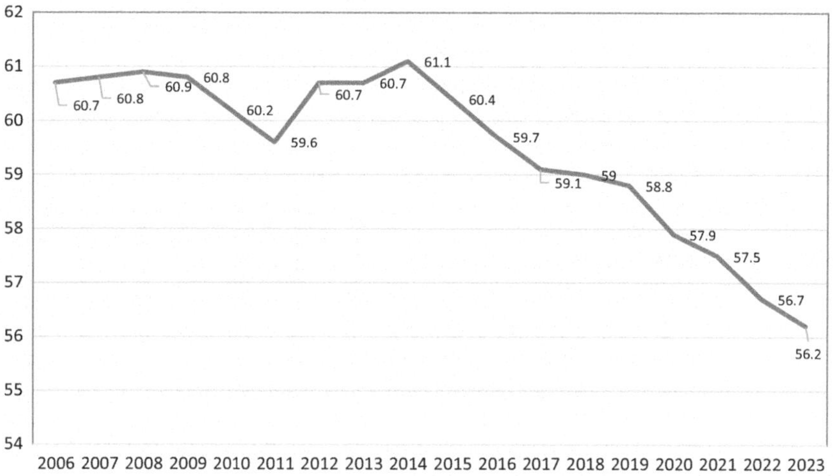

Fig. 5.14 Homeownership rates in Türkiye (Trading Economics, 2024; Tuncer, 2024)

lowest inflation and interest rates. Since then, consecutive local and global economic and political turbulences and wrong monetary policies have resulted in the decline of homeownership. The lowest rate of the last two decades was recorded in 2023 at 56.2%. Figure 5.14 shows the decline in homeownership rates in the last decade (Trading Economics, 2024; Tuncer, 2024).

Despite the rising population and demand, the decline in housing supply was also an important factor in the price increase and the decreased homeownership rates. We can take a closer look at the reasons behind this decline.

Mortgage as a Percentage of Income & Loan Affordability Index

Mortgage as a Percentage of Income is a ratio of monthly mortgage costs to take-home family income. The lower this ratio is, the better the affordability. While calculating the mortgage payment, a 100% mortgage loan is used for 20 years for a house or apartment of 90 square meters by using the average of the unit prices in the city center and outside of the city center.

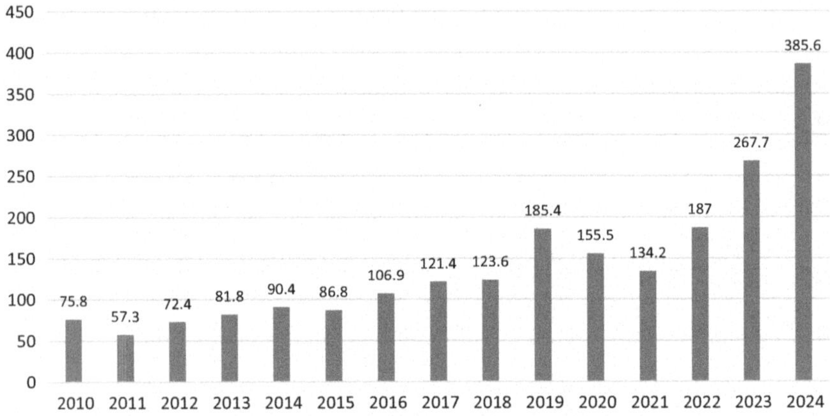

Fig. 5.15 Mortgage as a percentage of income (%) (Numbeo, 2024)

Traditionally, 28% of monthly gross income or 25% of net income is accepted as a *rule of thumb* that should go to the mortgage payment. To get a mortgage, borrowers must also consider their regular ongoing debts over their income (debt-to-income ratio) of up to 43%, preferably 36%. Türkiye, as shown in Fig. 5.15, although the ratio was far above the globally accepted rates, the mortgage as a percentage of income ratio was relatively better in the early 2010s. This ratio exceeded 100 in 2016, increasing until 2024, reaching 386, making Türkiye the 10th least affordable country globally (Numbeo, 2024).

The Loan Affordability Index is defined as the inverse of the mortgage as a percentage of income. The used formula is: (100/mortgage as a percentage of income). The higher the loan affordability index, the better affordability is. Figure 5.16 exhibits the loan affordability index in Türkiye since 2010. Despite a minor increase in 2015 and 2021, affordability has declined in Türkiye in the last 14 years.

Price-to-Income Ratio

The price-to-income ratio is a crucial gauge of housing affordability for potential buyers. A lower price-to-income ratio indicates improved affordability. This ratio is usually computed as the median apartment prices

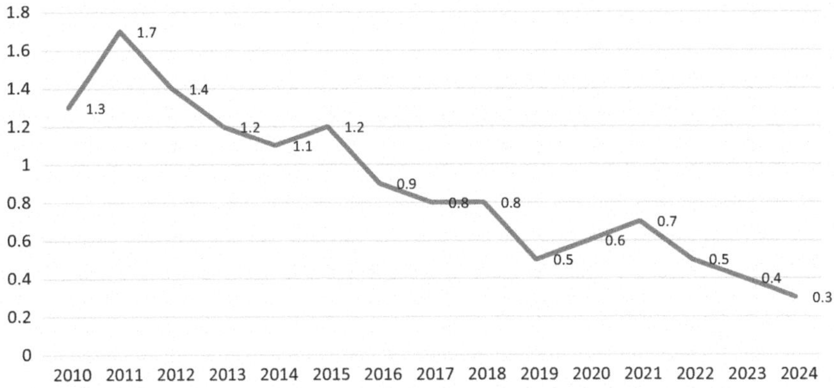

Fig. 5.16 Loan affordability index (Numbeo, 2024)

divided by the median familial disposable income, expressed in terms of years of income.

While the median size of the apartment is accepted as 90 square meters, net disposable family income is defined as 1.5 of the average net salary of the family. The price per square meter is calculated as the average price in and outside the city center.

As shown in Fig. 5.17, the price-to-income ratio in Türkiye was 5.6 in 2010. This ratio is 2.23 times its value in 2010 and reached 12.5 in 2024. This ratio is another bad indicator that shows that the housing affordability in Türkiye is worse than ever.

Price-to-Rent Ratio

The price-to-rent ratio is the housing price ratio to the property's annualized rent. It is a benchmark tool for estimating whether renting or owning a property is cheaper. The price-to-rent ratio also indicates whether the housing markets are valued or in a bubble. The price-to-rent ratio in the city centers of Türkiye is higher than the outside of the centers, except for the year 2021, where people tend to live outside of cities during the COVID-19 pandemic. While the price-to-rent ratio peaked in 2019, it fell to 16.3 for city centers and 14.6 for outside-of-city centers in 2024. This decline may be due to the slowed down of housing prices compared to the ongoing faster rise in rental prices nationwide.

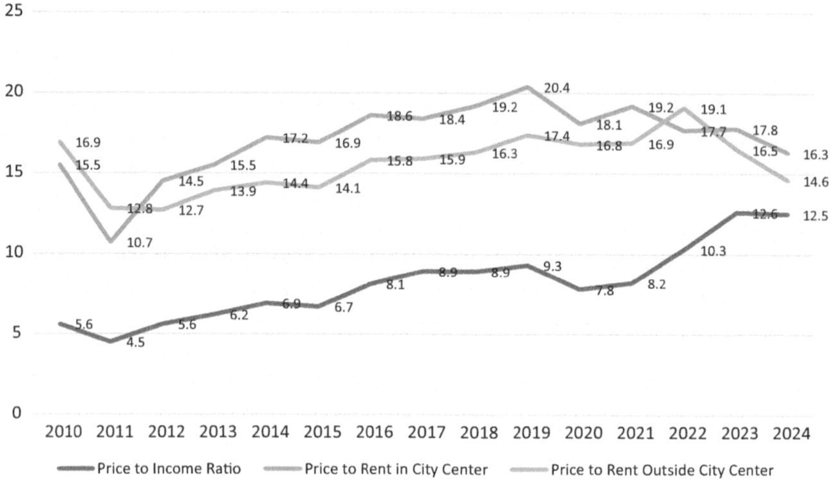

Fig. 5.17 Price-to-rent & price-to-income ratios (Numbeo, 2024)

Housing Policies in Türkiye

Providing sustainable housing policies has always been an important issue for policymakers. The current facts and figures that indicate a housing affordability crisis in Türkiye make this issue even more significant nowadays. Since its foundation in 1923, Türkiye has implemented several policies and housing schemes to match the accommodation needs of its citizens. While between 1923 and 1950, the main target of the government bodies was restructuring the country and getting rid of the negative impacts of two world wars through state-oriented policies, the beginning of the 1950s were the years of the intervention of private enterprises in many industries, including the housing sector. Within almost 30 years after its foundation, the total population living in cities had increased by only 3% and became 19% of the total population (İçduygu & Sirkeci, 1999).

During the first 27 years period, granting half salaries of the government employees as an advance to establish housing cooperatives in 1925, authorizing the Ministry of Finance to build apartments for government employees in 1928, and granting compensation for housing to the public officials, which lasted until 1951 and allowing municipalities to construct affordable housing and sell them to their employees were the primary laws and regulations that the government acted to overcome the housing issue (Uzun, 2022).

The establishment of state-owned Real Estate and Orphans Bank in 1926 (later renamed the Real Estate and Credit Bank of Türkiye) to offer housing loans and support construction initiatives, the issuance of mortgage loan of the Worker's Insurance Institutions to members of housing cooperatives in 1950, and the issuance of home loans by the State Railways Workers Pension Fund and the Military Factories Retirement and Assistance Fund were the primary funding mechanisms of the government to stimulate housing production and homeownership.

The 1950s were the years of accelerating migration from rural to urban areas due to the modernization of agriculture, change in the land ownership regime, the development of transportation, and the consolidation of lands (İçduygu & Sirkeci, 1999). Lack of sufficient housing supply in larger cities like Ankara, İstanbul, and İzmir, which received many internal immigrants, caused unlawful housing construction. Indeed, starting in 1948, many laws enacted to prevent squatter housing settlement could not be successful. After the 1960 coup and the new constitution was put in force, housing needs were defined as the condition of its citizens' physical and mental health, which he stated he was responsible for taking the necessary steps to meet. The Five-Year Development Plans and the Flat Ownership Law (634) were also needed steps to resolve the housing problems of society between 1960 and 1980.

In the 1980s, the National Housing Policy aimed to enable lower- and middle-income groups to become homeowners, improve infrastructure, expand the rehabilitation areas in the squatter housing settlements, provide sustainable financing solutions, provide cheaper land to minimize the cost of development, review the standards of all building components, and to give priority to mass housing and industrial construction. In 1984, the Mass Housing and Public Partnership Board was established as the Housing Development Administration (TOKİ) today.

Housing Development Administration of the Republic of Türkiye (TOKİ)

The Housing Development Administration of the Republic of Türkiye (TOKİ) is one of the leading institutions regarding housing and settlement issues in Türkiye. TOKi produces housing projects on its land, which is granted by the treasury to low- and middle-income groups who have limited sources of income to finance the purchase of a house.

Despite the criticism that the projects TOKİ develops are not affordable for the low- and mid-income groups due to high sales prices, as of January 2022, 86% of TOKİ's project portfolio is social housing projects with these disadvantaged target groups (Solak, 2024). The beneficiaries of the social housing projects make their down payments when the construction starts and make their monthly payments based on a single-indexed repayment plan, mainly the official public sector wage index announced by Turkstats. While the constructions are completed within 36 months on average, the maturities of the loans are set as 10–20 years on average, depending on the income levels of the homebuyers. Public banks primarily provide the loans, and since the title deed is not transferred to the homebuyers until the repayment is completed, TOKİ also acts as the loan guarantor.

Sales prices, including construction costs, social facilities, infrastructure costs, consultancy services, and units' land, are set by TOKİ without adding a profit. To keep the sales prices lower, the housing units produced for the lowest income do not cover the land cost. TOKİ also sells some of its lands to real estate developers using the *income (revenue) sharing model*. It targets high-income groups to generate funds for housing projects for low- and middle-income groups. The projects are constructed on the land of TOKİ, and the private developers offer a percentage of the total sales revenue to TOKİ. Despite the targeted high revenue, the model is criticized for its impact on increasing land costs and sales prices (TOKI, 2024).

Hence, the government's housing policies from its foundation in 1923 to today sometimes resulted in partial success. Still, the combined effects of the internal macro and micro monetary policies and the global and local political and economic conditions impacted the housing market in Türkiye negatively. Currently, the housing sector is urgently in need of sustainable solutions.

Non-Governmental Organizations

There are several non-governmental organizations (NGOs) in Türkiye, including the Real Estate Investors Association (GYODER), Housing Developers and Investors Association (KONUTDER), Istanbul Contractors Association (INDER), Urban Transformation and Urbanism

Foundation (KENTSEV), International Project Management Institute (UPYE), and many others that publish statistical reports regarding the real estate industry, provide training services, develop and recommend policies to attract more investors and capital inflow and offer sustainable solutions to overcome the difficulties in the country including the current housing affordability problems. The largest real estate developers and contractors are members of these NGOs, and government officials consider their forecasts and recommendations.

For instance, GYODER offers a public–private partnership (PPP) model in which the government is involved in housing development by providing land and tax incentives to developers. These incentives could help decrease the sales price as they contribute to lowering development costs. They also ask for long-term rental guarantees to housing developers but do not address how the construction will be financed (GYODER, 2023). Moreover, despite the latest statistics revealing a negative picture of the industry, according to a very recent report of the Housing Developers and Investors Association (KONUTDER) published in July 2024, housing sales in the second half of 2024 are expected to perform better compared to the first half figures. The report indicates a decline in mortgage rates, which may trigger more mortgaged sales in the third and fourth quarters of 2024. Despite their expectation that the construction costs will increase, it is estimated that the sales prices will remain the same, but the rents will keep rising. Based on the report, an increase in new home sales is also expected (KONUTDER, 2024b).

Housing Financing Models

The earliest financial institution, Real Estate, and Orphans Bank, that granted home loans was established in 1926, three years after the foundation of the Türkiye Republic. This bank was renamed Real Estate and Credit Bank of Türkiye in 1946. The Turkish home financing system is mainly based on fixed-rate bank loans. Whenever the interest rates are relatively low, the number of housing units sold and the residential property prices increase. The rise in the interest rates results in the opposite consequences.

Several alternative home financing models were implemented in the past, such as housing certificates and real estate certificates, enabling homebuyers to invest in square meters of a property purchased and sold in the stock market. At the end of the project completion, the certificate holder has the right to acquire the rest of the square meters and buy the house (either cash or by using a loan) or sell his certificates to a potential homebuyer and make his return. Although this was an innovative and sustainable financing model, it did not work well due to the high initial price of the certificate, five years of construction period returns below expectations, and insufficient marketing. Another innovative financing tool was launched in 1989 under the name of *land certificate*. The General Directorate of Land Office gave municipalities the right to sell land certificates that are zoned and ready to construct housing. Unfortunately, this tool did not attract many people due to the negative campaigns of land speculators (Coşkun, 2015).

Another financing scheme that the government initiated through public banks was the "housing account." A housing account is a product that enables customers to accumulate long-term savings by increasing their savings tendencies and encourages society to save by adding the State contribution to savings, provided that the conditions are met. The minimum maturity period of this account that accumulates savings is three years. After three years, the state contribution is deposited, and the account holder may be eligible for a home loan with interest rates below the market rates. This scheme also did not work as the maturity period was too long to save enough money. Yet, the housing prices were sharply increasing, and the savings would not be enough to accumulate enough money to match even the down payments.

One of the government's main policies that is put into force occasionally is decreasing the interest rates independent from the central bank funding rates. The public banks grant low-interest rate mortgage loans to stimulate the housing market. However, this policy does not seem relevant as it weakens the central bank's power over market stability, housing sales, and price increases. A temporary solution seemed to be reached, yet this policy postpones the problem by enlarging its size and impact.

Under high inflation periods, where the interest rates are also rising, a low-interest rate policy does not work. In Türkiye, another alternative financing method is used, which is called the "*My Home-Evim*" model.

My Home-Evim Model

In Turkish tradition, whenever an individual or a family is financially in need, relatives and friends support that person or family. This solidarity has always been a valuable social unity for building a strong society. Purchasing a house in that context was easier when there were such unities and helps. People have started using bank loans for the last few decades to finance their home purchases. As a result, this tradition was replaced by banks because most of the population had to pay bank loans and did not have enough savings to support others. Individualism took precedence over social and collective benefit.

In that context, the "My Home-Evim" model was developed as a *collective social housing system* in the Turkish housing market. This model is defined as a social finance system where individual savings are pooled and converted into a mass pool of funds. Thus, it becomes possible to meet the housing needs of participants by using the savings accumulated in the fund pool. Individuals do not need to take out a bank loan; they can get their houses in a shorter time and at a cheaper price than the conventional mortgage system.

Until 2021, many companies were providing such a service. Still, since they did not have a legal framework, it was too risky for the participants to deposit money as there was no guarantee of receiving their houses. Then, the Banking Regulation and Supervision Agency (BDDK) issued a regulation, and only six companies were licensed to operate and implement this system. In addition to housing finance, these companies provide financial services for vehicle and office space purchases. Nowadays, they also offer to purchase the land with the participants and do the construction. With this approach, they also aim to decrease the development cost and make the housing sales price more affordable. While this is also a good alternative solution, it is essential to underline that no regulated mechanism enables the participants to purchase the land without risking their savings. Thus, a platform, fund, or entity must regulate such operations (Birevim.com, 2024).

Urban Transformation

Türkiye is a country with a high risk of earthquakes of high magnitude. Several earthquakes in the past, including the 1999 Marmara Earthquake, 2023 Kahramanmaraş, and Gaziantep Earthquakes, revealed that millions of units need to be replaced by new ones or strengthened. Scientists warn of the potentially devastating social, economic, environmental, and psychological consequences of the upcoming earthquake in Istanbul soon. The potential İstanbul earthquake is an urgent and severe issue that requires immediate action. There are 6 million housing units and 1.5 office units at risk of collapse in an earthquake. 600,000 of these 6 million residential units are in İstanbul (NTV, 2023). According to the Istanbul Planning Agent (IPA), 450,000 to 750,000 units are vacant (Massink, 2023). Ironically, this figure is more than the risky units that may collapse in a severe earthquake.

On the other hand, KONUTDER (2024a) reports that Istanbul will need 1,230,000 new housing units within the next ten years, 123,000 on average yearly. In addition, the rent of a 100-square-meter apartment is 18,570 TL, more than the base wage, which is 17,000 TL (Emsal.com, 2024). Even renting an apartment for low-to mid-level income families has almost been impossible in Istanbul. The alarm bell is ringing loudly for the Turkish housing market.

The current economic conditions, high inflation, and interest rates make it impossible to take such actions as the construction costs are rising and people's affordability keeps declining. The existing banking-dependent home financing models and the housing policies in force seem not to provide a sustainable solution as the affordability problem deepens.

The following chapter discusses the global practices of housing financing models, policies, and schemes. The solutions recommended in chapter VII may also bring long-term solutions to the housing affordability crisis in Türkiye.

References

Aydın, K. (2019). Türkiye'de Konut Sahipliği, Konut Koşulları ve Konut Kalite Endeksi. *İstanbul Üniversitesi Sosyoloji Dergisi, 39*(2), 277–301. https://doi.org/10.26650/SJ.2019.39.2.0107

BDDK (2024). *Weekly Banking Sector Data*, https://www.bddk.org.tr/BultenHaftalik/en, Last Accessed on July 21, 2024.

Birevim.com. (2024). *Birlikte Tasarruf Finansı ile Neler Mümkün?* https://www.birevim.com/birlikte-tasarruf-finansi/. Last Accessed on July 22, 2024.

CBRT. (2024a). *Weighted average interest rates for banks' loans*. https://www.tcmb.gov.tr/wps/wcm/connect/EN/TCMB+EN/Main+Menu/Statistics/Interest+Rate+Statistics/Weighted+Average+Interest+Rates+For+Banks+Loans/. Last Accessed on July 21, 2024.

CBRT. (2024b). *Consumer price index*. https://www.tcmb.gov.tr/wps/wcm/connect/EN/TCMB+EN/Main+Menu/Statistics/Inflation+Data/Consumer+Prices. Last Accessed on July 22, 2024.

CBRT. (2024c). *Mortgage loan interest rates*. https://evds2.tcmb.gov.tr/index.php?/evds/serieMarket. Last Accessed on July 22, 2024.

CBRT. (2024d). *Housing unit prices*. https://evds2.tcmb.gov.tr/index.php?/evds/serieMarket. Last Accessed on July 22, 2024.

Coşkun, Y. (2015). *Türkiye'de Konut Finansmanı: Sorunlar ve Çözüm Önerileri*. TBB. İstanbul. ISBN 978-605-5327-54-5

Egeeye.com. (2024). *International banks upbeat on Turkish inflation*. INFLATION. https://theegeeye.com/economy-international-banks-upbeat-on-turkish-inflation/. Last Accessed on July 22, 2024.

Eğilmez, M. (2021). *Faizi Düşürdükçe Faiz Yükseliyor*. https://www.mahfiegilmez.com/2021/12/faizi-dusurdukce-faiz-yukseliyor.html. Last Accessed on July 22, 2024.

Emsal.com. (2024). *Konut Kira Artışları 4 Yıldan Sonra Düşüşe Geçti*. https://emsal.com/konut-kira-artislari-4-yildan-sonra-dususe-gecti/. Last Accessed on July 22, 2024

Endeksa. (2024a). *Türkiye'de Konut İmarlı Arsa m2 Birim Fiyatları*. https://www.endeksa.com/tr/analiz/turkiye/endeks/satilik/arsa. Last Accessed on July 22, 2024.

Endeksa. (2024b). *Türkiye'de Kiralık Konut m2 Birim Kiraları*. https://www.endeksa.com/tr/analiz/turkiye/endeks/kiralik/konut. Last Accessed on July 22, 2024.

Erikli, R. (2015). *The December 17–25, 2013 Corruption/Coup Incident in Turkey in the Eyes of Islamic Social Movement*. Central European University, Master Thesis. Budapest.

GYODER. (2023). *GYODER'den kiraları düşürecek formül*. https://gyoder.org.tr/files/202307/a2e898f8-3e5d-4f01-8ef6-df9df1bb4be2.pdf. Last Accessed on July 22, 2024.

İçduygu, A., & Sirkeci, İ. (1999). *Cumhuriyet dönemi Türkiye'sinde göç hareketleri*. 75 Yılda Köylerden Şehirlere. Tarih Vakfı Yayınları, 249–259. İstanbul.

Igan, D., & Loungani, P. (2012). Global Housing Cycles. IMF Working Paper. https://www.imf.org/en/Publications/WP/Issues/2016/12/31/Global-Housing-Cycles-26229. Last Accessed on July 22, 2024.

Kanat, K.B., & Duran, B. (2022). *Ak party years in Türkiye domestic and foreign policy*. SETA Publications. https://www.setav.org/en/assets/uploads/2023/05/K69En.pdf. Last Accessed on July 22, 2024.

KONUTDER. (2024a). *İstanbul'da Gelecek 10 Yılda Konut İhtiyacının Tespiti*. https://konutder.org.tr/files/pwckonutderistanbul-konut-ihtiyaci-calismasi17012024-basin-lansmani-sunumvf4-1705649938724.pdf. Last Accessed on July 22, 2024.

KONUTDER. (2024b). *6 Aylık Beklenti Göstergeleri*. https://konutder.org.tr/raporlar. Last Accessed on July 22, 2024.

Massink, W. (2023). *İstanbul grapples with housing crisis while thousands of homes remain vacant*. https://bianet.org/haber/istanbul-grapples-with-housing-crisis-while-thousands-of-homes-remain-vacant-278091. Last Accessed on July 22, 2024.

NTV (2023). *İstanbul'da kaç riskli konut var? Bakan Özhaseki açıkladı*. https://www.ntv.com.tr/turkiye/istanbulda-kac-riskli-konut-var-bakan-ozhaseki-acikladi,heSTBpfE_EyMqCWKZ1YDqg. Last Accessed on July 22, 2024.

Numbeo. (2024). *Property prices in Turkey*. https://www.numbeo.com/property-investment/country_result.jsp?country=Turkey. Last Accessed on July 22, 2024.

Presidency of Migration Management. (2024). *Temporary protection*. https://en.goc.gov.tr/temporary-protection27. Last Accessed on July 22, 2024.

Solak, A. O. (2024). Housing policies in Turkey post 2002. *International Journal of Housing Policy, 24*(2), 372–387. https://doi.org/10.1080/19491247.2022.2154905

TOKI. (2024). *Housing programs*. https://www.toki.gov.tr/en/housing-programs.html. Last Accessed on July 22, 2024.

Trading Economics. (2024). *Turkey home ownership rate*. https://tradingeconomics.com/turkey/home-ownership-rate. Last Accessed on July 22, 2024.

Tuncer, A. C. (2024). *Türkiye evsizleşiyor: Konut sahipliği oranı yine düştü*. https://www.politikyol.com/turkiye-evsizlesiyor-konut-sahipligi-orani-yine-dustu. Last Accessed on July 22, 2024.

Turkstat. (2024a). *The results of address based population registration system, 2023*. https://data.tuik.gov.tr/Bulten/Index?p=The-Results-of-Address-Based-Population-Registration-System-2023-49684&dil=2. Last Accessed on July 22, 2024.

Turkstat. (2024b). *İnşaat Maliyet Endeksi, Mayıs 2024*. https://data.tuik.gov.tr/Bulten/Index?p=Insaat-Maliyet-Endeksi-Mayis-2024-53664. Last Accessed on July 22, 2024.

Turkstat. (2024c). *Total housing sales*. https://data.tuik.gov.tr/Bulten/Index?p=Konut-Satis-Istatistikleri-Haziran-2024-53760. Last Accessed on July 22, 2024.

Uzun, N. (2022). *Housing policies in Turkey policy, planning, practice* (Ö. Burcu Özdemir Sari, E. Aksoy Khurami, & N. Uzun, Eds.). Routledge. https://www.routledge.com/Housing-in-Turkey-Policy-Planning-Practice/Sari-Khurami-Uzun/p/book/9781032003269. Last Accessed on July 22, 2024.

Wang, Y., & Kinugasa, T. (2022). The relationship between demographic change and house price: Chinese evidence. *IJEPS, 16*, 43–65. https://doi.org/10.1007/s42495-021-00068-z

CHAPTER 6

Housing Financing Models, Schemes, and Policies: Global Practices

Each experience teaches us new things if we learn from the outcomes of these experiences, and the next time, we aim not to repeat our mistakes. Unfortunately, when we look back and analyze the past housing bubbles and crises, we observe *repetitive mistakes* such as insisting on wrong monetary policies, being stuck to conventional banking-dependent financing methods, being trapped in the box, and being unable to think out of it. That is why the global housing sector is in a deadlock and struggling with many recurring problems. People need shelter, but either they don't have enough funds to purchase a house as we experience in the west side of the world due to high interest rates and rapid rise in housing prices, or people can't move to their flats due to unfinished constructions because of the financial defaults of the developers in the east side, especially in China.

In that context, the housing industry, which primarily uses conventional financing methods that are highly dependent on inflation and interest rate spiral, needs alternative and sustainable models not only to overcome the current affordability problems under high financing costs to both the developers and potential homebuyers but also to minimize the risks of the global economy as we are all aware that any crisis in the housing industry may trigger another global financial crisis as we experienced in 2008.

L. Sümer, *The Global Housing Crisis*,
https://doi.org/10.1007/978-3-031-72604-0_6

Besides the bank loans, households in countries such as China, Türkiye, and Italy support each other when purchasing a house. The increasing volume of mortgage loans and decrease in wages and purchasing power also diminish the effect of this tradition, as most families' income and savings are not even adequate for their expenses.

Various factors can influence the implementation of the most appropriate home financing approach. The economic environment, financial structure, the economic system of the country, and the individual's financial status are essential determinants in employing the most suitable housing financing model.

Mortgage System

Some countries use traditional mortgage loans, where a homebuyer obtains a loan from a bank or financial institution to purchase a home and repays the capital plus financing cost (interest payment) over a specified period, mostly 15 to 30 years. In some other countries, such as the US, the governments provide insurance and guarantees to lenders, as we call government-backed loans, and allow homebuyers to get loans with loose conditions by paying lower down payments. This method is mainly used to help lower-income groups access affordable houses. Sometimes, the mortgage rates are fixed for the entire loan term, enabling the borrowers to manage their cash flows more efficiently since they know their monthly repayments. Instead of fixed-rate mortgages, adjustable-rate mortgages (ARMs) are preferred where the interest rates change based on market conditions. ARMs help the borrowers pay less at the beginning due to lower interest rates applied; the rates may increase over time, and the repayment amount may rise. Another mortgage type is the interest-only mortgage, where the borrowers pay the financing cost of the loan over a certain period, 5 to 10 years, and thereafter, the interest and principal are paid, which relaxes the cash flow of the homebuyers. Another option for low-income individuals is microfinance institutions or informal lenders, which provide housing loans to those who may not qualify for traditional bank loans.

Fannie Mae

The Federal National Mortgage Association (FNMA), known as Fannie Mae, is a leading supplier of mortgage financing in the US. The history of

Fannie Mae dates back to the 1930s, the post-Great Depression period, when nearly 25% of America's homeowners lost their homes to banks. Fannie Mae was established to fund local banks by using federal money to finance home loans to improve homeownership rates and increase the availability of affordable housing (Alford, 2015).

Fannie Mae, a government-sponsored enterprise (GSE) and a publicly traded company since 1968, purchases mortgages from lenders to release the money they need to make other mortgage loans to ensure the continuity of affordable mortgages. Fannie Mae facilitates reasonable and sustainable access to homeownership and affordable rental housing (Fannie Mae, 2024). Fannie Mae does not originate mortgage loans or lend money directly to borrowers. Instead, they buy mortgage loans made by lenders, who can then use those funds to offer mortgage loans to more people. Fannie Mae borrows money at low rates, then reinvests into mortgage loans and mortgage-backed securities. It sells bonds and provides liquidity to loan originators by buying whole loans. It purchases whole loans and then securitizes them for the investment market by creating mortgage-backed securities that are either retained or sold. With over USD 4.3 trillion in assets, Fannie Mae is the largest company in the US and the fourth largest company globally.

Freddie Mac

The Federal Home Loan Mortgage Corporation (FHLMC), known as Freddie Mac, was chartered by Congress in 1970 to support the US housing finance system and help ensure an affordable and trustable supply of mortgage funds. Like Fannie Mae, Freddie Mac operates in the US secondary mortgage market, buying loans from approved lenders rather than lending directly to borrowers. Those lenders provide more loans to qualified borrowers and keep money flowing into the housing market. Freddie Mac then pools the mortgages it buys into securities, which they sell to investors globally (Freddie Mac, 2024).

Ginnie Mae

The Government National Mortgage Association (GNMA), known as Ginnie Mae, is a government-owned corporation of the US Federal Government within the Department of Housing and Urban Development (HUD) (USA.gov, 2024). Ginnie Mae was founded in 1968 to grow affordable housing by ensuring housing loans and lowering financing costs by guaranteeing investors the on-time payment of mortgage-backed securities (MBS) even if homeowners default on the underlying mortgages and the homes are foreclosed upon. Ginnie Mae securities are the only MBS that carries the credit guarantee of the US government. Therefore, investing in Ginnie Mae MBS is one of the safest investments that can be made.

Ginnie Mae does not buy or sell loans or issue MBS. Ginnie Mae guarantees investors the timely payment of principal and interest on MBS backed by federally insured or guaranteed loans. These loans are insured by the Federal Housing Administration (FHA) or guaranteed by the Department of Veterans Affairs (VA) (Ginnie Mae, 2024).

Malaysian Cagamas Berhad

Cagamas Berhad (Cagamas) is a Malaysian government-partnered (20% owned by Bank Negara Malaysia (BNM), and 80% by commercial and investment banks) institution that was established in 1986 as the national mortgage corporation that plays a critical role in the country's housing finance sector by operating as a secondary mortgage market company that purchases housing loans from banks and primary lenders to provide liquidity and promote the availability of housing finance (Cagamas.com, 2024).

These purchased loans are securitized into mortgage-backed securities (MBS) or other debt securities by Cagamas to help free up capital for lenders to issue new loans and manage their balance sheets more effectively. Purchasing mortgage loans from primary lenders ensures a steady flow of funds to the housing market, and access to financing becomes easier for homebuyers. The diversified portfolio of housing loans also helps financial institutions to manage credit risk. Its government-backed structure provides trust and increases the credibility and accessibility to cheaper financing costs by getting lower interest rates. Stabilizing the mortgage rates, providing market liquidity, promoting affordability, and supporting economic growth are significant impacts of Cagamas.

Shared Equity and Co-ownership

Besides the conventional bank loan financing options, some alternative models exist. In the shared equity and ownership approach, a housing association or a government agency owns the house with the homebuyers. The homeowners own a share of the property, pay rent on the remaining portion, increase their shares over time, and decrease their rents. This model is known as diminishing musharakah (partnership) and is based on Islamic finance principles. The landlord may offer the potential homebuyer the opportunity to rent the property with the option to buy it before the lease term ends, typically at a set price. These rent-to-own agreements consist of a standard lease and a provision for purchasing the property later. Lease-option contracts grant the potential homebuyer the right to buy the home at the end of the lease, whereas lease-purchase contracts obligate the homebuyer to purchase the property. There are also non-profit organizations named community land trusts that hold land in trust for the benefit of the community and sell or lease homes at below-market prices while retaining ownership of the land (Financialislam.com, 2024).

Timeshares (Vacation Ownership)

The OECD (2024) reports that vacancy rates in seasonal/holiday houses are higher than in regular houses. Most of the year, these houses are unoccupied as people use their seasonal houses only in some periods of the year. Timeshare, also called shared vacation ownership, is a solution for those who use their seasonal properties only for a predetermined period of the year. Timeshares are divided among the shareholders in ownership or use of rights. Condominiums, villas, or apartments are shared among multiple parties who hold the rights to use the same property and use it in the preset period.

Timeshare was first used in Switzerland and the UK in the early 1960s. It became popular after Second World War II as a vacation system. In 1963, a developer named Hapimag and his partner, Dr. Guido Renggli, constructed a 13-unit resort in Graubuenden, Switzerland, after purchasing multiple resort properties in the area. They started selling right-to-use packages while pioneering the first points program (Trask, 2019). In the UK, four European families purchased a vacation cottage jointly, each having exclusive use of the property for one of the four seasons by rotating the season each year to enjoy the nice seasons equally. In the early years of timeshare use, no property manager was involved, so related families mostly used the concept as joint ownership requires trust. Since the families did not use the property for an entire season, these shared properties were again vacant for long periods. Then, the system was used as a commercial business model by British entrepreneurs, who divided a resort room into 50 shares, and each shareholder had the right to use the property for one week. Two weeks a year were left for repairs and upgrades, which are charged to each owner.

The global vacation ownership market was valued at USD 19 billion in 2022 and is anticipated to reach USD 29 billion by 2029, witnessing a CAGR of 7.3% during the forecast period 2023–2029 (Kingpinmarketresearch, 2024). The title deeds in timeshares are divided into the number of owners, but in practice, people may transfer their right of use or sell it to a third party. It is a flexible tool, yet it requires professional management and trust.

Housing Funds & Schemes & Initiatives

Over the past few decades even before, many developing and emerging countries, including Germany, China, Brazil, Mexico, Singapore, Uruguay, the Netherlands, Sweden, and many others, have launched large-scale public housing programs. The success of these programs and approaches depends on government regulations and long-term sustainable housing schemes. These schemes may include direct payments, low-interest loans, tax incentives, deductions or exemptions, joint financing, housing development funds, rent subsidies, or microfinance for low-income groups. Social housing institutions, mostly as government entities or government-backed organizations, play an important role in the housing industry. Providing rental housing units at below-market rates to eligible households, owning and managing housing properties directly, providing rent subsidies, tenant-based vouchers, or capital subsidies to support the development or rehabilitation of affordable housing units, offering counseling, job training, childcare facilities, or healthcare services to tenants to improve their well-being, enhancing the quality of residents by engaging in community development initiatives, such as neighborhood revitalization projects, infrastructure improvements, or social programs are significant roles and contributions of these institutions.

Saiz (2023) underlines the importance of behavioral responses of individuals, companies, governments, and markets when designing effective housing programs and emphasizes the significance of unideological and professional implementation for their success. Analyzing different case studies and best practices in housing programs implemented in various countries may be beneficial or inspirational for others. Let's start with one of the oldest housing schemes, the German Bauparkasse System.

German Bausparkassen System

The term *Bausparkasse* in Germany historically refers to a type of financial institution that provides long-term savings and loan services primarily for housing purposes. These institutions were common in Germany during the early to mid-twentieth century and significantly facilitated homeownership by offering specialized savings plans and mortgage financing. Indeed, the history of the *Bauspar* concept starts in 1775 with the establishment of Kettley's Building Society in Birmingham. The members of this society contribute their monthly savings to a pool of capital, which enables them to get a loan to build their homes. In 1885, pastor Freidrich von Bodelschwingth founded a German type of Building Society in Bielefeld under the idea of "Bausparkasse für Jedermann" ("Bausparkasse for Everyone"). In 1921, the establishment of Gemeinschaft der Freunde (GdF) (Society of Friends) by the author Georg Kropp, which aimed to promote home ownership in Wüsternrot, speeded up the organization's activities. After World War II, Bausparkassen was the driving force in rebuilding the homeownership sector. The system was successfully introduced into the new federal states in East Germany in 1990.

Bausparkassen are particular credit institutions established to help individuals save money toward purchasing or constructing a home that operates on the principle of collective saving, where members contribute regular savings into a shared pool. Members sign a contract called Bauspar. Bausparkassen plays a significant role in fostering homeownership and providing accessible housing finance in Germany's housing market.

In the model, the members of a Bauparkasse make regular deposits into their savings accounts, accumulating interest over time. The savings collected in the fund are then used to finance the purchase or construction of a home. The model is simply based on *"help for self-help."* Bausparen is a closed and flexible system, and it is independent of capital markets.

Members, depending on their credit scores and the amount of their savings, may also be eligible to use lower interest rate mortgage loans from Bausparkassen than the rates of commercial banks. Bausparkassen receives governmental support, including guarantees on savings deposits or incentives for individuals to join these savings plans (Bausparkassen.de, 2024).

Affordable Housing Programs in the US

Affordable housing in the US is structured in a decentralized, privately led system. Affordable housing is defined as housing that is rented or sold at below-market prices or can be occupied only by households below a defined income level. The root of the affordable public housing programs goes back to the post-Great Depression period, which was initiated primarily to put contractors back to work and clear shanty-towns (nlihc.org, 2015). After 1960, the Department of Housing and Urban Development (HUD) started providing subsidies for the development of affordable housing to be privately owned. Low Income Housing Tax Credit (LIHTC) was adopted in 1986, and investors in affordable housing developments received tax breaks for ten years. Property tax abatement schemes were also implemented as the scheme forgives part or all the property tax liability for a property if affordable units are included in the project (Freeman & Lei, 2017).

After the GFC, federal agencies implemented various initiatives to strengthen affordable rental housing. These programs encompass rental assistance payments, grants, loan guarantees, and tax incentives. Additionally, the government aids homeownership through mortgage insurance, loan guarantees, direct homeowner loans, and grants or loans for home repairs (Gao.gov, 2024).

For instance, Inclusionary Zoning (IZ) uses zoning regulations to incentivize or expect developers to include affordable housing in new developments alongside market-rate units either mandatorily or voluntarily, whereby developers receive a density bonus or some other development-related benefit in exchange for including affordable housing units as part of the development.

Another program, the Sect. 8 Housing Choice Voucher Program, is administered by HUD and provides rental assistance vouchers for eligible low-income households to rent privately owned housing. Another HUD Program, the Housing Counseling Assistance Program, provides financing to approved counseling agencies advising purchasing, renting, maintaining, or avoiding housing foreclosure.

Local public housing agencies (PHAs) manage public housing, providing affordable rental housing for qualified low-income families, elderly people, and persons with disabilities. To finance different affordable housing activities, including construction, purchasing, and rehabilitating affordable housing for rent or homeownership, the Investment Partnerships Program (HOME) offers block grants to states and localities. Other programs, named the US Department of Agriculture (USDA) Rural Development Housing Programs, also support affordable housing in rural areas by providing direct loans, grants, and loan guarantees for housing development.

The Housing Trust Fund federal program, established during GFC in 2008, offers grants to states to increase the supply of rental housing for extremely low-income families, including homeless people. HUD also administers a federal grant program, the Self-Help Homeownership Opportunity Program (SHOP), that grants funds to eligible non-profit organizations to help develop affordable housing units for purchase by low-income families. Buyers contribute "sweat equity" to the project by helping build their own homes (Gao.gov, 2024).

Singapore Central Provident Fund (SCPF)

Singapore Central Provident Fund (SCPF) is a compulsory savings scheme for Singaporean citizens and permanent residents. It covers employed individuals, including self-employed ones, who contribute their accounts to fund their retirement, healthcare, and housing needs.

The participants contribute to three accounts, subject to the rates depending on their age and wage levels, as shown in Table 6.1. The first one is the *Ordinary account*, which accounts for retirement, housing, and investment plans. Participants use these funds to finance home purchases and repay housing loans. The second one is the *Medisave account*, which accounts for individuals' medical insurance, healthcare, and hospitalization expenses. The *Special account* is also designed to invest in for retirement periods. The fourth one, the *Retirement account*, accounts for monthly retirement payouts (CPF.gov.sg, 2024).

The government guarantees competitive interest rates in SCPF accounts. By enrolling in the system, the participants make long-term savings that support them in their retirement in terms of healthcare

Table 6.1 Singapore Central Provident Fund (CPF) Types (CPF.gov.sg, 2024)

Ordinary Account	*For retirement, housing, insurance, and investment*
Medisave Account	For hospitalization expenses and approved medical insurance
Special Account	For old age and investment in retirement-related financial products
Retirement Account	For monthly retirement payouts (age 55 and above)

affordability, housing affordability, future income security, and financial stability.

China Housing Provident Fund

Inspired by the Singapore Central Provident Fund, after testing it for three years, China launched the Housing Provident Fund (HPF) in 1994 as a national housing initiative to promote homeownership in China. HPF is governed centrally, and employers and employees contribute a mandatory predetermined percentage of their salaries to an HPF account. Workers can obtain around 1% lower interest rate mortgage loans than the market rates for self-construction, home remodeling, or acquisition. After the government announced that it would stop the old housing allocation system in 1998, the employees' income level was insufficient to purchase private houses. The China Housing Provident Fund is only established in urban areas for in-service employees. Unemployed urban residents and retired employees do not participate in the system. Participants can withdraw savings from the system to purchase houses or for other emergencies. The remaining part is considered the retirement savings (HRone.com, 2023).

The HPF was designed as a savings program to enable mid- and low-income groups to buy houses and help its members retire. The program became successful over the past decade in assisting in privatizing Chinese urban housing. Singapore, India, and Thailand have implemented similar systems. The majority of the population is required to participate in the Chinese and Singaporean plans, while large sections of the population in Thailand and India can choose to join voluntarily. In the Chinese and Indian programs, a fixed rate of return is offered on funds invested. In contrast, in the Singaporean and Thai plans, individuals have the option to invest in different asset classes, such as stocks, bonds, and gold (Chen & Wu, 2006).

Mexico National Workers' Housing Fund Institute (Infonavit)

In Mexico, the National Workers' Housing Fund Institute, known as Infonavit (Instituto del Fondo Nacional de la Vivienda para los Trabajadores), which was established in 1972 under Mexico's Ministry of Social Development is a government agency plays a crucial role in easing access to affordable housing for Mexican workers. The main objective of Infonavit is to manage a housing savings fund that enables participants to access affordable housing through loans and subsidies. Contributions to this housing fund through a certain percentage of the salaries are mandatory. AFORE, a retirement fund manager, manages savings to increase the returns (Guerrero, 2023).

Like other housing schemes, Infonavit also provides mortgage loans with competitive interest rates, using the savings accumulated in the fund for home purchases, renovations, and repairs. Infonavit also offers subsidies to low-income workers, and it collaborates with private real estate developers, financial institutions, and government agencies to improve affordability and expand housing options. Infonavit values sustainable housing development by emphasizing eco-technologies and energy-efficient housing solutions. Digital platforms are also offered to participants to increase accessibility and enable them to manage their accounts, apply for loans, and access information online (OECD, 2015).

Overall, Infonavit plays an important role in fostering homeownership in Mexico, supports social inclusion by providing housing opportunities to low-income groups, and stimulates economic growth by supporting the construction and real estate industries.

Uruguay Housing Schemes

Uruguay has various housing schemes and initiatives, such as providing financial support and assistance and improving housing conditions to address housing affordability and promote homeownership in its nation. For rural housing development, the Mevir Program is designed to improve the living standards of rural populations by renovating and constructing new homes. Mevir collaborates with residents by getting labor and resource support and builds houses for low-income families in rural areas (Mevir.org.uy, 2024).

Plan Juntos means Together Plan, a version of Mevir for extremely low-income groups in urban areas. Like Mevir, the government collaborates with beneficiaries to build houses or apartments under the Plan Juntos program. While families provide and contribute labor, materials, or financing, the government provides technical assistance and subsidies (Latinno.wzb.eu, 2024).

Another housing program in Uruguay is the Más Cerca Program, which focuses on improving current housing conditions and infrastructure in banished urban neighborhoods to reduce spatial segregation and improve living standards. In addition to these schemes, the government provides financial support to developers for affordable housing construction. The beneficiaries also have access to low-interest-rate mortgage loans to purchase social housing. Low-income families are also included in rental housing programs such as subsidies offered by Uruguay state. Nonprofit organizations and real estate developers also financially support the development of rental housing units.

Philippine Pag-IBIG Fund

Established in 1978, the Philippine Pag-IBIG Fund, also known as the Home Development Mutual Fund (HDMF), was created to address the affordable housing needs of Filipino workers' financing. The fund was initially administered by two agencies: The Social Security System (SSS) managed the funds of private employees, and the Government Service Insurance System (GSIS) oversaw the savings of government workers. After one year, the fund's administration was transferred to the National Home Mortgage Finance Corporation (NHMFC). In 1979, the Pag-IBIG Fund was created, and one year later, it became independent from the NHMFC. Following this, Pag-IBIG membership was mandatory for all SSS and GSIS member-employees. Self-employed individuals and voluntary members can also join the program. Pag-IBIG Fund encourages savings and offers housing loans at lower interest rates than commercial banks. Both employers and employees make monthly contributions to the fund, and the accumulated money earns dividends to finance housing loans for qualified members (pagigibfund.gov.ph, 2024).

Pag-IBIG offers several housing loan programs. Affordable housing loans are provided for the purchase of residential units and houses, home construction loans are granted for the construction of a new residential unit on a member's owned lot, and home improvement loans are provided for repairs, renovations, or improvements on existing residential units, refinancing loans are offered to pay off an existing housing loan from an accredited developer or financing institution, calamity loan used for the assistance for members affected by disasters with relaxed eligibility and payment terms during such periods. The interest rates offered by Pag-IBIG are competitive with longer payment terms than commercial banks, making housing more accessible to its members. Pag-IBIG declares annual dividends and increases its members' savings based on its financial performance. Pag-IBIG has an online portal that makes it easy for its members to access their contributions, apply for loans, and perform other transactions.

The Netherlands Social Housing Associations (Woningcorporaties)

The Netherlands is one of the countries in the EU with the largest share of social housing. Even though there is no specific definition of social housing, about 29% of the total housing stock and some 75% of the rental units in the country are categorized under social housing (Van Deursen, 2023). It is also remarkable that 35% of the total housing stock is covered by the Dutch social rented sector, compared with the UK (20%) and most European countries (less than 10%) (Whitehead & Scanlon, 2004).

In 2010, the European Commission defined the social housing system as the housing provided below-market price to disadvantaged or socially less advantaged groups and categories of key workers.

The history of social housing in the Netherlands dates back to 1860. Social housing organizations, named *Woningcorporaties,* are private non-profit organizations with a legal task to prioritize housing households with lower incomes. Social housing played a vital role in matching the housing needs after World War II. Until 1990, the Dutch government mostly managed the operations and financing of housing associations. These institutions had hierarchical solid connections with the government (Van Bortel & Elsinga, 2007). Around 425 registered social housing entities in the Netherlands build, maintain, sell, and rent social housing stock and provide other kinds of services directly related to the use of the dwellings to the occupants.

Woningcorporaties have been financially independent of the central government since 1993, and they can benefit from a three-level security structure: The first element is the Central Fund of Social Housing (CFV). This independent public entity supervises the organization's financial situation and supports the organizations with financial difficulties. The Netherlands Central Housing Fund (Centraal Woningfonds Nederland or CWN) is a critical player in the Dutch housing market and provides mortgage loans with competitive interest rates to individuals purchasing houses in the Netherlands. The operations of CWN are subject to regulations of the Dutch central bank; it primarily acts as a lender and aims to enable homeownership by offering affordable mortgage options, including fixed- and variable-rate mortgages. Income requirements, creditworthiness assessments, and compliance with legal and regulatory standards are the main criteria for eligibility for the mortgage loans that CWN offers.

The Guarantee Fund for Social Housing (WSW) is the second security instrument, and it is a private organization established by housing organizations to serve as a solidarity fund. This fund allows social housing organizations to access favorable interest rates to finance their activities and make Dutch owner-occupied housing industry more resilient during the financial crisis (Priemus, 2013). If the first two instruments are inadequate in addressing the economic issues of the organizations, the State and local authorities step in as a last resort. (Van Bortel & Elsinga, 2007).

Sweden Housing Finance Schemes

The traditional Swedish housing market was designed to minimize speculation and instability, featuring a significant rental sector and cooperative tenures instead of condominiums (Holmqvist & Turner, 2014). More than 30% of 10 million Sweden's population lives in rental housing. Half of them live in houses owned by municipalities (Spolander, 2024). The evolution of the welfare state model and higher levels of mortgage debt indicate that Sweden's housing market may now be more vulnerable to macroeconomic pressures.

Sweden has numerous housing finance schemes focusing on supporting its citizens in affording houses. Fixed or variable-rate mortgage loans *(Bolån)* require the borrowers to pay the principal and interest together over a long period that extends until retirement or 50 years, subsidizing housing (Statligt Subventionerad Bostad) both for rental and owner-occupied units to make the housing more affordable, housing allowance (Bostadsbidrag) to help low-income individuals and families for housing purchases, home insurance subsidy (Bostadsförsäkringsbidrag) to help cover the cost of home insurance premiums for certain groups, cooperative housing (Bostadsrätt) which enables the residents to own a share (rather than the property itself) in a cooperative housing association and pay a monthly fee to cover operating costs and mortgage payments, rent control programs to ensure fair pricing in rental market to protect the tenants, and providing tax incentives to promote new housing are the main housing schemes of Sweden put in place to overcome housing-related problems (Fox & Syvixay, 2020).

Brazilian Housing Program (My House, My Life Program—Minha Casa, Minha Vida)

Brazil started an ambitious national social housing program named "My House, My Life Program" (Minha Casa, Minha Vida—MCMV) in 2009 to initially develop 1 million affordable housing units. From its first establishment until 2016, MCMV developed more than 4.5 million units. Even though it helped reduce the country's housing supply deficit, the program was criticized for the completed units' planning, design, and quality (Biderman et al., 2018; UN-Habitat, 2013). The location of the houses built, which were far from the city center, lacking public transit and utilities, the distance from jobs, education facilities, lack of health facilities, parks, shops, and libraries was also a significant criticism of the MCMV Program.

Summary of the Housing Programs and Schemes

The housing programs, schemes, and funds used in different countries have common approaches. They all aim to increase the homeownership rate of low-mid-income level groups. While some of them use conventional mortgage approaches, such as Cagamas acting as a secondary mortgage company which is providing market liquidity, some others focus on using savings, as in the case of German Bausparkassen, Philippine Pag-IBIG Fund, and Singapore Central Provident Fund. Sweden Housing Scheme encourages co-ownership, and Woningcorporaties in the Netherlands are private non-profit organizations. Most programs provide low-interest rates below the market rates to facilitate purchasing and tax

Table 6.2 Standard features of housing schemes, programs, and funds

Encouraging and categorizing savings
Providing low-interest rate
Providing market liquidity
Targeting the low-mid-income level groups
Including rental housing programs
Including renovation and self-constructions
In line with non-governmental organizations
Providing housing allowance
Tax incentives and subsidies
Co-ownership approach
Aiming to reduce the shortage of supply
Increasing the rate of homeownership

incentives; these programs' housing allowances and subsidies are also important common points, as summarized in Table 6.2.

Criticism of the Programs

On the other hand, these programs are criticized in different ways. For instance, in the Bausparkassen system, it may be challenging to save enough money while the housing prices are rising, and the integration of savings and the low-interest rate subsidies may cause problems under dire economic conditions. The system also receives criticism as it does not target the needy groups but brings a partial solution for the upper middle classes (Diamond, 2002). The location of the affordable houses constructed, which are far from city centers and lacking infrastructure and social services, is a critique of the Minha Casa Minha Vida Program of Brazil. The Central Provident Fund of Singapore is also criticized for not being a social security welfare model but a tool that encourages self-reliance where the participants receive back what they put in with interest (Selvam, 2023). Difficulties in qualifying for Infonavit loans, high interest rates applied, limited housing options, the bureaucracy of the application and approval process, the quality of construction, infrastructure problems, security issues, lack of support services, and political influence are the issues that Mexico's housing finance institution Infonavit receives.

While policymakers focus on subsidies, providing subventions sometimes works for low-income groups but puts mid-income households into a dilemma. Due to their income levels, these families are not qualified for subsidies but don't have enough income to purchase a non-subsidies house (Hoekstra & Marais, 2016).

In Poland, the *Family's Own Home* program, which was launched in 2007 and terminated in 2012, aimed to increase homeownership but failed due to a public finance crisis. In addition, the subsidized mortgage loan did not increase the supply. The necessity of homeownership was also questioned, as many young people do not have stable incomes, and more rental units are required (Radzimski, 2014).

On the other hand, Milligan et al. (2006) conducted a research that exhibited interesting findings. Australia's housing policy is based on promoting homeownership with a small intervention of the public housing system, and the Netherlands, which has a diversified and large social housing system, has similar consequences for the housing affordability of low-income households. The authors also underline that the case in Australia is worse due to its dependency on private housing development.

To conclude, we observe efforts in many countries to overcome housing problems no matter what they are caused by. Internal and, to some extent, external dynamics sometimes help policymakers to be partially successful or cause them to fail. While some of the factors are controllable, others are beyond the control of the states. Mass migrations, demographics, political development, conflicts, nearing or post-elections, the impact of climate change and natural disasters, and monetary policies as responses to local or global economic circumstances may influence the success and endurance of the policies.

Effective monitoring and reporting, in some cases being flexible and acting agile depending on the situation's urgency, may also enhance getting better results. Having analyzed different housing financing models, policies, and schemes, we can discuss the details of the new sustainable housing financing model in the following chapter.

References

Alford, R. (2015). *What are the origins of Freddie Mac and Fannie Mae?* https://www.hnn.us/article/what-are-the-origins-of-freddie-mac-and-fannie-mae. Last Accessed on July 22, 2024.

Bausparkassen.de (2024). *What we do.* https://www.bausparkassen.de/en/about-us/what-we-do/. Last Accessed on July 22, 2024.

Biderman, C., Hiromoto, M. H., & Ramos, F. R. (2018). *The Brazilian housing program Minha Casa Minha Vida: Effect on Urban Sprawl*. Lincoln Institute of Land Policy (Working Paper WP18CB2). https://www.lincolninst.edu/publications/working-papers/brazilian-housing-program-minha-casa-minha-vida/. Last Accessed on July 22, 2024.

Cagamas.com. (2024). *About us*. https://www.cagamas.com.my/about/about-us. Last Accessed on July 22, 2024.

Chen, C., & Wu, Z.G. (2006). *China's housing provident fund: Inequitable and inefficient*. The CRIOCM 2006 International Symposium on "Advancement of Construction Management and Real Estate". https://www.irbnet.de/daten/iconda/CIB5819.pdf. Last Accessed on July 22, 2024.

Cpf.gov.sg. (2024). *How CPF works*. https://www.cpf.gov.sg/member/cpf-overview. Last Accessed on July 22, 2024.

Diamond, D. B. (2002). *Comments on the Bauspar system and proposal for Lithuania*. Round table discussion on the Bauspar system. http://pdc.ceu.hu/archive/00001144/01/19.pdf. Last Accessed on July 22, 2024.

Fannie Mae. (2024). *Who we are*. https://www.fanniemae.com/about-us/who-we-are. Last Accessed on July 22, 2024.

Financialislam.com. (2024). *Diminishing Musharakah*. https://www.financialislam.com/diminishing-musharakah1.html. Last Accessed on July 22, 2024.

Fox, R., & Syvixay, J. (2020). *Sweden's public housing and rent control strategy lessons for planners in a Canadian context*. Case-in-Point 2020. https://umanitoba.ca/architecture/sites/architecture/files/2023-02/CP_cip2020_Fox.pdf. Last Accessed on July 22, 2024.

Freddie Mac. (2024). *About Freddie Mac*. https://www.freddiemac.com/about, Last Accessed on July 22, 2024.

Freeman, L., & Lei, Y. (2017). *An overview of affordable housing in the United States*. https://penniur.upenn.edu/uploads/media/An_Overview_of_Affordable_Housing_in_the_United_States_Updated.pdf. Last Accessed on July 22, 2024.

Gao.gov. (2024). *Affordable housing*. https://www.gao.gov/affordable-housing. Last Accessed on July 22, 2024.

Ginnie Mae. (2024). *Funding government lending*. https://www.ginniemae.gov/about_us/who_we_are/Pages/funding_government_lending.aspx. Last Accessed on July 22, 2024.

Guerrero, O. (2023). *Understanding INFONAVIT and AFORE: Benefits for foreign workers in Mexico*. https://vegaguerrero.com/labor-law/understanding-infonavit-and-afore-benefits-for-foreign-workers-in-mexico/?lang=en. Last Accessed on July 22, 2024.

Hoekstra, J., & Marais, L. (2016). Can Western European home ownership products bridge the South African housing gap? *Urban Forum, 27*, 487–502. https://doi.org/10.1007/s12132-016-9279-7

Holmqvist, E., & Turner, L. M. (2014). Swedish welfare state and housing markets: Under economic and political pressure. *Journal of Housing and the Built Environment, 29*, 237–254. https://doi.org/10.1007/s10901-013-9391-0

Hrone.com. (2023). *China's housing provident fund*. https://hrone.com/blog/housing-provident-fund-in-china/. Last Accessed on July 22, 2024.

Kingpinmarketresearch.com. (2024). *Global vacation ownership (timeshare) professional market insights, players, region, type & application analysis 2019–2030*. https://www.kingpinmarketresearch.com/global-vacation-ownership-timeshare-professional-market-27807479. Last Accessed on July 22, 2024.

Latinno.wzb.eu. (2024). *Plan together*. https://latinno.wzb.eu/en/case/18047/. Last Accessed on July 22, 2024.

Mevir.org.uy. (2024). *Mevir*. https://www.mevir.org.uy/. Last Accessed on July 22, 2024.

Milligan, V., Dieleman, F., & van Kempen, R. (2006). Impacts of contrasting housing policies on low-income households in Australia and the Netherlands. *Journal of Housing and the Built Environment, 21*, 237–255. https://doi.org/10.1007/s10901-006-9047-4

Nlihc.org. (2015). *A brief historical overview of affordable rental housing*. https://nlihc.org/sites/default/files/Sec1.03_Historical-Overview_2015.pdf. Last Accessed on July 22, 2024.

OECD. (2015). *Better housing policy for Mexico: What role for INFONAVIT?* https://www.oecd-ilibrary.org/better-housing-policy-for-mexico-what-role-for-infonavit_5js7x2rq1pq1.pdf?itemId=%2Fcontent%2Fcomponent%2F9789264227293-6-en&mimeType=pdf. Last Accessed on July 22, 2024.

OECD. (2024). *Housing stock and construction*. https://www.oecd.org/els/family/HM1-1-Housing-stock-and-construction.pdf. Last Accessed on July 22, 2024.

pagigibfund.gov.ph. (2024). *Affordable housing loan for minimum-wage earners*. https://www.pagibigfund.gov.ph/AffordableHousingLoan.html. Last Accessed on July 22, 2024.

Priemus, H. (2013). Public mortgage guarantee: Instrument to cope with impacts of the financial crisis on the owner-occupied housing market evidence from the Netherlands. *Journal of Housing and the Built Environment, 28*, 345–362. https://doi.org/10.1007/s10901-012-9315-4

Saiz, A. (2023). *The global housing affordability crisis: Policy options and strategies* (IZA Policy Paper, No. 203). Institute of Labor Economics (IZA). https://docs.iza.org/pp203.pdf. Last Accessed on July 22, 2024.

Selvam, P. (2023). *Is now the time to review the Central Provident Fund?* https://www.ey.com/en_sg/tax/is-now-the-time-to-review-the-central-provident-fund. Last Accessed on July 22, 2024.

Spolander, P. (2024). *Public housing in Sweden*. https://www.sverigesallmannytta.se/in-english/public-housing-in-sweden/. Last Accessed on July 22, 2024.

Trask, J. (2019). *The history of timeshare ownership | Part 1: 1960's and 70's*. https://vacationownershipconsultants.com/history-of-timeshare-ownership-in-the-1960s-1970s/. Last Accessed on July 22, 2024.

UN-Habitat. (2013). *Scaling-up affordable housing supply in Brazil: The "My House my Life" Programme (Programa Minha Casa Minha Vida)*. https://unhabitat.org/scaling-up-affordable-housing-supply. Last Accessed on July 22, 2024.

USA.gov. (2024). *Ginnie Mae*. https://www.usa.gov/agencies/government-national-mortgage-association-ginnie-mae. Last Accessed on July 22, 2024.

Van Bortel, G., & Elsinga, M. (2007). A network perspective on the organisation of social housing in the Netherlands: The case of urban renewal in The Hague. *Housing, Theory and Society, 24*(1), 32–48.

Van Deursen, H. (2023). *The people's housing: Woningcorporaties and the Dutch social housing system Part 2: The mechanics*. Harvard University Joint Center for Housing Studies. https://www.jchs.harvard.edu/sites/default/files/research/files/harvard_jchs_the_peoples_housing_mechanics_van_deursen_2023.pdf. Last Accessed on July 22, 2024.

Whitehead, C., & Scanlon, K. (2004). *International trends in housing tenure and mortgage finance*. Council of Mortgage Lenders Research Report. https://www.iut.nu/wp-content/uploads/2017/07/International-trends-in-Housing-Tenure-and-Mortgage-Finance.pdf. Last Accessed on July 22, 2024.

CHAPTER 7

Time to Change the Rules of the Game: Introducing a Sustainable Home Financing Model

The global housing industry is running into a new crisis. The current outstanding mortgage loans are more than the value of the 2008 Global Financial Crisis (GFC) initiated by the subprime mortgage crisis. Interest rates and inflation rates are also above the GFC's level. Housing prices are more expensive, yet people's purchasing power is lower, access to financing is more difficult, and the cost of funding is too high. Within the last two decades, average real housing prices increased by around 46% in OECD countries (Van der Drift et al., 2023). Sixteen years have passed since the GFC, and the global economy has experienced new local and regional financial crises and the Great Recession in 2020 due to the COVID-19 pandemic.

A housing bubble and subprime mortgages mainly described the 2008 GFC. A rapid increase in the US housing market alongside easy access to financing ended with the housing bubble burst, foreclosures, and a significant decline in housing prices. The crisis affected the global economy due to the interconnection of the economies and the high leverage used by the financial institutions, which enlarged the impact level of the crisis after the decline of asset prices. The crisis resulted in a decrease in interest rates, and many central banks applied monetary expansion policies.

The case we are currently experiencing is the outcome of the low-interest rates and quantitative easing policies of central banks during the COVID-19 pandemic, which resulted in high inflation rates. The ongoing

L. Sümer, *The Global Housing Crisis*,
https://doi.org/10.1007/978-3-031-72604-0_7

war between Russia and Ukraine and additional political risks have made inflation higher than expected by the central banks. Until the monetary tightening decisions of the Federal Reserve (FED), European Central Bank (ECB), and other central banks regarding fighting against inflation, housing prices had already risen sharply in many countries. We can say that the housing crisis was the reason behind the 2008 GFC. Today, the crisis in the housing industry is a consequence of the great lockdown during COVID-19, prolonged monetary expansion policies of central banks, and high inflation rates.

In 2008, there was an oversupply of homes in the market, but today, the situation is reversed. There is a demand for housing, and it is even hard to find an apartment to rent in many cities. In addition, the subprime mortgage crisis, a key driver of the 2008 crash, was fueled by inconsiderate lending practices, but today, lending standards are far more rigorous.

Comparing the 2008 and 2024 housing crises, the 2024 crisis is expected to end with a market price correction. This approach may be correct, and I hope it is, but high interest rates keep the stagnation risk, and high financing and construction costs due to prolonged high interest rates and low wages put additional threats on the future of the housing industry. Additionally, the housing market is very highly dependent on the banking sector. In 2023, 5 banks (Silicon Valley Bank, Signature Bank, First Republic Bank, Heartland Tri-State Bank, and Citizens Bank) with around USD 750 billion asset size collapsed in different US states (FDIC, 2024). The bankruptcy of Silicon Valley Bank was recorded as the second-largest bank collapse in US history and the largest since 2008 GFC. Noting that 15% of Silicon Valley was mortgage and commercial loans, this collapse may not directly affect the housing industry as the Silicon Valley Bank primarily funded tech start-up companies but may indirectly impact the mortgage repayments due to potential job losses in the technology market (Tracey, 2023).

Bank-dependent funding mechanisms may have a different impact on the housing market. Decreasing the interest rates may stimulate the housing market's growth and increase sales but mainly results in a rise in housing prices (Sümer, 2022). On the other hand, high interest rates halt the development of housing prices (Thom, 1983) and a decline in the long run when the mortgage rates are high (McGibany & Nourzad, 2004; Reichert, 1990).

While it seems the easiest way to finance the housing industry is through banks, the interest rate-dependent mortgage systems cannot regulate the industry due to the ups and downs in crisis periods. We must find alternative financing solutions for a more stable and sustainable housing market. The solution may be possible by implementing the four pillars (*developing, balancing, saving, and sharing*) of the new sustainable economic and financing system I recommended in my previous book. With its dynamics and direct touch on people's lives, the real estate industry is an important sector in which this model can be applied.

4 Pillars of Housing Development: Developing, Balancing, Saving and Sharing

Planning the cities based on their potentials and capacities, determining their needs, planning the population, projecting growth, and constructing sustainable towns are the starting points of implementing the four pillars in the real estate industry. This approach takes us to a *sustainable development* of the cities, which replaces the current too debt-oriented consumerist system. On the other hand, instead of accumulating all the living opportunities in big metropolitan cities and congesting people there, investing in different towns may create new job opportunities and better living conditions that may bring a *balance among cities*. The balancing may even be employed by constructing eco-villages where the comfort of cities is provided, but the spirit of the villages is not spoiled. Eco-villages may be possible by the combination of technology use and production in these eco-villages.

The hybrid working options after the COVID-19 pandemic may also positively impact this balance as many people prefer to work remotely from their houses, which are not necessarily in the same city where the offices are located. The balance provided among cities may result in real estate developers' decision to invest in different cities. The supply and demand balance in the housing market takes place, bringing price stability and preventing speculative increases in housing prices. When stability occurs, affordability also increases, and a societal balance is provided. This balance increases *savings* as people do not have to pay high bank financing costs. The increase in savings may shift the paradigm from a banking-oriented financing approach to a collective, participating, and *sharing economic system* where the people become the funder and the investor of the investment projects. The role of the banks in the financial system is redefined.

We can shift the mindsets from a conventional mortgage financing system to a collective and cooperative approach. In that case, we may contribute to the price stability of the housing market, increase the affordability and homeownership rates, decrease the financing costs, and help more people live in better conditions.

Before describing the details of the new sustainable housing financing model I developed, it is helpful to discuss the real estate capital market instruments, including real estate investment funds, real estate investment trusts, real estate certificates, pension funds, and the diminishing musharakah (partnership) approach that the different variations of the model are structured on.

Real Estate Investment Trusts

Real estate investment trusts (REITs) are investment companies with closed-end structures. They act as financial intermediaries and oversee portfolios of real estate, real estate-based projects, and other capital market instruments related to real estate. According to Brueggeman and Fisher (2011), a REIT is defined as a real estate trust or company that distributes most of its taxable earnings and any capital gains derived from property sales or dispositions to its shareholders. REITs play a crucial role in facilitating fund flows within real estate markets.

Given the high cost of property ownership, investors often turn to REITs as an alternative to investing directly in real estate. Equity REITs manage and trade physical real estate, while mortgage REITs specialize in selling commercial and residential mortgages. Hybrid REITs, on the other hand, offer a mix of both. Equity REITs primarily earn revenue from property rents, whereas mortgage REITs generate their income from interest earned on mortgage loans (Sümer & Ozorhon, 2016). REITs specialize in different asset classes, including residential, commercial, office, tourism facilities, logistics, healthcare, and industrial. Innovations in artificial intelligence and the growing demand for computing power have made data center REITs very popular and profitable. Figure 7.1 shows the distribution of REIT investments in the US.

REITs are considered profitable investment tools that compete with other stock indices. Since REITs have a low correlation with different

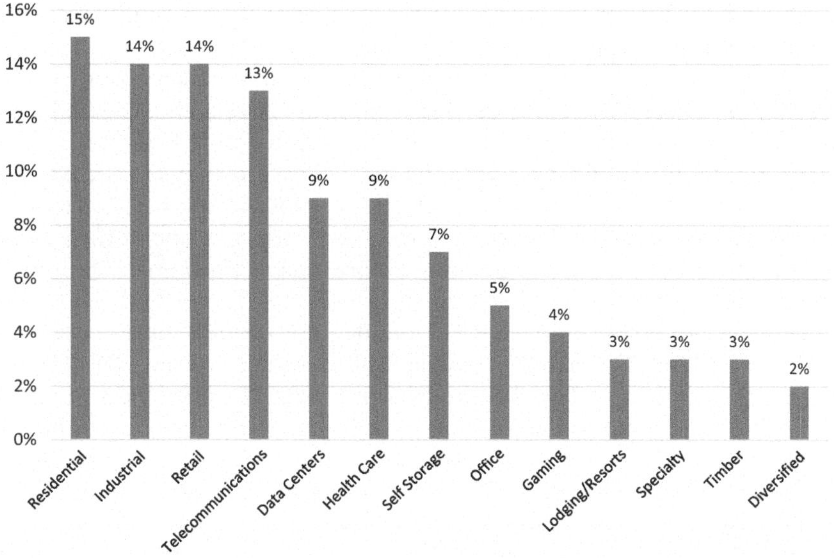

Fig. 7.1 Property sector share in FTSE nareit all equity REITs index (Reit.com, 2024)

assets, they help reduce investors' portfolio risk and increase their returns. It is recommended that the optimal REIT portfolio allocation be between 5 and 15%. Hence, 64% of the top 25 largest US and global institutional investors use REITs in their portfolios. Additionally, in times of economic downturn, the real estate securities listed provide a hedge against inflation in developed markets (Marcato & Brounen, 2015).

As of 2023, the total global size of REITs is USD 3.22 trillion, and the US, with an approximately USD 1.4 trillion market size, has the largest REIT market. Mortgage REITs help finance one million homes in the US, and approximately 170 million people in the US own REITs through pension funds or other investment funds. The US REITs own more than USD 4 trillion of gross real estate, and public REITs own USD 2.5 trillion in assets. REITs deliver competitive returns based on high, steady dividend income and long-term capital appreciation. In 2022, REITs paid its shareholders approximately USD 110 billion in dividends (REIT.com, 2024).

Regarding market size, the US was followed by Japan, Singapore, the UK, and Australia. As shown in Fig. 7.2, the REITs market in the Asia Pacific consists of 35.1% of the total market, with a market size of USD 1.13 trillion. While the REIT market volume in Europe, the Middle East, and Africa is USD 640,1 billion, Latin America has only USD 42 billion (Statista, 2024a). Table 7.1 shows the major REIT markets in the world. While the history of REIT dates back to the 1960s in the US, it is a new instrument in Germany, France, and the UK. Türkiye is one of the countries that adopted REIT regulation before major European developed countries.

Globally, 44 countries have REIT regulations. Among these countries, such as Türkiye, Germany, Malaysia, Bulgaria, and Ireland, REITs are corporate tax exempt. The shareholders of the REITs are subject to taxation. The tax exemption applies only to dividend payments in countries including the US, Japan, Singapore, and South Korea. The shareholders of these REITs again shall pay taxes. Tax exemption is applied in the UK, France, Brazil, Belgium, and Italy based on certain conditions, such as passing the income tests (Tolu, 2024).

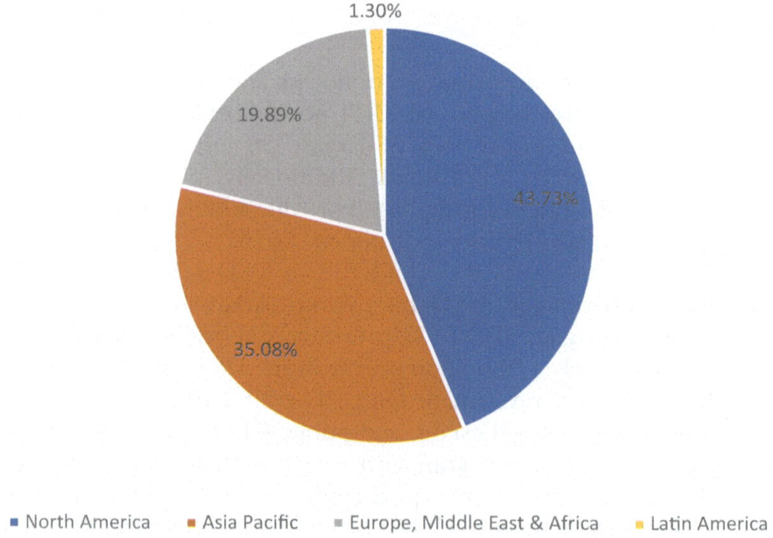

Fig. 7.2 Global listed real estate market size 2023 by region (Statista, 2024a)

Table 7.1 The REITs in the world (Sümer, 2017)

Country	*Enacted year*	*REIT Type*
United States	1960	Corporate type
Australia	1985	Trust type
Japan	2000	Trust or corporate type
UK	2007	Corporate Entity
Canada	1994	Trust type
Netherlands	1969	Corporate type (only for corporate taxpayers)
France	2003	N/A
Singapore	1999	Trust type
Hong Kong	2003	Trust type
South Africa	2013	Legally, a company or trust
Mexico	2004	Trust
Belgium	1995	Corporate type
Spain	2009	Corporate type
Türkiye	1995	Corporate type National Stock Exchange Commission
Germany	2007	Corporate type
Malaysia	2002	Trust type

From investment, return, and tax perspectives, REITs are crucial real estate capital market instruments in the real estate industry.

Real Estate Investment Funds

A real estate fund invests in securities offered by public real estate companies. It can include REITs and real estate operating companies, with some funds also directly investing in real estate properties. Investing in real estate funds offers a broader range of assets and diversification than purchasing individual REITs. There are three main types of real estate funds: real estate exchange-traded funds (REIT-ETF), which own shares of real estate corporations and REITs and trade like stocks on major exchanges. Additionally, real estate mutual funds can be open- or closed-end and actively or passively managed. Another type is private real estate investment funds, professionally managed funds that invest directly in real estate properties (Hayes, 2023).

A real estate investment fund (REIF) enables its investors to make a return on capital gain or rental income from the assets included in the portfolio. A property called REIF is set up by asset management companies and real estate portfolio management companies to manage a portfolio of real estate assets and transactions as determined by the Capital Markets Board. The fund accumulates money from qualified investors and directs these investments into different real estate and money market instruments with certain conditions and limitations. Investors who are interested in real estate investment but prefer to avoid dealing with physical issues, purchase and sale transactions, or real estate leasing can find a liquid investment opportunity in REIFs. Funds also provide risk management to their investors by diversifying their portfolios. REIFs are also considered an option for those who do not have enough cash to invest in direct real estate. The unit value of the funds is determined based on these two main return items.

The Property Funds Research and Institutional Real Estate, Inc. (2023) report that the global real estate assets under management reached USD 6.09 trillion based on 2022 AUM figures. As of May 2023, 2,035 private equity real estate funds are in the market, managing a total of USD 547.5 billion. Like REITs, real estate investment funds are also corporate or income tax exempt in some countries such as Türkiye, Germany, and Italy.

As of December 2022, the ten leading real estate investment managers worldwide held nearly USD 1.9 trillion in assets under management (AUM), as shown in Fig. 7.3 (Statista, 2024b).

Real Estate Certificates

A real estate certificate is an innovative way of investing in real estate in small portions. It can be compared with crowdfunding, but the main advantage of real estate certificates is that they provide two-way financing for developers and investors who want to purchase their houses. The regulations for real estate certificates were introduced in Türkiye in 1995, but trust in the tool has not been enough to use such an important tool since then. Private companies can use real estate certificates to fund up to 50% of their residential and commercial projects, except for urban transformation projects, which can be fully financed through these instruments (Communique on Real Estate Certificates SPK, 2017). It was 2017 when additional regulations came into force, and the real estate certificate was used for a specific real estate development project. Despite its success, it was not used for further real estate development projects.

The real estate certificate investment tool allows investors to acquire partial ownership of a property if the purchaser of the certificate meets

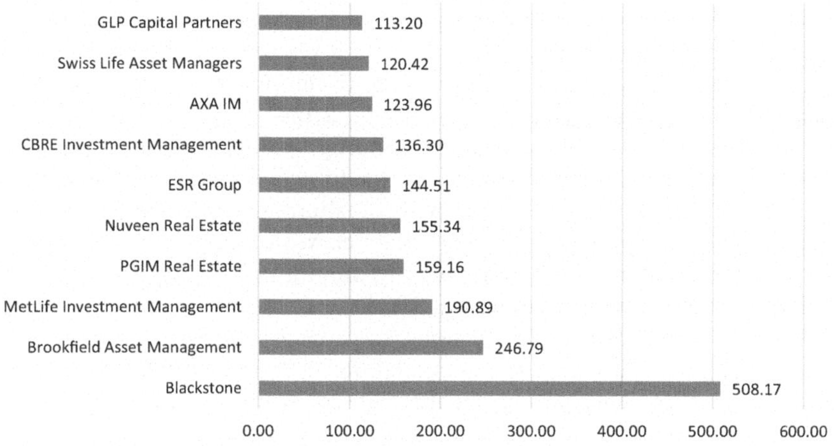

Fig. 7.3 Top 10 real estate investment managers worldwide in 2022 by assets under management (Statista, 2024b)

the required investment size of square meters. Investors can choose to hold onto the certificate until it reaches maturity or sell it to another investor in the stock market. Additionally, investors have the option to sell the real estate certificates on the stock exchange before they reach maturity or request liquidity from the issuer. The issuer of real estate certificates will offer investors a repurchase guarantee at specific predetermined intervals. Furthermore, the issued certificates can be traded on the stock exchange directly by the issuer's construction firm or through an intermediary financial institution. Trading in the stock market enables real estate certificates to gain a liquid characteristic through continuous transactions on the stock exchange.

Crowdfunding

Real estate crowdfunding (RECF) is a quickly expanding, technology-driven advancement that has sparked considerable discussion in global real estate finance (Montgomery et al., 2018). Crowdfunding involves seeking financial support from the public to kickstart new projects. Potential investment opportunities are showcased on websites, allowing ordinary internet users to engage with and consider these proposals directly. Individuals interested in the projects contribute to a collective pool of capital, which other investors form. This pooled capital then serves as financial support for current or potential real estate investments, whether residential or commercial and can encompass the development of new real estate or a stake in existing properties (Steinberg, 2024).

Investors can use real estate crowdfunding to fund real estate projects through online platforms, aiming to profit from either capital appreciation or passive income. As a type of alternative investment that is becoming increasingly popular, real estate crowdfunding may have significant barriers to entry, including meeting minimum funding requirements and accreditation status (Friedberg, 2024).

Crowdfunding can help with housing project financing, starting with land purchasing. Participants can contribute to a pool of funding during the construction phase. Financing through crowdfunding may reduce the total development costs and decrease housing prices.

Diminishing Musharakah (Partnership)

Diminishing Musharakah, an Islamic finance tool, operates on the principles of partnership. It involves two parties initiating an investment with different shares, and the partnership concludes with one partner acquiring complete ownership by buying out the other partner's share based on mutually agreed conditions. This financing method is commonly used when one party aims to purchase an asset like a house but lacks sufficient funds to cover the entire cost, seeking financial support from the other party. The supporter's share is divided into multiple units, and the other party gradually purchases these units from the financier's share. The partnership ends when the purchaser gets all the financier's shares and becomes the asset's owner. Until the whole shares pass to the purchaser, the asset is co-owned by both parties at the rates of their shares.

Shirkah al-aqd, also known as contractual partnership, allows for this type of collaboration. It involves any party contributing capital, service, goodwill, or reputation. As a result, the distribution of profits for each partner may not match their equity ratio and must be agreed upon when the contract is executed. However, if there is a loss, it is shared based on the equity ratio at the time the loss occurred. The partner leasing the assets may agree to buy the financier's share periodically at market value or a predetermined price. The price of share units cannot be fixed in the promise to sell.

Diminishing Musharakah may also be carried out through ***shirkah al-milk***, a form of joint ownership partnership, allowing for the distribution of profits without needing prior agreement. Each partner assumes the risk and reward in proportion to their ownership stake in the property or asset. Under this method, the financing partner has the option to lease its share to the other party and receive rental income for the leased portion. The lessee continues paying rent while acquiring a share of the financing partner through ownership units. As the lessee increases her stake, the rental payment decreases. One partner can't buy ownership units representing the other partner's share at a predetermined price.

Several areas of finance utilize Diminishing Musharakah, especially for financing assets eligible for leasing. Transactions for long-term financing can incorporate a floating rate of return, even in economies experiencing high inflation rates. Examples of applications include house financing, auto financing, plant and machinery financing, and financing for all other fixed assets. Specifically for home financing, Diminishing Musharakah can be employed to purchase a house for occupancy, construct a house, renovate an already occupied house, and replace interest-based housing mortgages with a balance transfer facility. In addition, both the bank and the homebuyer share the asset risk in proportion, and even if the homebuyer is unable to buy the bank's ownership units for a specific period, the bank does not suffer a loss because the homebuyer will continue to pay rent (Financeislam.com, 2024).

A new program known as "buy as you go" was also introduced in the UK. Similar to diminishing partnership approach, this program allows individuals renting homes to pay around 90% of the local market rate, with the payment split between rent and equity. The equity payments change over time until the tenant eventually becomes the complete owner of the home (Rama & Andoni, 2017).

Pension Funds

Everybody wants to live a good life, now and when getting older. Nobody knows when to die, but make savings to keep the quality of life in retirement years. Pension accounts are those where people make investments through different *pension funds*. As shown in Fig. 7.4, in 2023, the total size of pension funds was 51,32 USD, with a 14% decline compared to the previous year (OECD, 2023). Higher interest rates and falling equity valuations were the main reasons for investment losses in 2022.

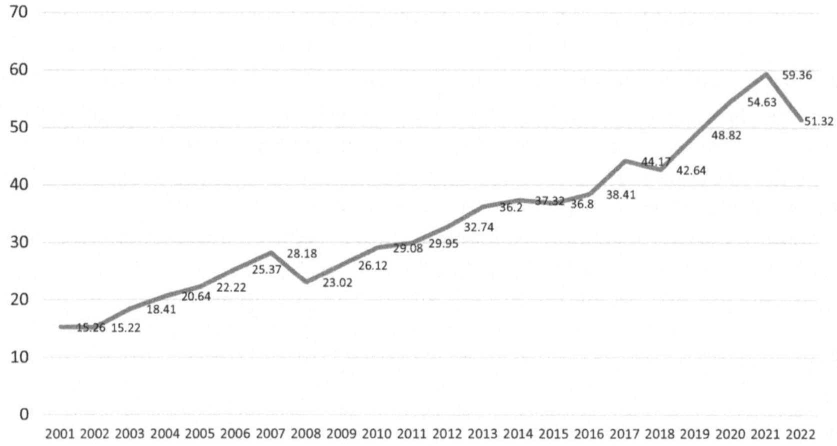

Fig. 7.4 Total assets in pension plans (trillion USD) (OECD, 2023)

Bond and equities accounted for more than 70% of the investments of pension plans in 2021, but both bond and equity prices fell in 2022 (i.e., S&P500 (19%), Nikkei 225 (9%), and DAX (12%). Figure 7.5 shows asset-backed pension systems' nominal and real investment rates of return (IRR) in 2022 (OECD, 2023).

During an increasing interest rate, pension schemes in the Netherlands and the UK experienced setbacks on their interest-rate derivatives that they had used to safeguard against the possibility of interest rates dropping. Additionally, Dutch pension funds incurred losses on their investments in real estate. As a result of these losses, coupled with those on bonds and stocks, pension schemes in the Netherlands and the UK reported the lowest nominal returns compared to all other reporting jurisdictions (−21.1% and −18.5%, respectively). On the other hand, while Türkiye has 50% nominal IRR, the real IRR is 9%, for instance. Table 7.2 also shows the geometric average annual real investment rates of selected OECD countries over the last 5, 10, 15, and 20 years, and Table 7.3 exhibits the asset allocations of the OECD countries.

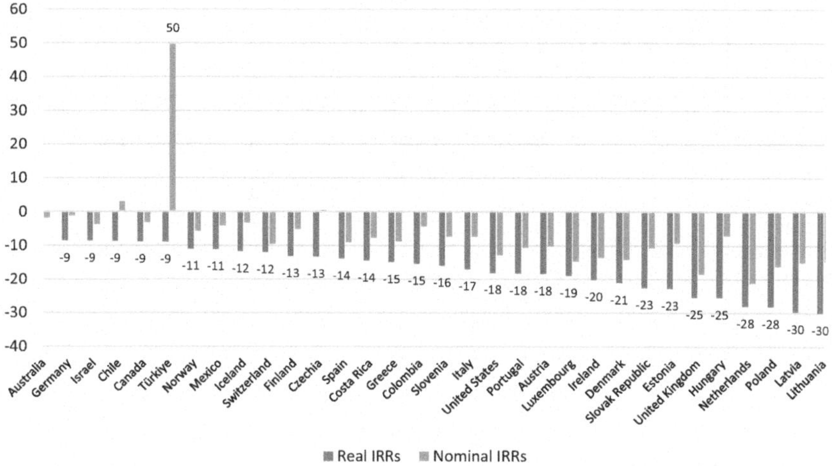

Fig. 7.5 Nominal and real investment rates of return (IRR) of asset-backed pension systems (OECD, 2023)

Model Framework

The housing industry needs a sustainable alternative financing solution. The sector is in a deadlock from both developers' and homebuyers' sides. While financing costs are too high for a feasible housing development project, access to finance is limited. On the other hand, although there is a demand to purchase houses, the affordability is too low under current high interest rates globally. The new model I proposed in this book is structured to find sustainable solutions to problems of both sides.

For a stable housing market, the International Monetary Fund (IMF) (2011) suggests enhanced risk management, funding standards and administration, proactive and careful government participation, and improved participant incentive alignment while utilizing capital market funding.

Current bank-oriented housing financing models were discussed in the previous chapters. Some important real estate capital market instruments widely used in many countries were also listed. Creating an investment and financing ecosystem among these capital market instruments can bring a new approach that homebuyers, developers, and investors can benefit from.

Table 7.2 Geometric average annual real investment rates over the last 5, 10, 15, and 20 years in % (OECD, 2023)

Selected OECD countries	*5-yr average*	*10-yr average*	*15-yr average*	*20-yr average*
Australia	3,3	5,4	2,8	4,0
Austria	−2,9	0,2	−0,3	0,8
Canada	1,7	3,9	3,6	4,1
Chile	0,1	2,0	1,4	3,1
Colombia	0,2	1,4	3,8	4,8
Costa Rica	3,8	5,1	3,7	...
Czechia	−4,7	−2,4	−1,7	−1,0
Denmark	−0,8	1,9	2,6	3,3
Estonia	−4,1	−1,0	−2,2	−1,1
Finland	1,6	3,6	...	...
Germany	−0,6	1,2	1,6	1,9
Greece	−0,7	...	...	...
Hungary	−6,3	−0,3	...	...
Iceland	3,6	4,2	1,7	3,3
Ireland	1,1	...	...	...
Israel	3,5	4,7	3,8	...
Italy	−2,5	0,2	0,3	0,9
Latvia	−6,3	−2,2	−1,8	−1,9
Lithuania	−4,6	−0,5	...	...
Luxembourg	−3,2	−0,2	−0,2	...
Mexico	0,3	0,5	1,4	...
Netherlands	−3,2	1,3	1,8	3,1
Norway	0,2	2,4	2,2	3,5
Poland	−7,2	...	...	...
Portugal	−1,8	0,8	0,0	1,6
Slovak Republic	−4,4	−1,4	−1,7	...
Slovenia	−2,6	1,2	2,0	...
Spain	−1,8	1,1	0,6	...
Switzerland	0,8	2,9	2,3	2,8
Türkiye	−3,5	−2,2	−0,3	...
United States	−1,4	1,4	−0,1	1,0

The new model is based on sharing economy principles, fundamentals of asset-backed financing, and collective investment and return mindset. Conventional banks, participating banks, and investment and development banks are also integrated into the model by redefining their role in the system.

Table 7.3 Allocation of assets earmarked for retirement in selected asset classes and investment vehicles at the end-2021 (%) (OECD, 2023)

OECD countries	*Equities*	*Bills and bonds*	*Cash and deposits*	*Collective investment schemes*	*Other*
Czechia	2,4	81,8	12,0	2,5	1,3
Costa Rica	15,2	72,7	5,9	...	6,2
Mexico	23,6	72,6	1,2	...	2,6
Portugal	15,8	71,8	3,6	...	8,8
France	18,3	63,8	7,4	...	10,5
Türkiye	17,9	62,1	8,6	...	11,4
Israel	24,1	56,7	7,0	...	12,1
Hungary	30,7	55,6	6,0	...	7,7
Luxembourg	28,2	54,4	4,2	...	13,2
Chile	43,9	54,3	1,7	...	0,1
Latvia	41,5	52,0	3,1	...	3,5
Slovak Republic	4,0	51,8	2,7	39,1	2,4
Norway	41,0	51,1	1,7	...	6,2
Slovenia	5,1	50,8	7,6	35,1	1,5
Spain	30,1	49,1	7,8	...	13,1
Ireland	24,5	45,1	2,8	...	27,6
Germany	7,6	43,5	2,7	...	46,2
Belgium	49,7	43,2	2,4	...	4,7
Italy	25,1	42,7	6,1	...	26,1
Netherlands	30,8	42,6	2,0	...	24,6
United Kingdom	26,8	40,4	1,8	...	31,0
Colombia	41,1	39,4	1,8	...	17,8
Greece	19,3	39,3	17,7	23,7	0,1
Korea	3,2	36,2	20,4	9,8	30,3
Iceland	41,9	35,8	5,4	...	16,8
Estonia	59,1	34,1	4,7	...	2,1
Switzerland	31,7	27,8	4,5	...	36,0
Austria	33,0	27,2	2,0	...	37,8
Canada	40,6	26,9	4,0	...	28,4
Japan	10,1	26,0	7,5	...	56,4
Denmark	25,8	26,0	1,5	2,5	44,2
New Zealand	45,6	24,0	4,8	21,2	4,4
Finland	45,6	19,5	4,6	...	30,3
United States	36,7	19,0	2,0	31,7	10,6
Lithuania	74,6	18,9	3,4	...	3,1
Australia	47,3	13,2	12,0	...	27,6

(continued)

Table 7.3 (continued)

OECD countries	*Equities*	*Bills and bonds*	*Cash and deposits*	*Collective investment schemes*	*Other*
Sweden	14,6	12,3	0,9	68,9	3,3
Poland	91,0	6,0	1,6	0,0	1,3

People have money in different accounts such as banks, pension funds, investment funds, stocks, bonds, and even cash or gold in the safes at their houses. Banks use this money to connect fund seekers with fund owners. From a housing financing perspective, the bank provides mortgage financing to the homebuyer by using the savings of other individuals or institutions. The money you need to finance your house may be the money of your neighbor who keeps his savings in the same bank you are asking for to finance your house. On the other hand, homebuyers keep making savings in pension funds where asset managers invest the money in different investment tools.

To design a new financing model, the first question to answer is:

Can I direct my savings in different accounts to an account or a fund to purchase my house without asking for a bank loan?
The simple answer is, "*why not?*"

The second question comes then:

How?

The answer is:

By creating a real estate investment fund designed to make you invest in it to purchase a specific unit, you would like to live in.

Then, the third question comes:

How are the real estate developers involved in this financing mechanism?

There are different options for this. First, we need to determine the developers' expectations. Do they have unsold completed units that they want to sell these units to homebuyers, or do they want to finance their newly started housing development projects through the fund? We are experiencing problems with both issues. Real estate developers need alternative, sustainable, and inexpensive financing solutions to decrease sales, and they also want homebuyers to purchase the houses they build with cheaper financing, which helps them reduce their purchasing price. The developers may be the investors of the real estate investment fund by developing new units or selling the completed units to the fund. This fund can also be designed as a platform where the parties' partnership collectively starts from the land purchase stage and contributes to the construction cost through periodic payments to the homebuyers.

The fourth question arises:

How is the sales price determined, and how are the parties protected?

Asset management companies that operate under capital market board regulations establish the real estate investment fund. Independent audit companies audit all the financial tables. On the other hand, the asset manager manages all properties subject to independent valuation reports. The audit and valuation reports protect the rights of the fund parties and avoid any speculation over the prices, which eventually regulates the market and brings stability.

Fifth question:

What is the role of the pension plans in this new model?

Pension plans can play an essential role in economic growth and price stability. As I have been proposing and underlying in many of my previous studies published since 2017, OECD (2023) also states that directing the savings in pension funds to invest in infrastructure projects, hospitals, schools, renewable energy facilities, and real estate, including housing projects can provide good returns, mitigate risks, create jobs, and deliver tangible assets that fuel long-term economic growth. Thus, considering the size of pension funds and the total outstanding mortgage loans, creating an investment and financing ecosystem that enables homebuyers to direct their savings in their pension accounts to purchase their houses can provide a considerable amount of financing to replace the debt financing both for financing the construction activities and the purchase of the house.

The next question is:

How is diminishing musharakah (partnership) integrated into the new model?

The model is structured on sharing economy and partnership principles where the interest rates are not the main determinants of the prices. The ownership rate of the property that the homebuyers partially own at the beginning of the process by paying a down payment, and the share gradually increases until the full payment is made to the fund. This approach matches the method of DM in Islamic home financing, with the main difference being that the model is implemented under a real estate investment fund umbrella rather than a bank structure.

Figure 7.6 shows the outline of the model. The steps of this new model are described below:

- An asset/portfolio management company establishes a housing fund as a real estate investment fund.
- Real estate developers and investors sell their housing units to this housing fund.
- Homebuyers directly or indirectly (through their pension accounts) invest in the housing fund and become shareholders of the fund for the specific housing unit they are willing to buy.

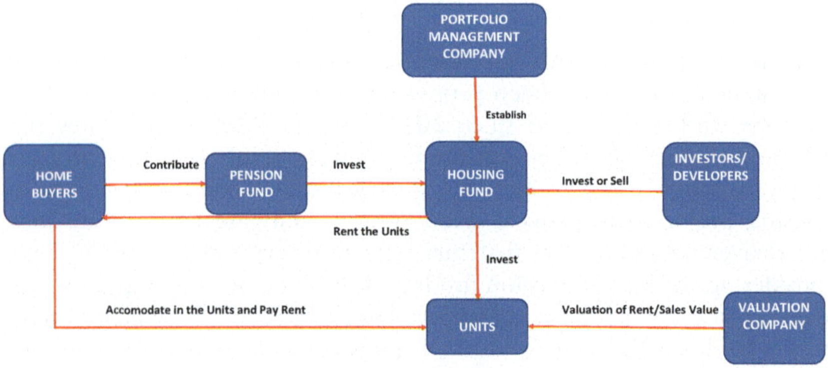

Fig. 7.6 The model framework (By Author)

- The housing fund rents the unit to the homebuyer and starts getting rental income from the homebuyers.
- Diminishing musharakah is integrated into the model from a partnership perspective. The homebuyers pay the rent in the proportion of their shares in the house. For instance, if the initial investment (we can consider it as the down payment of the house) is 20%, then the homebuyer pays only 80% of the rent as she owns the 20% of the house through the fund share she has. Homebuyers keep investing in the fund and increasing their shares (house ownership rate). The more the homebuyers increase their shares in the fund, the less rent they pay.
- Independent valuation companies determine the sales and rent prices to avoid price bubbles and speculation.
- The capital market board regulates the whole process, and the funds submit periodical independent audit reports.

As shown in Fig. 7.6, the real estate investment funds are the model's core, but how will other real estate capital market instruments mentioned (REITs, real estate certificates, etc.) be involved in the model?

When discussing an ecosystem, we need to ensure that the real estate capital market instruments are interconnected to produce sustainable expected benefits for all stakeholders so we can design alternative models to the main framework introduced above.

Alternative 1: Financing Through the Integration of REITs and REIFs

A real estate investment trust may develop a housing project. Potential homebuyers can directly invest in the housing fund or indirectly by way of contributions they made to their pension accounts. In the second option, the pension funds invest in the housing fund. The money accumulated in the housing fund can be invested in REITs and purchase units from the projects that the REIT developed. The housing fund owns the properties and rents them to potential homebuyers. The rent price the homebuyers need to pay is calculated based on the proportion of the total payment they made over the total sales price of the house. Diminishing partnership is again integrated into the system here. The homebuyers keep investing/contributing to the housing fund. The more they increase their shares, the

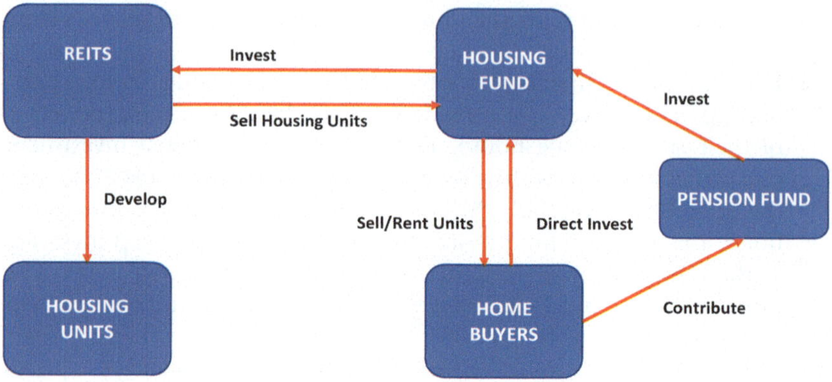

Fig. 7.7 Alternative-1: financing through the integration of REITs and REIFs (By Author)

less rent they pay. The fund will hold the title deed until the homebuyers make the last payment.

Alternatively, depending on the market interest rates and financing costs, if the homebuyers want to get their title deeds, they can use a mortgage loan and exit the fund earlier. Figure 7.7 exhibits the fund transfer and the investment scheme of the model.

Alternative-2: Financing Through the Integration of REITs, REIFs, and Real Estate Certificates (by Author)

Another model can be structured based on integrating the REITs, real estate certificates, and the housing fund (REIF). A REIT or a real estate development company may issue real estate certificates to finance their development projects. Homebuyers may directly purchase these shares and become homeowners gradually. Another option can be implemented by directing the savings of homebuyers accumulated in their pension accounts to a housing fund, which will be an investor in the real estate certificates issued by REITs. Alternatively, the homebuyers may directly become investors in the housing fund. By accumulating the real estate certificates, the homebuyers purchase their house and opt out of the system by getting their title deeds (Fig. 7.8).

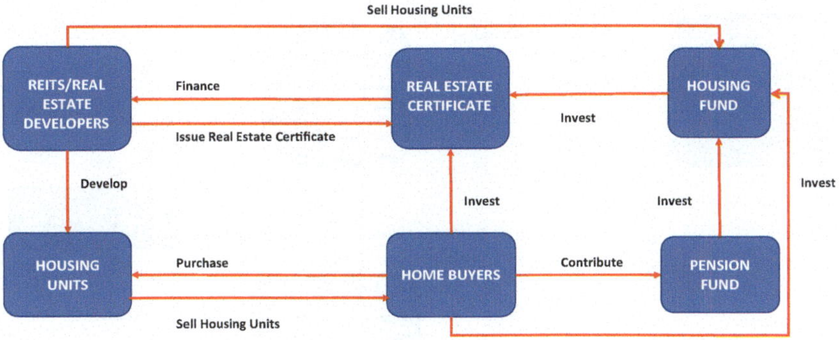

Fig. 7.8 Alternative-2: financing through the integration of REITs, REIFs, and real estate certificates (By Author)

Alternative 3—Developing Directly Through Real Estate Investment Fund (Housing Fund)

Real estate investment funds are investment tools that invest in completed projects or lands. REIFs do not carry the risks of the construction. These risks may include financial risks, completion risks, safety risks during construction, regulation risks, etc. Suppose a new housing fund type is structured, the land is purchased, and the project is developed. The houses are constructed with direct or indirect contributions (through pension funds). In that case, the homebuyers may collectively purchase their houses cheaper under the Capital Market Board's regulations. The housing fund may also rent the units to potential homebuyers in this model (Fig. 7.9).

Alternative 4—Integration of Timeshares to REIF Model

Timeshares are also important investment tools for co-ownership a tourism facility, such as a resort, hotel, condominium, or apartment. Timeshares, also known as vacation ownership, provides the opportunity to share the ownership of the properties and the right to accommodations during vacations in a predetermined week.

Integrating the timeshare concept with the real estate investment fund mechanism is possible. Instead of purchasing the 1/50th of the unit (two

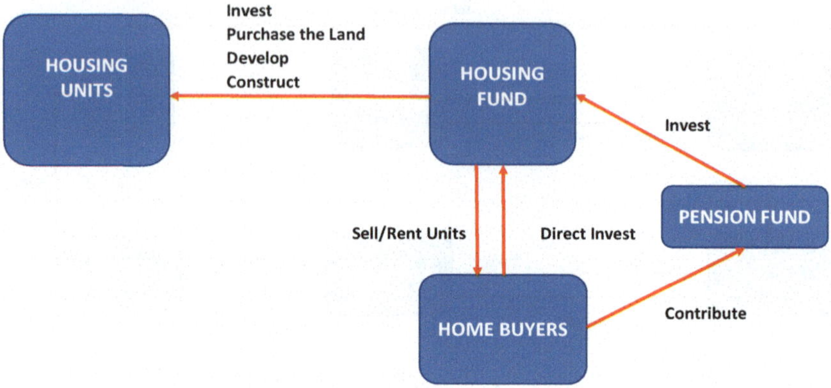

Fig. 7.9 Alternative-3: developing directly through real estate investment fund (housing fund) (By Author)

weeks left for maintenance and repair), the potential timeshare investors invest in a real estate investment fund. The REIF either purchases a completed property or builds it from scratch. The property is rented to a professional hospitality management company. The fund's shareholders make a return on their investment, and they still have the right to use the property in a preset week of the year. The model is schematized in Fig. 7.10.

Tokenization of the Model

Tokenization involves creating a digital representation of an asset within a blockchain. This can be applied to various investments such as bonds, stocks, physical items like art and real estate, and intangible assets like identity and data. To tokenize, the property's value is divided into fractions, and the process is automated using smart contracts. The property's value is then broken down into smaller units, allowing investors to purchase these fractions through tokens, individually or collectively. Enhanced liquidity, fractional ownership, transparency, flexibility, reduced settlement time, and reinforced security brought by blockchain technology can be implemented into the real estate industry.

There are five stages of tokenization. The first stage is the deal structuring phase, in which the terms and conditions of the tokenized securities

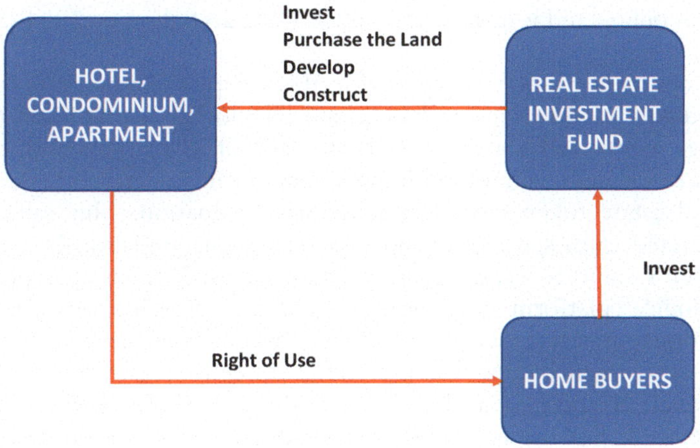

Fig. 7.10 Integration of timeshares to REIF model (By Author)

are set. In the digitization stage, the information is uploaded from paper or document to the blockchain, coded in smart contracts, and security tokens are issued. In the third stage, the primary distribution phase, tokens are distributed to investors in exchange for investment capital, and the collected information from investors is recorded on the digital ROM. In the post-tokenization management phase, which continues throughout the token's life until maturity or redemption, dividend distribution, shareholder voting, and many other management processes are automated by smart contracts coded on the token. Finally, the value of tokenization in enhancing liquidity is realized, and tokens are traded among investors (Pang et al., 2024).

The main advantage of tokenizing real estate is the opportunity to open the real estate market to smaller investors. The real estate properties become more liquid, and the investors can make investments or transfer their shares to each other through the tokens created (Baum, 2020).

Lack of regulation is one of the main obstacles that needs to be resolved for the tokenization process. Another barrier is a lack of knowledge of blockchain technology, but the more people have information about the blockchain, the faster real estate tokenization will be widespread. As of 2022, the size of the tokenized real estate market is

USD 3.8 billion and is projected to reach USD 26 billion by 2034 (Singh, 2024).

The alternative models suggested in this Chapter can be implemented in the digital world by using blockchain technology. In addition to the obstacles mentioned above, such as the lack of regulations and knowledge of blockchain technology, it is also important to determine the value of a real estate token based on actual asset valuation. This value shall be protected from speculative movements and manipulation by pegging the token's value to capital market board-licensed valuation reports. A technological platform that monitors millions of valuations and sales transactions can decrease the volatility of the values of the tokens.

No matter which model is preferred, either the main framework or alternatives, if there is a shared ownership, then this ownership can be tokenized. For instance, a real estate developer may issue tokenized real estate certificates, the potential homebuyers may directly or indirectly (through their pension accounts) invest in the housing fund, and the housing fund may invest in these tokens and exchange them with the housing units when the construction is completed. In the model proposed, the homebuyer does not directly buy or sell tokens, but portfolio management companies make all the transactions under the regulations of the capital market board to avoid any speculations or manipulations over the values of the tokens. Figure 7.11 shows the tokenization framework.

Implementing such innovative models requires strong regulation backed by capital market boards. The funds shall be established and

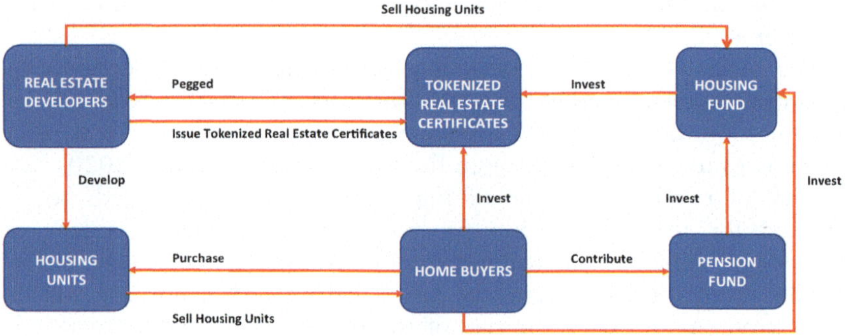

Fig. 7.11 Tokenization framework (By Author)

managed by licensed portfolio management companies. Professional valuation firms shall make regular valuations. The independent audits shall be made regularly. The tokenization process also needs stable regulations issued and monitored by banking regulatory authorities.

Bringing the homeowners and home builders together in one ecosystem under a fund's umbrella is difficult and requires straightforward marketing language. Fund mechanisms typically target qualified investors, but the models introduced aim for any individual to be a fund investor (shareholder) regardless of the adequacy of his financial knowledge. In that context, describing the benefits of the model is critical. In addition, if developing the housing project directly under the fund umbrella (alternative 3) is implemented, the project management and monitoring services shall be required as the fund will bear the construction risks.

The models I developed do not offer a *magical touch* to resolve the housing industry's affordability and debt-oriented problems with a *silver bullet* but encourage policymakers to *think out of the box*.

If the model and its derivatives are implemented, as suggested in this Chapter, many loan-free alternatives will be developed soon. The housing market will find its equilibrium and become more stable in the long run. The banks will reposition themselves in the new system. They will probably become either shareholders of the fund or interim loan providers for those who would like to use the traditional mortgage system, with the condition that the interest rates become reasonable.

References

Baum, A. (2020). *Tokenisation—The future of real estate investment? The future of real estate initiative*. Saïd Business School, University of Oxford. https://www.sbs.ox.ac.uk/sites/default/files/2020-01/tokenisation.pdf. Last Accessed on July 23, 2024.

Brueggeman, W., & Fisher, J. (2011). *Real estate finance & investments*. The McGraw-Hill/Irwin Series in Finance, Insurance, and Real Estate, McGraw-Hill Education.

Communique on Real Estate Certificates SPK. (2017). *Real estate certificates*. https://cmb.gov.tr/data/628162651b41c617eced0fc9/905b0ff52b8eac0e91551c1646bce656.pdf. Last Accessed on July 23, 2024.

FDIC. (2024). *Bank failures 2023 in brief*. https://www.fdic.gov/resources/resolutions/bank-failures/in-brief/bfb2023.html. Last Accessed on July 23, 2024.

Financialislam.com. (2024). *Diminishing Musharakah*. https://www.financialislam.com/diminishing-musharakah1.html. Last Accessed on July 22, 2024.

Friedberg B.A. (2024). *Best real estate crowdfunding platforms for July 2024*. https://www.investopedia.com/best-real-estate-crowdfunding-sites-5070790. Last Accessed on July 23, 2024.

Hayes, A. (2023). *REIT vs. real estate fund: What's the difference?* https://www.investopedia.com/ask/answers/012015/what-difference-between-reit-and-real-estate-fund.asp. Last Accessed on July 23, 2024.

IMF. (2011). Housing finance and financial stability-back to basics? In *Global financial stability report, durable financial stability: Getting there from here*. https://www.elibrary.imf.org/display/book/9781616350604/ch003.xml. https://doi.org/10.5089/9781616350604.082. Last Accessed on July 23, 2024.

Marcato, G., & Brounen, D. (2015). *The liquidity of international real estate securities* (EPRA Research, pp. 1–27).

McGibany, J. M., & Nourzad, F. (2004). Do lower mortgage rates mean higher housing prices? *Applied Economics, 36*(4), 305–313. https://doi.org/10.1080/0003684041000l674231

Montgomery, N., Squires, G., & Syed, I. (2018). Disruptive potential of real estate crowdfunding in the real estate project finance industry: A literature review. *Property Management, 36*(5), 597–619. https://doi.org/10.1108/PM-04-2018-0032

OECD. (2022). *Strengthening asset-backed pension systems in a Post-COVID world*. OECD Publishing.https://doi.org/10.1787/288cb3cf-en

OECD. (2023). *Pensions at a glance 2023: OECD and G20 indicators*. OECD Publishing.https://doi.org/10.1787/678055dd-en

Pang, P., Tang, H. F., Lam, J., Chan, S., Hobler, N., Kan, K.K.K., Jeong, H., Lau, R. (2024). Real Estate Tokenization. Available at https://assets.kpmg.com/content/dam/kpmg/cn/pdf/en/2020/04/real-estatetokenization.pdf, Last Accessed on July 21, 2024.

Property Funds Research. (2023). *Global investment managers 2023*. https://propertyfundsresearch.com/wp-content/uploads/2023/10/2023_PFR_IREI-REPORT-Euros.pdf. Last Accessed on July 23, 2024.

Rama, B., & Andoni, D. (2017). Affordable Housing and Housing Affordability in Europe. *Connection—The Architectural and Design Journal of the Young Architects Forum*, 1–6.

Reichert, A. K. (1990). The impact of interest rates, income, and employment upon regional housing prices. *Journal of Real Estate Finance and Economics, 3*, 373–391.

Reit.com. (2024). *REITs by the numbers*. https://www.reit.com/data-research/data/reits-numbers. Last Accessed on July 23, 2024.

Singh, B. (2024). *Real estate tokenization market: An in-depth analysis*. https://www.linkedin.com/pulse/real-estate-tokenization-market-in-depth-analysis-bobby-singh-rdr7f/. Last Accessed on July 22, 2024.

Statista.com. (2024a). *Value of listed real estate market worldwide as of December 2023, by region*. https://www.statista.com/statistics/1189675/listed-real-estate-market-size-global/. Last Accessed on July 23, 2024.

Statista.com. (2024b). *Assets under management of leading real estate investment managers in 2022*. https://www.statista.com/statistics/1193064/leading-real-estate-investment-managers-ranked-assets-under-management-worldwide/. Last Accessed on July 23, 2024.

Steinberg. S. (2024). *Real estate crowdfunding: What it is and how it works*. https://www.rocketmortgage.com/learn/real-estate-crowdfunding. Last Accessed on July 23, 2024.

Sümer, L. (2017). *Developing a real estate-pension fund investment ecosystem: Turkey real estate fund*. Ph.D. Thesis, Boğaziçi University, Istanbul.

Sümer, L. (2022). An alternative interest-free home financing model. *International Journal of Housing Markets and Analysis, 16*(2), 408–425.

Sümer, L., & Ozorhon, B. (2016). *A comparative return analysis of real estate investment trust (REIT) index and major indexes in Istanbul stock exchange*. 12th International Congress on Advances in Civil Engineering, 2008, Bogaziçi University.

Thom, D. R. (1983). House prices, inflation and the mortgage market. *The Economic and Social Review, 15*, 57–68.

Tolu, A. (2024). *GYO'ların kurumlar vergisi istisnası kaldırılabilir mi?* https://www.ekonomim.com/kose-yazisi/gyolarin-kurumlar-vergisi-istisnasi-kaldirilabilir-mi/746295#google_vignette. Last Accessed on July 23, 2024.

Tracey, M. D. (2023). *How 3 recent bank failures could impact housing market*. https://www.nar.realtor/magazine/real-estate-news/how-3-recent-bank-failures-could-impact-housing-market. Last Accessed on July 23, 2024.

Van der Drift, R., de Haan, J., & Boelhouwer, P. (2023). Mortgage credit and house prices: The housing market equilibrium revisited. *Economic Modelling, 120*, Article 106136. https://doi.org/10.1016/j.econmod.2022.106136

CHAPTER 8

What the Future Holds: The Roadmap for a Sustainable Housing Industry

A house is a need for everyone, regardless of their income level or the part of the world they live in. Irrespective of their education level, occupation, economic development, or cultural differences, everybody needs shelter to protect themselves from external conditions, create a peaceful environment, collect memories, socialize, actualize their self-esteem, and more.

In the twenty-first century, housing, one of the basic needs of humans, still seems to be a serious problem for many countries in the world, unfortunately. While around 1.6 billion people live in insufficient housing conditions, 150 million people are homeless worldwide (Sümer, 2023). Local or international conflicts that force people to leave their hometowns and migrate, natural disasters such as earthquakes, floods, or hurricanes that destroy homes and leave families homeless, the inability of people to afford a house due to low income, and the government policies lacking the regulating the housing markets in terms of balance in supply and demand and bad economic conditions of countries may be the reasons for homelessness (Filipenco, 2023).

The global economy is struggling with many challenges that are affecting the housing markets widely. The US and Europe have been experiencing a high inflation period after the COVID-19 pandemic. Challenges like income inequality, difficulties accessing financing, and rising

L. Sümer, *The Global Housing Crisis*,
https://doi.org/10.1007/978-3-031-72604-0_8

housing prices but relatively low wage increases affect housing affordability. In contrast, where uncompleted constructions created ghost cities with more than 50 million vacant units, China is experiencing deflation, and housing prices are decreasing (US-China Today, 2023). In Africa and Latin America, houses built without proper permits or meeting regulatory standards and low-quality housing create urbanization problems. Infrastructure problems caused by rapid urbanization due to mass migration to urban areas, especially in African or South American countries, are another problem, along with inadequate housing supply. In addition, Australia is also suffering high prices due to housing shortages.

The fact that several markets experienced similar housing problems in the past makes us question the adequacy and correctness of the current housing systems and the policies implemented. As Al Rifai (2015) defines the global financial system as structured on a boom-and-bust cycle, the housing industry, whose financing models are highly dependent on the banking sector, is also built on a boom-and-bust vicious circle. Penrose Stairs would be the best description of the global housing market situation. The crises we have been experiencing over the past decade reveal that increasing evictions, overcrowding, unaffordability, inadequate housing conditions, rise in homelessness, and displacement have become the new normal of our lives (Fields & Hodkinson, 2018).

Housing bubbles and crises have social, economic, environmental, and psychological impacts on people's lives and communities. The financial or economic crises are sometimes the outcome of such cycles or, in some cases, the initiator of housing crises. If not avoided or at least effectively handled, the effects of housing bubbles might still be felt years or even decades after the first outburst.

These impacts may be felt both on micro and macro levels. On an individual level, while many homeowners feel like increasing their wealth at the peak of a housing bubble and making them consume more, the bubble burst may erase the whole gain. The value of the property may even become less than the outstanding loan amount of the homebuyer, as experienced in the 2008 mortgage crisis, which led many families to defaults and psychological problems, including depression, anxiety, and physical sickness, and even took them to suicide.

From a macro perspective, the mortgage default may result in significant financial damage to lending institutions, and banks may go bankrupt due to liquidity problems. As construction and real estate industries are important sources of employment in an economy, the crises in these sectors may increase the country's unemployment rates, leading to an economic recession. The decline in consumer spending during such crisis periods may cool down the economy, contributing to the downturn, prolonging it, or creating a stagnation period as experienced in Japan's lost decade in the 1990s asset bubble. After the bubble burst, the ongoing housing projects may remain uncompleted due to the lack of financing. This issue may create environmental problems, such as the ghost cities of Spain in the 2010s or China in the 2020s. Security problems may arise in neighborhoods close to these ghost towns because the abandoned houses provide cover and unoccupied spaces. Removing such houses decreases the crime rates (Porter et al., 2019).

Roadmap

Life is structured on a balance. Adabre et al. (2021), based on their scientometric analysis of the housing affordability literature, underline the most significant factor in overcoming the housing affordability problem is reducing poverty and decreasing income inequality globally. Circular economy, modular housing, prefabricated housing, cooperative housing, collective self-build housing, and the application of artificial intelligence are important points for ensuring housing affordability globally.

Suppose we create a balance among individuals, societies, and even cities. In that case, we can discuss more livable cities for most of the population where the housing prices are more stable and affordable.

Knowing the root cause of a problem is the starting point to resolve it. The first step is learning from past mistakes. The second one is initiating a reverse migration from metropolitan cities to other cities that we can promote or to smaller towns or even ecovillages that we can build. Next, we can find solutions to reduce the cost of development. Finally, we can shift traditional bank loan-oriented financing models to alternative sustainable collective approaches and benefit from digital technologies.

Learning from Past Mistakes

Buying a house may be the most expensive investment for people in their lifetime. Without making an accurate financial analysis considering current income levels, future projections, and economic conditions, this investment may turn into a disaster that destroys people's lives. Paying high financing costs or being unable to pay the monthly installments may turn the housing investment into a total loss and decline in wealth. Financial literacy is essential when making important investment decisions in that context. Owning a house is a dream for everyone, but renting a house is sometimes more rational than buying it under bad economic circumstances.

On the other hand, financial institutions shall have proper risk identification and management practices when granting loans to customers. Past crises revealed how bad background checks and improper documentation may lead to distress in mortgage loans. Thus, loan approval and monitoring processes are critical for banks. Market conditions may change occasionally, so banks should follow economic developments to set their loan strategies. Adjusting the interest rates by following central banks' decisions is essential, yet it is not the only criterion for a sustainable and stable housing market. Indeed, the housing industry is too large to be financed solely or mainly by bank loans, which are highly dependent on interest rate policies. Hence, alternative financing models are needed to be developed.

Designing Sustainable Cities and Ecovillages

The world's population is rapidly increasing, and resources are quickly consumed. In 2023, the rate of urbanization worldwide reached 57%. 4,52 billion people are living in cities. That was only 1 billion in 1960 and 2 billion in 1985. Around 25% of people living in urban areas live in slums. (Ritchie et al., 2024). North America (83%), Latin America and the Caribbean (82%), and Europe (75%) are the regions with the highest level of urbanization. On the other hand, in Africa, less than half of the population in Asia is in cities, and 53% of the people live in cities. By 2050, around 70% of the global population (7 billion people) is projected to live in cities (Statista, 2024). Adequate housing, infrastructure, connectivity, green spaces, public transport, and community facilities are essential to the inhabitants' good quality of life.

People prefer to live in cities as their level of income increases. Higher access to electricity, improved sanitary and drinking water, access to clean fuel, and lower child malnutrition are important factors for people preferring to live in urban areas. On the other hand, cities are more exposed to organized crimes, terrorism, natural disasters, ethnic conflicts, mass events, and violence of all types (Li et al., 2012). Inadequate infrastructure, lack of green areas, climate change, expensive cost of living, air pollution, traffic congestion, and high population density are other significant problems in cities.

The cities shall be planned based on the balance between the planned population and the resources. This balance may avoid mass migration and speculative property bubbles. A balance provided among cities, making different cities centers of attraction by investing in them and creating equal life standards, may also help avoid property bubbles as the cluttering of a few cities may be prevented. A reverse migration from urban areas to rural settlements shall be initiated and incentivized. Indeed, the COVID-19 pandemic was the turning point and could trigger this mindset shift. During and after COVID-19, people tend to live in larger houses with balconies and move outside city centers, suburbs, or smaller cities due to the hybrid working model. Shopping behaviors also changed as e-commerce speeded up during lockdown days.

Remote working changes the mindset of office development as well. Employees do not need to go to offices five days a week. The office spaces are decentralized, so we don't need big headquarters that occupy thousands of square meters of leasable areas. If we can create a new settlement idea that enables people to have the chance to live, work, and entertain in smaller communities, more livable towns can be constructed. This new development concept may soften the demand for expensive urban property markets. Hence, a market equilibrium is provided, and excess, sudden, and speculative increases in housing prices may be prevented or at least diminished. Vacant offices or shopping malls where visitors decreased may also be converted into residential units, green areas, schools, or community centers. Regenerating and renewing existing urban spaces, strengthening the historical buildings, and making them more livable, sustainable, and community-friendly would also help the housing market find its balance.

Another focus shall be on designing ecovillages structured on circular economy principles. In ecovillages, people can find the comfort of cities on a smaller scale and enjoy village life by replacing the consumption approach with a production-oriented perspective. An ecovillage is a community in an urban area intentionally planned by local residents to create sustainable social, cultural, ecological, and economic environments to rejuvenate natural and social surroundings (Ecovillage.org, 2024). Although it is emphasized that ecovillages are not islands for the rich and middle-income groups, it may be considered a new way of creating communities that share common values, vision, culture, and interests. Designing ecovillages and promoting people to live by integrating the technological benefits with a circular economy approach may help regulate the housing market.

Reducing the Cost of Housing Development

The housing prices consist of two primary costs: land and construction costs. The governments may provide land subsidies to decrease land costs. Regulating the construction market by emphasizing the ESG (environment, social, and governance) principles, supporting the use of renewable energy, designing energy-efficient greenhouses, promoting passive houses, rainwater harvesting, green roofs, and the use of sustainable construction materials would help to increase the quality standard of dwellings. Implementing modern construction technologies such as building information modeling (BIM), prefabricated units, and 3D printing can reduce construction costs, improve building efficiency, and shorten the duration of housing development. The more affordable housing units are produced, the more people become homeowners.

Financing Through Savings and Partnerships

Can we buy a house without getting a mortgage loan? Yes. The first step is changing the mindset of policymakers from banking-dependent financing models to collective financing approaches. People have savings in banks either in deposit accounts or interest-free accounts. They also accumulate money in pension funds or invest in stocks, gold, and other investment funds. Insurance companies collect cash from policyholders to insure their houses, cars, health, and other goods and services. The collected money also accounts for a large amount of money that can be used for the benefit of people.

A new housing financing model can be structured based on people's money for their needs. Creating an investment and financing ecosystem that both the developers and the homebuyers meet in a capital market board-regulated platform (this could be a real estate investment fund, a crowdfunding mechanism, venture capital investment fund, real estate investment trust, real estate certificate, land certificate, or a combination of these real estate capital market instruments) can resolve the funding of the home builders to finance the construction cost. By directing people's savings to this real estate investment ecosystem, homebuyers can start paying first for the land of their houses and then the construction cost. This approach may reduce the sales prices of the units. Using the savings as a down payment and enabling the fund participants to make monthly payments according to their income levels may also increase homebuyers' affordability.

The diminishing partnership, a co-ownership model, can also be integrated into the system from a sharing economy perspective. Until the unit's total price is paid, the fund and the homebuyer become shareholders of the unit. The fund can also rent the unit to the homebuyer and get the rent of its share (suppose that the monthly rent is USD 2,000, and the fund owns 70% share of the house, so the homebuyer pays only USD 1,400 monthly rent). In further stages, after the new model is implemented, the banks can also be involved in interim or bridge financing for those who would like to get their title deeds earlier. Indeed, even though the house's total price is paid, the homebuyers may prefer to keep renting the unit from the fund and become a fund investor by comparing the potential return and the rents to be paid. To run such a model successfully, proper valuation, professional asset management companies, and strong regulations monitored by the capital market board are essential.

Digitally Securitization (Tokenization) of Housing Industry

Technological advancement makes it a must to digitalize the housing sector. Virtual property tours, Artificial Intelligence (AI) in property investments, and blockchain-based property registries are being used in the housing industry and will be used widely in the future. Collecting big data, converting them into smart data, and using AI to predict future market trends and behaviors may also help to take the required steps when the risks are determined.

On the other hand, securitization of the housing industry is also an alternative for investors who do not want to deal with the risk of single housing investments separately but rather invest in real estate capital investment tools such as real estate investment funds, real estate investment trusts, and real estate certificates. Digitalizing such tools through *tokenization* would make it easier for homebuyers to access such investment tools through digital platforms. If people could purchase their houses with small savings through tokens, becoming homeowners would be much faster. There is a need for strong regulation to overcome any speculation, as we know that, with their current situation, cryptocurrencies are very volatile and risky to invest in, as they are not backed by government regulations yet.

Policy Recommendations

The ongoing individualization of responsibility in all social life has conceptual and political implications. It is becoming increasingly difficult to assume that the private sphere of a home provides individuals with freedom and security from societal forces, pressures, and compulsions. We may be in a transitional phase where a home's meaning and psycho-social foundation are transforming. Understanding these processes is not just an epistemological pursuit but also a political one, as comprehending the psycho-social implications of the housing crisis allows us to recognize its connection to the societal processes of individualization and the potential to create pathways for the emergence of a transitional community (Wolf, 2022).

A house is not just a brick and mortar but a place where its inhabitants feel peace and call it a "home." The booms and busts, bubbles, crises, and their long-term consequences taught us that the housing industry needs to be handled carefully by overlooking it from macro perspectives as it touches many social, economic, cultural, environmental, historical, and political factors. Policymakers should learn from past mistakes and not repeat them. A wrong decision will not only affect the country itself but may also result in a domino effect, as we experienced in the 2008 subprime mortgage crisis, which became the most severe global financial crisis in history. The impacts of such crises may be too heavy to recover for many years, and such a prolonged crisis may cause another local or global crisis.

While discussing housing policies, we need to understand that there is no single solution to the increasing threat of housing affordability. The history of housing development, political climate, and socioeconomic conditions are important city-tailored determinants. On the other hand, community outreach, commitment, and flexibility are the common strategies to be implemented for each city. Moreover, implementing a housing policy may not have an immediate outcome, so we must go step by step and reach milestones first. Setting the land use regulations that control the type of housing to be built based on the homebuyers' preferences and demographic structures is also a significant determinant of the housing policies. Cooperation of the state and the community and strong will and dedication are also critical for sustainable solutions (Wood et al., 2020). Rental housing policies are also crucial for a regulated housing market. A decentralized and more private sector involvement in rental housing policy, getting full support from inside of the government bodies and outside such as the builders, housing associations, non-governmental organizations, and special commissions, and finding the most appropriate language and campaign to explain the benefits of the policies are significant success factors of the policies (Von Hoffman, 2012). Developing rental houses in neighborhoods with a high concentration of job opportunities may also help tackle the increasing distance of commutes Blumenberg & Siddiq, 2023).

Policies addressing affordability problems encompass rent control, public or social housing, housing vouchers, low-income tax credits, inclusionary zoning, mortgage subsidies, and government equity loans. Their design, local market conditions, and broader economic adjustments influence these measures' impact and social welfare consequences. Even though numerous housing policies are ineffective, costly, or result in unwanted distributional consequences, policymakers often favor them because the households they target may not fully comprehend the adverse indirect effects. This is partly because the primary recipients are frequently influential property owners who are not explicitly aimed at but profit through increases in property values and rents. It is a significant challenge for policymakers to create policies that address the fundamental issues behind the housing affordability crisis and assist those in need (Hilber & Schöni, 2022).

I recommend 20 policies and strategies to overcome the ongoing affordability problems and design a new sustainable housing system.

(1)Developing policies that aim to resolve the problems of today, and avoid the potential risks of tomorrow, (2) developing and implementing standard borrowing mechanisms with a proper customer investigation, strong credit monitoring, (3) adjusting (making it stricter or softening) the regulations by following the market conditions and trends carefully, (4) understanding the psychology and the expectation of the society, (5) decreasing the link between the home financing and banking industry (untying the housing financing with interest rates), (6) implementing alternative financing solution by promoting co-ownership and collective financing models, valuing sharing economy and using the money of people for helping them purchase their houses, (7) providing land subsidies, tax incentives and low-interest rate financing to enhance affordability, (8) directly intervening in developing affordable housing for low-income groups, (9) promoting the developers to build houses for renting instead of selling, (10) emphasizing the importance of financial literacy for making the rent or buy decision, (11) as the world is very interconnected to each other and the economy is globalized, developing proactive responses to a potential nearing crisis, (12) by designing sustainable smaller cities and ecovillages initiating a reverse migration from metropolitan cities to smaller ones, (13) encouraging homeowners to rent their vacant houses by providing incentives, (14) analyzing the supply and demand balance by following the demographic changes such as the population, gender, age group distributions, marriages, divorces, (15) promoting the fractionally securitization of the real estate and enabling homebuyers to purchase houses by using land or housing tokens, (16) emphasizing the circular economy, renewable energy, ESG and sustainability in housing development phases, (17) replacing public–private-partnership (PPP) models with public–private-people-partnership (4P) model by focusing on the needs and the contribution of people, (18) depending on the geography, using alternative, faster and reliable construction techniques such as modular construction, (19) using the strengthening, renovation and rehabilitation options for existing buildings instead of demolishing and rebuilding, if possible, and (20) avoiding the housing boom-and-bust cycle by implementing a stable investment and financing ecosystem structured on the real estate capital market instruments supported by savings accumulated in pension or other saving accounts are the main policies that the policymakers shall focus on developing a more sustainable housing market.

Last Words

As an extension of my first book, in which I outlined the new and sustainable economic and financial system to replace the current flawed capitalism, which frequently creates crises, this book suggests a paradigm change and a mindset shift from the current banking-dependent system to a new sustainable housing financing model. This model is structured to create an investment and financing ecosystem where people's savings are the primary source of financing.

The book covered many aspects of the housing industry, including the psychology of homeownership, dynamics of the industry, causes and consequences of past housing crises as well as lessons learned from past mistakes, the outlook of the housing sector based on the market data, statistics and forecasts, the past and ongoing housing policies, funding mechanisms and schemes, the best practices, their pros and cons, and proposed a sustainable home financing models with different alternatives.

I hope the policymakers implement these ideas and the models proposed in this book and trigger better and more sustainable housing policies.

References

Adabre, M. A., Chan, A. P. C., & Darko, A. A. (2021). Scientometric analysis of the housing affordability literature. *Journal of Housing and the Built Environment, 36*, 1501–1533. https://doi.org/10.1007/s10901-021-09825-0

Al Rifai, T. (2015). *Islamic finance and the new financial system: An ethical approach to preventing future financial crises*. Wiley. ISBN: 978-1-118-99063-6

Blumenberg, E., & Siddiq, F. (2023). Commute distance and jobs-housing fit. *Transportation, 50*, 869–891. https://doi.org/10.1007/s11116-022-10264-1

Ecovillage.org. (2024). *Global ecovillage network*. https://ecovillage.org/. Last Accessed on July 23, 2024.

Fields, D. J., & Hodkinson, S. N. (2018). Housing policy in crisis: An international perspective. *Housing Policy Debate, 28*(1), 1–5. https://doi.org/10.1080/10511482.2018.1395988

Filipenco, D. (2023). *Homelessness statistics in the world: Causes and facts*. https://www.developmentaid.org/news-stream/post/157797/homelessness-statistics-in-the-world. Last Accessed on July 21, 2024.

Hilber, C. A. L., & Schöni, O. (2022). *Housing policy and affordable housing*. https://cep.lse.ac.uk/pubs/download/occasional/op056.pdf. Last Accessed on July 23, 2024.

Li, J., Liu, Q., & Sang, Y. (2012). Several issues about urbanization and urban safety. *Procedia Engineering, 43*, 615–621.

Porter, L. C., De Biasi, A., Mitchell, S., Curtis, A., & Jefferis, E. (2019). Understanding the criminogenic properties of vacant housing: A mixed methods approach. *Journal of Research in Crime and Delinquency, 56*(3), 378–411. https://doi.org/10.1177/0022427818807965

Ritchie, H., Samborska, V., Roser, M. (2024). Urbanization. Available at https://ourworldindata.org/urbanization. Last Accessed on July 21, 2024.

Statista.com. (2024). *Share of urban population worldwide in 2023, by continent*. https://www.statista.com/statistics/270860/urbanization-by-continent/. Last Accessed on July 23, 2024.

Sümer, L. (2023). *The world economy and financial system: a paradigm change offering a sustainable approach*. Palgrave Macmillan.https://doi.org/10.1007/978-3-031-27530-2

US-China Toda. (2023). *Cities lost in Limbo: Are China's ghost cities here to stay?* https://uschinatoday.org/features/2022/01/11/cities-lost-in-limbo-are-chinas-ghost-cities-here-to-stay/. Last Accessed on July 23, 2024.

Von Hoffman, A. (2012). *History lessons for today's housing policy: The political processes of making low-income housing policy*. Joint Center for Housing Studies, Harvard University. Wl2-5. https://www.jchs.harvard.edu/sites/default/files/w12-5_von_hoffman.pdf. Last Accessed on July 23, 2024.

Wolf, H. (2022*). "Trying as hard as I can"—Narratives of failure and success in the experience of housing insecurity*. Human Arenas.https://doi.org/10.1007/s42087-021-00268-1

Wood, J., Eskic, D., Benway D. J., & Macdonald-Poelman, K. (2020). *Housing affordability: What are best practices and why are they important?* https://d36oiwf74r1rap.cloudfront.net/wp-content/uploads/Best-Practices-Dec2020.pdf. Last Accessed on July 23, 2024.

Index

L. Sümer, *The Global Housing Crisis*,
https://doi.org/10.1007/978-3-031-72604-0

The manufacturer's authorised representative in the EU is Springer Nature Customer Service Centre GmbH, Europaplatz 3, 69115 Heidelberg, Germany. If you have any concerns regarding our products, please contact ProductSafety@springernature.com

Printed and bound by CPI Group (UK) Ltd, Croydon, CR0 4YY
30/09/2026
02225591-0003